Church, Book, and Bishop

EXPLORATIONS
Contemporary Perspectives on Religion

Church, Book, and Bishop:
Conflict and Authority in Early Latin Christianity
Peter Iver Kaufman

Religion and Politics in America:
Faith, Culture, and Strategic Choices
Robert Booth Fowler and Allen D. Hertzke

Birth of a Worldview:
Early Christianity in Its Jewish and Pagan Context
Robert Doran

FORTHCOMING

New Religions as Global Cultures
Karla Poewe and Irving Hexham

Images of Jesus
L. Michael White

Religious Ethos and the Rise of the Latino Movement
Anthony Stevens-Arroyo and Ana María Díaz-Stevens

Transformations of the Confucian Way
John Berthrong

Ancient Israelite Religion
Saul Olyan

Church, Book, and Bishop

CONFLICT AND AUTHORITY IN EARLY LATIN CHRISTIANITY

Peter Iver Kaufman

University of North Carolina–Chapel Hill

WestviewPress

A Division of HarperCollinsPublishers

Explorations: Contemporary Perspectives on Religion

Copyright © 1996 by Westview Press, Inc., A Division of HarperCollins Publishers, Inc.

Published in 1996 in the United States of America by Westview Press, Inc., 5500 Central Avenue, Boulder, Colorado 80301-2877, and in the United Kingdom by Westview Press, 12 Hid's Copse Road, Cumnor Hill, Oxford OX2 9JJ

A CIP catalog record for this book is available from the Library of Congress.
ISBN 0-8133-1816-5 (hc.) — ISBN 0-8133-1817-3 (pbk.)

The paper used in this publication meets the requirements of the American National Standard for Permanence of Paper for Printed Library Materials Z39.48-1984.

10   9   8   7   6   5   4   3   2   1

Contents

Acknowledgments

It has been a strange two years writing about conflict and writing rather favorably about the management strategies of the early churches' executives while pressing the executives at my university for substantial change. I owe much to the dozens of colleagues who participated in that latter initiative, educators who insist that values they impart in their classrooms—inquiry, honesty, and excellence—be reflected in the management of their campus. I dedicate this book to my two closest collaborators and good friends, Melissa Bullard and Terry Evens, and to Professor Robin Scroggs of Union Theological Seminary in New York, who awakened my interests in the earliest Christians.

Trent Foley of Davidson College threw caution to the wind and assigned an early draft of *Church, Book, and Bishop* to the students in his class on Christian antiquity in 1994. Their comments and criticisms enabled me to improve the text, as did Trent's interest and suggestions. Bart Ehrman, Maureen Tilley, Carolyn Wood, John Headley, and Kim Haines-Eitzen gave invaluable advice. At Westview, Spencer Carr's encouragement, patience, and counsel were all an author could wish for. I am grateful to them all; defects that remain are my own doing.

Peter Iver Kaufman

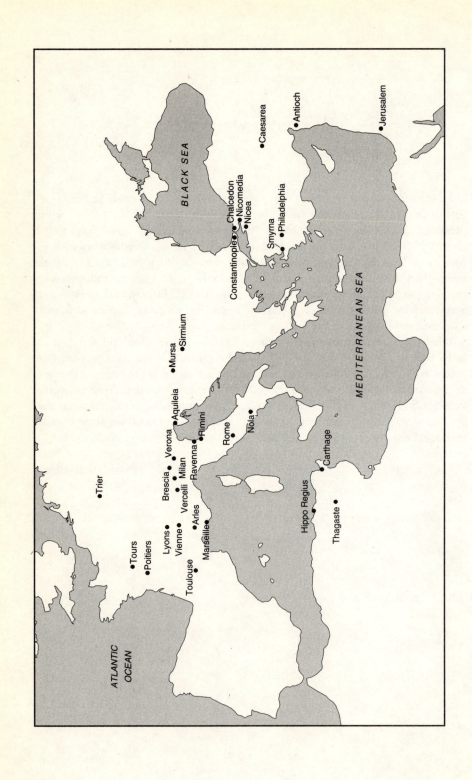

BLACK SEA

MEDITERRANEAN SEA

ATLANTIC
OCEAN

Caesarea

Antioch

Jerusalem

Chalcedon
Nicomedia
Nicea
Constantinople
Smyrna
Philadelphia

Mursa
Sirmium

Aquileia
Verona
Rimini
Rome
Nola

Brescia
Milan
Vercelli
Ravenna

Trier

Arles

Carthage

Lyons
Vienne
Marseille
Hippo Regius
Thagaste

Tours
Poitiers

Toulouse

Introduction

Cranbrook in Kent was a rather sleepy small town in 1583, slightly more than twenty miles southwest of Canterbury. Dudley Fenner was twenty-five when he arrived there that year, having just returned to England from Antwerp. He had been ordained a priest on the Continent yet was pleased to have been assigned a parish close to his birthplace. Later in the year, Bishop John Whitgift of Worcester came to Canterbury to be consecrated as archbishop, the principal administrator of the reformed English church. These two men were a mere twenty miles apart, but they did not see the same prospects when they looked back at Christian antiquity. Whitgift found that the apostles had been the church's first bishops. He and his friends inferred God had authorized the concentration of power in the church in the hands of a few able, distinguished administrators. Fenner protested that the earliest churches had been governed differently, more democratically. Popular consent had been required, elders consulted, councils called. Not one to pull his punches, Fenner pronounced that Whitgift and other apologists for the established church order in England, wanting to retain their salaries and privileges, "faleslie father[ed] upon the apostles . . . a false and bastard distinction of ministries."[1]

Origins seem sacred in many, if not most, religions. What happens at the start and the meanings that originators give to what happens acquire tremendous authority. Appeals to the very beginnings of this or that practice argue for its continuation. Memories of the first shoots of an idea argue for its repetition and ramification. For nearly two millennia, Christians have been ascribing normative status to Christian antiquity, to all or the earliest part of the religion's first six centuries. Looking back is hard, Christians have learned; what was thought, done, and meant usually defies precise determination. And looking back is competitive, as Whitgift and Fenner discovered; those who search for origins must reinvent them while trying to reappropriate them.

My interests were like those of Fenner and Whitgift, though I was not looking to reappropriate, to find patterns in what was for what is or ought to be. Even so, disclaimers of this sort do not diminish all difficulties. Although historians may not have to contend with resistances to reappropriation, they must nevertheless narratively reinvent a past that has left only modest stocks of evidence, and they

1

must always compete with rival explanations. My interests in the early church's management strategies further complicated this enterprise because management is a monster category. It compasses liturgical and teaching responsibilities as well as political initiatives ranging from recrimination to reconciliation. To tame the monster, I tried to put many rituals and doctrines in contexts dominated by more overtly political strategies devised to keep order and maintain discipline, to prevent diversity from generating divisions and hostilities among Christians, and, when that failed, to resolve conflict and crisis.

If successful, *Church, Book, and Bishop* should register a sense of the challenges Christians faced as they sought to order their lives together in this world while awaiting their rewards in the next. And if successful, the book's many stories of conflict and resolution should suggest how and why Christians designated certain texts as sacred literature; how and why they interpreted select passages, traditions, and experiences to define and extend the reach of their churches; and how and why they distributed authority within those churches to elders (later priests) and bishops, whom I call "executives" to distinguish them from itinerant preachers and prophets whose attachments to local settled communities were generally more tenuous.

Strategies of selection, interpretation, and distribution can hardly be understood apart from the struggles that occasioned them. Sacred literature and leadership were initially defined in and by the struggles of small and sectlike communities to establish uniform doctrine, discipline, expectation, and organization. The jurisdictions of authorities within those communities were later determined by the struggles of churches and networks of churches to defend conformity against nonconformists and secessionists, to combat diversity and perceived novelty, and, to that end, to enforce policies of exclusion and reintegration. It was not my purpose to detail every struggle or give every known detail of any struggle. I did not try to be comprehensive because, in part, my students regularly informed me that too many strange-sounding names, faraway places, and long-ago dates obscured the drama of leadership development. So I set out to tell stories that would introduce and illustrate representative struggles and management strategies.

It is prudent, however, to be rather tentative about each story's representative status, for what most students perceive as an avalanche of names and dates historians know as a modest drift, and we know too little, for instance, about the fourth-century episcopacy to say that any single pontificate represents the others. I hope only that my stories and illustrations exhibit the virtues Annabel Patterson recently ascribed to the anecdotes of early modern chroniclers: that they "have a nonarbitrary relationship to the project" and "possess all the attributes of good fiction (shapeliness, thrift, vitality, the capacity to speak to social issues of importance, particularly those not yet fully or widely understood)." I can only hope that they "finesse the problem of *representativeness* by virtue of their *representational* solidity, their sense of being statistics come alive."[2]

I hope that *Church, Book, and Bishop* will be a congenial companion piece. It seeks no greater sphere. To get the largest possible picture of Christian antiquity, readers must hear more directly from and about nonconformists and discuss doctrines, rehearse rituals, and interrogate theorists and texts unmentioned here. Readers may want to consult instructors, pastors, more compendious narratives, and, ideally, some of the specialized studies commended in the Suggestions for Further Reading. But this book will be a useful companion if it effectively blends with most stories of crisis, conflict, and consensus standard assessments and informed, revisionary guesses to discover how church, book, and bishop were defined and why they acquired such authority.[3]

Although I have tried to take into account what colleagues have learned from bottom-up interpretive approaches to the transfer of authority, imposition of discipline, and maintenance of congregational solidarity, this is a book about the elites. Chapter 1 investigates their formation in the first and second centuries. Chapter 2 scans the literary career of a late-second-century apologist for church authority and one of the more outspoken critics of those executives who wielded it, Tertullian of Carthage. Chapter 3 considers church leadership during the third and fourth centuries by examining several executives' responses to prominent, contested issues: the identity of Jesus, the relationship between Christianity and secular politics, the determination of standards for conduct becoming and unbecoming the Christian, and the nature and extent of penance and pardon. Chapter 4 belongs to Augustine of Hippo, who from 400 until his death thirty years later influentially adjusted the churches' frontiers, defining what it meant to be a member and an official in the universal church. All of the first four chapters report conversations and arguments about church, book, and bishop, but Chapters 2 and 4 concentrate, respectively, on the sacred book and the Catholic Church. Chapter 5 looks at how bishops managed conflicts and built consensus during the fifth and sixth centuries and at the increasing importance of the one apostolic see or seat of church government in the western portion of the empire, the church (and bishop) of Rome.

Church, Book, and Bishop, then, reviews a number of early arrangements and initiatives against nonconformity and anarchy, inspecting a series of executives' decisions to exclude or absorb Christians who trusted other than "the right" churches, canonical books, and orthodox bishops. Historians once imagined they could tell all and tell it objectively. At the very least, they thought they could retrieve and piece together enough information to give an integrated, accurate view of the past. Theirs was a splendid, "noble dream," as Peter Novick recently admitted in a study of the profession that was something of a wake-up call, a ringing repudiation of those dreamers' ambitions.[4]

Of course, we need not borrow Novick's lens to see that the ideals of objectivity, consensus, comprehensiveness, and closure or completion are under siege. We need only look at the sea of competing interpretations of nearly all historical phenomena or count the growing number of historians who have graduated from a discreet, sage, and candid acknowledgment of the problematic character of all historical knowledge (can we ever know?) to join the militantly critical assault on the very possibility of historical knowledge (we can never know). The criteria for evaluating a historian's findings and the narratives that present them have never been less consensual than they are now. Indeed, it seems odd to be writing about early Christian integration and reintegration within, and with, a disintegrating discipline. Yet there are good reasons to press ahead—and to do so selectively and simply, because, as Novick insisted, overspecialization and "arcane terminology" contribute to historians' failures to communicate with all and cooperate with each other.

And, readers are those good reasons.

I do not presume readers' intense interest in the history of the early churches. Nor do I expect that readers are alike and that close resemblances would permit me to pose a family portrait on the other side of these pages. Yet would it be all that unfair or tremendously presumptuous to say that humans are irrepressibly historical and that reading makes them so? We read, as Fenner and Whitgift did, though perhaps not with their sense of purpose and urgency, to discover roots, origins, the whence as well as the whither, because the knowledge of origins and developments, as imperfect as it may be, often explains why, how, and even what. We are usually undeterred, then, by our intimation that stories written after the fact are prejudicial, that the after always plays havoc with the fact. Fascination survives our skepticism about the noble dream. No cure I know has yet been found for curiosity. And curiosity beckons our intuitive and imaginative powers, the exercize of which is good in and of itself, even if we are left only with a familiar, yet disagreeable sense of how much we may never know. Those materials from which historical narratives and seemingly substantiated conclusions are crafted defy conquest, but they compel lively conversation and endless argument.

And that, too, is an excellent reason to press ahead and look behind. Controversies over authority and leadership in the early churches enlivened the history of the Christian traditions in virtually every generation. Fenner and Whitgift could hardly be called exceptional. To be sure, the ground has shifted since their time and tussle, but it is still contested. *Church, Book, and Bishop* intends to specify where some contemporary scholars stand and to volunteer a few fresh interpretations of an elite's predispositions and behaviors. The principal objective, however, is to kindle readers' curiosity and invite their contributions to the conversation about the nature and distribution of religious authority.

I work from texts and think of them as working texts because they do not lay back, so to speak, and reflect prepackaged parts of culture—namely, what happened or was happening around them. Involved and almost unconscionably abstract theological treatises, businesslike and confessional correspondence, admiring lives of saints, and angry, extended accusations shaped what happened, tried to affect what would happen, composed cultures, and contained (in both senses of the word) antagonisms and anxieties of which the authors may have been only partially aware.

Historians have to locate contexts to decode texts, to save those texts from superficial readings but also to keep them from becoming infinitely interpretable.

But here is the rub: We learn about contexts by decoding texts, artifacts, sites, and silences. Contexts are little more than what we are able to tease, extort, and accumulate from texts of all kinds. But must we circle until driven by dizziness to a standstill? Or are we on the threshold of an adventure requiring a constant commerce between texts and plausible contexts? The dilemma will either paralyze us or launch us into a process of relentless correction and argument with our archives, our colleagues, and ourselves.

I vote against paralysis. I mentioned the circularity only to lift the hood for a moment and remind readers of the difficulties that historical narratives, present company included, will often screen. Other difficulties will arise; they are featured in what follows. They are not the difficulties and dilemmas of historians but those of the churches' executives. So the hood must now close, the latch click, so we can press forward with conflict management, leadership, and authority—with church, book, and bishop—in early Latin Christianity.

❀ 1 ❀

Order over Error

Had Jesus left explicit instructions about how to organize, or even what to organize, the lives of many of his early admirers probably would have been much simpler than they were. Their conflicts over authority—over who had it and over how far it extended—could then have been avoided altogether or at least easily resolved, and this short study of conflict management would be much shorter. But conflicts there were, often spirited ones.

These controversies were decades and more ahead when Jesus first started talking about God's will and human well-being. He appears to have concentrated principally on emancipation rather than organization. Perhaps he and his disciples thought that there was neither need nor time to organize. There was no need because everyone, on hearing of freedom from sin and from God's vengeance, would behave benevolently and resolve disputes with their neighbors before crises compelled authorities to intervene. It was senseless to covet and grasp and hoard on earth when treasures beyond measure were elsewhere: "Fear not, for it is your Father's good pleasure to give you the kingdom."[1] There was no time because the end and the "elsewhere" were at hand; those devotees whose faith in Jesus' message survived the shock of his "trial" and death would soon be snatched up, provided for, and given that promised kingdom, a wholly new and holy new order, when their savior returned.

To report that good news, that "fear not," devotees composed gospels. The first of the four that were later included in the New Testament was written more than thirty years after Jesus' death. It and the others were biographies: Their authors, the evangelists, patched together reminiscences to tell the story of Jesus' life, ministry, execution, and resurrection and to retell the stories Jesus had told. The evangelists sifted, selected, added, omitted—all to pass along the word effectively. Their gospels were seasoned with appeals and promises: "Seek first [God's] kingdom and righteousness," for thereupon "all these things"—the staples for life in this world, such as nutrition, clothing, shelter—"shall be yours."[2]

Also among "all these things" were good company, gratifying fellowship, and collegial worship. Or so it would seem from a reading of the gospels, the Acts of the Apostles, which rehearses the experiences of the first Christian missionaries, and the letters written by the apostle Paul before the composition of the gospels and Acts. But the very same texts also suggest how difficult it was to achieve collegiality and consensus. In fact, the postresurrection communities of Jesus' followers and admirers seem to have constantly courted crisis.[3]

"Not a God of Confusion"

Fairly late in the first century, the evangelists tried to resolve something of an identity crisis by articulating exactly what distinguished Jesus from the Pharisees who preached, as Jesus did, the resurrection of the dead. Some of the Pharisees were known to have protested strenuously when Jesus' brother James was stoned, so those wishing to minimize the differences and to identify or intern the early Jesus movement as a chapter in the history of Pharisaic Judaism had at least the beginnings of a case. The evangelists, however, featured objections that Jesus supposedly raised against the Pharisees' strict observance of ancestral laws, and they dramatized the Pharisees' refusal to acknowledge Jesus as the messiah. The author of Matthew's gospel vividly depicted a series of confrontations during which Jesus snapped at mean-spirited Pharisaic critics: They were shamelessly eager for notoriety, he said, and they were quick to find fault with all but themselves. Perhaps they were knowledgeable about custom and ceremony, Jesus conceded, but they did not comprehend justice, mercy, and faith.[4]

Some years before Matthew composed his characterization, Judaism had fallen on hard times. Its revolt against Rome had failed, and its fine temple at Jerusalem had been destroyed. Matthew and the other evangelists apparently thought it important, therefore, to emphasize, maybe even to exaggerate, Jesus' declaration of independence from his Pharisaic contemporaries, "blind guides" and "brood of vipers."[5]

Christians learned from their evangelists not only that the Pharisees were "blind guides" but also that the aristocratic Sadducees, who had supervised temple affairs, were shortsighted and skeptical about the resurrection of the dead. So it seemed to the early generations and communities of Jesus' followers that none of his Jewish critics saw things all that clearly. Late-first-century Christians harbored the hope that Jesus, perceiving this myopia as well, had offered an alternative plan for leadership. Certainly, they realized that there had been both time and need for organization; they were already squabbling among themselves. But evangelists, for their part, recorded no plan. They neither encouraged nor obliged the hope that there had been one. The closest that the author of Matthew's gospel came was to recall a few remarks that inclined toward some power-sharing arrangement: "You are not to be called Rabbi," Jesus was reported to have said; "neither be called masters." Indeed, "whoever exalts himself will be humbled." And nothing at all was mentioned in the gospels about the apostle Paul, who had tried for some time to reconcile such sentiments with the need to maintain order, manage conflict, and avoid error in the postresurrection communities.[6]

Paul had been a Pharisee, defending the ancestral Jewish traditions and raging against Jesus' disciples until his heart and mind were changed on the road to Damascus. He said that his conversion from Pharisee to friend of the friends of Jesus left him with a more generous will and a profound appreciation for the deference, patience, and mutual affection required of the faithful. Intent on conveying the meaning of Jesus' death and resurrection to new recruits, he allowed that power-sharing might work, but only if each Christian's conversion transformed his or her character. So Paul drafted instructions to perfect the conversions of his correspondents, structure and discipline their desires, and assure the solidarity of their communities. Yet as he did so, he inevitably called attention to his own authority. He fired off warnings, framed counsels, and issued commands. He professed humility but also, arguably, edged toward arrogance: "I became your father in Christ Jesus," he told the fractious Corinthians. "Be imitators of me."[7]

One of the several problems in Corinth was that too many Christians were imitating the apostle, counseling and commanding, presuming to set standards and to interpret Jesus' significance for their community. They spoke "in tongues," apparently in ecstasies as well as with unfamiliar languages, and they claimed considerable authority on the strength of that gift. Paul wanted to suppress a claim that had proven so divisive. "I speak in tongues more than you all," he wrote, declaring nonetheless that his contributions to the maintenance of peace were far more valuable than his ecstatic utterances. He praised all who worked for peace, "laborers" who knew the importance of ecstasies and prophecies but still agreed with him that "all things should be done decently and in order." These laborers, he said, were his genuine imitators, and their authority derived from their reconciling work. Yet inasmuch as that letter to Corinth concluded by naming laborers whom Paul had converted and with whom he continued to converse, we cannot shake the impression that their advantage and authority ("give recognition to such men") were also due to their acquaintance with the apostle.[8]

Paul recommended "recognition," but he did not elaborate. Earlier in his letter, he listed functions that could conceivably be taken as official positions: apostles, prophets, and teachers as well as "healers, helpers, and administrators" (at the bottom of his list he deposited those "speakers in various kinds of tongues"). "God has appointed" officials, Paul specified, but he did not imply that divine appointment was intended to give birth to bureaucracy. This inventory of responsibilities corresponded to personal powers. It was offered not as a blueprint for community rule, a layering of one set of responsibilities on another, but as a set of special God-given aptitudes and talents. In fact, another of Paul's letters explicitly made that point about service in the church and the "gifts which differ according to the grace given to us."[9]

Authority or recognition, therefore, appears to have been awarded those with notable personal powers—and was what some call "charismatic authority." If Paul had had his way, authority to refine doctrine, oversee worship, and arbitrate disputes would probably have been given to irenic managers and consensus-builders with personal connections to the apostles. Only once in those letters we know were his did Paul use titles later attached to church executives, only, that is, when he addressed "all the saints . . . at Philippi, with the bishops and deacons." That second plural, "bishops" *(episcopoi),* suggests that he did not anticipate monoepiscopacy, a subsequent arrangement providing one bishop in each church and, later still, one bishop for each regional cluster of churches. Possibly he had in mind a congress or team of superintendents, yet his correspondence never mentioned *presbuteroi,* elders of the church known through the next century to have met in council to deliberate and make decisions affecting their communities.[10]

The author of the Acts of the Apostles recalled that Paul and his companion Barnabas, traveling from town to town in the first century, "appointed elders . . . in every church." Such a recollection would carry greater weight, of course, if Paul had named those elders and called them *presbuteroi* in his authentic letters, for the silence (or omission) awakens a suspicion that Acts remembered incorrectly. Perhaps the author wanted to credit Paul and Barnabas with having made those arrangements that prevailed somewhat after their missions. There was indeed a need to arrange and organize, but an organization based predominantly on need was less likely to compel conformity than an organization prescribed or endorsed and thus dignified by the heroes of the faith.[11]

The author of Acts had Paul himself predict the problem that led to organization and the further definition of leadership: "I know that after my departure fierce wolves will come in among you, not sparing the flock; and from among your own selves will arise men speaking perverse things to draw away the disciples." Who were these wolves prowling for members? Were they ancestors of the Gnostic Christians who put a mystical spin on the apostle Paul's teaching, drew disciples into elite regiments of savants, and upset second-century bishops with their wolfish appetites for innovation and speculation?[12] Or were they Judaizers, new converts to Christianity who wished to drift back a bit toward Judaism and "draw away" members of the new Christian communities with them and who objected to the mixed Jewish-Gentile fellowship that resulted from the expanded Christian mission? The Judaizers lionized the apostle Peter, who reputedly voiced their objections and was consequently scolded by Paul. But the scolding did not end the apostolic disagreement; the issue of mixed fellowship divided Christian communities late in the first century and into the next.[13]

The author of Acts plainly favored mixed fellowship and redrafted the history of missionary initiatives, strategically drawing Peter to his and to Paul's side of that controversy with the Judaizers. Stories of mission and ministry, however, were no substitutes for scrupulous shepherds-in-residence, apostolically appointed elders stationed "in every church" and deputized to keep those "wolves" at bay. Acts did not press that point and trumpet Paul's alleged appointments more loudly, probably because its author knew that elders participated in the government of the Jerusalem church, which disapproved of mixed fellowship. Rather than risk associating shepherds on site with the opposition to mixed fellowship,

Acts entered only a muted plea for government by elders. The upshot is that the text moved only a little closer than the apostle Paul's authentic letters to a settled, explicitly defined church administration.[14]

The pastoral letters to Timothy and Titus, written in Paul's name early in the second century, suggested a somewhat more structured church government. Evidence for organization was certainly not overwhelming, but elders were doubly honored, once for teaching and preaching and once for "rul[ing] well." Perhaps their positions evolved from arrangements to which the apostle's authentic correspondence alluded. Some laborers distinguished themselves by taking greatest advantage of their gifts and were tremendously admired. With reputation came authority. They ruled well, and, as the first letter to Timothy reported, they were not easily impeached.[15]

The author of the pastoral letter to Titus seems to have used "bishop" and "elder" interchangeably, indicating that communities had not yet experimented with monoepiscopacy. Yet nothing about administration is nailed down with lawyerlike precision. Enough is said in the first letter to Timothy, however, to confirm, if not the elevation of a single bishop in each local church, at least the suspicion that bishops possessed more prestige and responsibility than elders.[16]

All the pieces of our puzzle are not in place. Itinerant prophets and apostles continued to wander throughout the territories from Athens to Antioch and around to Alexandria. But the deutero-Pauline pastoral letters show that executives-in-residence were critical parts of the new religion's local apparatus. There had been time to organize; the second coming of Jesus had not come as swiftly as some had expected. And there definitely had been a need or cause to organize, for many Christians passed that time in conflict with one another. In the early second century, there were still wolves among the sheep.

> But understand this, that in the last days there will come times of stress. For men will be lovers of self, lovers of money, proud, arrogant, abusive . . . treacherous, swollen with conceit, lovers of pleasure rather than lovers of God, holding the form of religion but denying the power of it. . . . Among them are those who make their way into households and capture weak women burdened with sins and swayed by various impulses. . . . As Jannes and Jambres opposed Moses, so these men also oppose the truth, men of corrupt mind and counterfeit faith.[17]

Charges of this character were not uncommon in religious controversies, which is not to say, however, that they did not stir up anxiety and insecurity. We can imagine that such accusations were also composed to expose beguiling charlatans who threatened any emerging consensus and to generate eagerness and initiatives to protect truth from "men of corrupt mind and counterfeit faith." The apostle Paul generally relied for protection on the power of the truth experienced in personal conversions. Those to whom he wrote had been profoundly touched or moved by Jesus' ministry and passion or by the good news of both. But the letters to Timothy and Titus were composed later; they were addressed to Christians who were decades, probably generations, removed from the most recent conversions in their friendship circles or families. Experiences familiar to persons of Paul's time must by then have seemed rare, if not unrepeatable. There was still a need to protect the truth from wolves, to alert the faithful to those who tried to mislead them. It therefore appears that the postresurrection communities, having already started down the road from ideology to institution, continued to develop from simple, separatist assemblies or sects with no fixed form of government into churches with resident executives and uniform organizations.[18]

Greetings in some early Christian correspondence suggest the existence of small conventicles, cozy cells and extended families gathered in "household churches." Were that the case, protection, as I have sketched it, would have required minimal precautions. But the presumed intimacy and informality are hard to document. Scholars now say that the greetings signal only that Christians sometimes congregated in the homes of more affluent members, that most left their homes and made their ways to worship with persons from different parts of their villages, from different villages, from different classes, and with different ideas.[19]

With differences came disagreements and with disagreements, charges like those we have just encountered. Church leaders could find no crawl space beneath controversy to hide. The cultic meals should have effaced differences and promoted sociability as well as solidarity, melding all participants into a single company or "body," but even those exercises turned out to be controversial.

The cultic meal was an occasion to offer thanks to God, hence the name "eucharist," thanksgiving. The apostle Paul provided a good but general description of the ceremony that recapitulated Jesus' last supper with his first disciples and commemorated Jesus' atonement, his sacrifice to emancipate others from sin. The cup of wine was "a participation in the blood of Christ"; bread, "a participation in the body of Christ." Breaking and sharing that bread coaxed devout and thankful Christians to contemplate the corporate character of their "participation," their communion: "We who are many are one body because all partake of the one bread."[20]

The idea of participation proved sufficiently ambiguous to trouble theorists for centuries, but earliest participants would not have missed the themes of sacrifice and judgment. They both celebrated their savior's sacrifice and sacrificed self-will so attitudes commended by Jesus would spread among members of their communities, whereupon all at communion might be spared divine retribution—"so that we may not be condemned along with the world." But the apostle was disappointed because liturgical opportunities to overcome differences and disagreements came instead to excite and intensify them—to perpetuate "divisions" and "factions" that plagued the church of his time. Judaizers in "the circumcision party" resented dining with Gentiles. Radical spiritualists, known now as Docetists, insisted that Jesus only appeared to have taken on flesh and blood; they grumbled about the claims made for the bread and wine. Then there were those Christians who ate and drank extravagantly, making even more conspicuous the differences between the community's haves and have-nots. Paul censured them for importing class distinctions into a ritual of religious solidarity. How could consensus-building survive the efforts of some to outclass and "humiliate" others? Something was awfully wrong with a community that could not celebrate its cultic meal congenially, harmoniously, "for [its] God is not a God of confusion but of peace."[21]

Confused communities could expect rapid deterioration of discipline and some collateral erosion of the consolation that Christianity promised. Indeed, discipline and consolation were paired in those commissions Jesus was remembered to have given his disciples, hence, his new religion. One report in Matthew's gospel awards priority to discipline or "binding": "Whatever you bind on earth shall be bound in heaven, and whatever you loose on earth shall be loosed in heaven." Another, in the gospel of John, speaks first of pardon: "If you forgive the sins of any, they are forgiven; if you retain the sins of any, they are retained." The disciples and their heirs purportedly received the divine spirit along with "the keys to the kingdom of heaven." Thereupon, they could judge, condemn, and absolve disruptive behavior, knowing that God would ratify their decisions.[22]

Considerable power was therefore at stake in the struggles to stave off confusion and create and preserve the fellowship of each community's eucharist. Insolent challengers were thought to contaminate the new religion with crazy ideas and disrupt the orderly transfer of spirit, keys, and authority. At least that was how those who first acquired and held power saw the situation, and until relatively recently most historians of first- and second-century Christianity endorsed their view. It looked to them as if a normative or orthodox Christianity resisted confusion while the challengers drove churches to or into it, either by objecting to widely held opinions about Jesus' identity and ministry (heresy) or by distancing themselves from those officials whose policy or personal conduct seemed disreputable (schism). Whereas orthodox Christianity stayed the course and, according to the conventional perspective, inched forward from Jesus' commission to and through the great councils of the church centuries later, heretics and schismatics went off and tried to pull the church in all directions.

But in 1934 Walter Bauer offered an influential alternative to that conventional perspective, and without subscribing to all he said about orthodoxy and heresy, scholars now generally agree that earliest Christianity was a cluster of competing religious insights. So we might just as well, or better, speak of earliest Christiani*ties* and look for "heresies" before the creation of an orthodoxy. To the Jewish Christians in Jerusalem, for example, the apostle Paul seemed a heretic. Then, as Bauer put it, "the arrow quickly flew back at the archer" when Paul all but charged the circumcision party with heresy. Conflict came first and often; consensus came later. To justify its emergence and remaining battles against heresies, the consensus crafted and perpetuated the illusion that an unaltered and unalterable orthodoxy had stayed the course from the start.[23]

Bauer alleged that consensus actually came from Rome, where Christians felt the full force of the first persecutions. Nero's name is most often associated with first-century intolerance and fanatical cruelty, but his predecessors and immediate successors hardly did the Christian community in Rome any favors. Bauer in-

ferred that the martyrdoms of the early apostles Peter and Paul made abundantly
clear what Christians could expect from citizens of the empire's capital. He
guessed that municipal and official hostility encouraged partisans of the new religion "to develop attributes of shrewdness, energy, and communal unity," and, he
continued, the Christian community's solidarity and its acquired survival skills
made Rome "the one church of dependable orthodoxy" in the second century.[24]

We stay a bit longer in Rome, looking first at the document that seems to substantiate Bauer's claims, a letter from Rome to the Christian community in
Corinth, then watching the leadership of the Roman church develop during the
second century. Despite stated opinion that their God was not a God of confusion, Christians appear almost addicted to confusion and conflict. And that ad-
diction helped them come to some self-definition, to define the authority of the
church, book, and bishop.

Clement of Rome and Ignatius of Antioch

There is still disagreement about the date of an important letter from the
Christians at Rome to those in Corinth. Estimates run from the last quarter of the
first century through the first quarter of the next. Clement's name was put on the
letter long after its completion and dispatch, and we cannot tell for sure who this
Clement was, what office he held, whether he wrote the letter, and, if he did, on
whose authority. Alas, in studies of early Christianity it is not unusual for so many
mysteries to attach to a single document. At least in Clement's case, we can be certain that we have an introduction of sorts to one or more representatives of the
Roman Christian community who were unable to stand idly by while Christians
quarreled among themselves many miles away.

What more do we know? The author of the letter—historians cite him as
"Clement" for convenience—was familiar with the apostle Paul's correspondence
with the Corinthians. He shared Paul's alarm about confusion and competition
among Christians, yet he also advised that the proponents of peace be carefully
screened. Some of them honorably pursued reconciliation; others, he noted, only
paraded peaceful intentions when convenient and were usually combative, always
"deceitful." Clement called down curses on those sham peacemakers who seemed
to him far more concerned with advancing the interests of their factions than
with serving the entire congregation.[25] They were impatient and irascible, he said,
suggesting that the slightest insubordination was inconsistent with peaceful intent. Terribly impressed by the discipline and obedience in the Roman legions, he
instructed all Christians to "observe those who were soldiering under our commanders and see how punctually, how willingly, how submissively they execute
the commands! Not all are prefects or tribunes or centurions . . . but each in his
own rank executes the orders of the emperor and the commanders."[26]

The Christians in Corinth seem not to have asked for Rome's or Clement's instruction and advice. The letter from the capital mentions no appeal from its re-

cipients. Clement said that sorrow had prompted him to write, to express his grief for consensus lost, and to reprimand rogue Christians who defied and deposed their blameless elders. The rebels were guilty of having forgotten the virtues of modesty, humility, and forbearance, which, Clement observed, were so much a part of the new religion, in theory, if not also in practice.[27]

Bauer believed that Clement's letter was a fledgling "call to orthodoxy." Strangely, however, it fails to specify the rebels' heretical opinions. Possibly restraint was tactical; Bauer said that by declining to debate abstract doctrinal issues, or even to identify them, Clement suggested the superiority of his much more "markedly moralistic approach" to religion.[28] This may be so, yet it is just as likely that Clement knew next to nothing about the Corinthian heresies. We learn from the letter only that squabbles resulted in schism. We do not hear whether jealousy or ideology sparked the rivalry. We read that the rebels were young upstarts, unreasonable, impulsive, conceited, but descriptions of that kind were probably scripted to brand the conspirators rather than to report on them responsibly.[29]

It is tempting to agree with Bauer that there was a battle brewing in Corinth between charismatic prophets and the church's executives, if only because Clement's letter rules out so very little and Bauer was shrewd to point out its relative silence about doctrine. But I suspect Clement's rhetoric and restraint can be interpreted differently. Arguably, his letter suppressed whatever Rome had heard about doctrinal novelty or jealousy in order to throw the evil of insubordination into greater relief. Admittedly, we know neither what there was to know nor what the Roman Christian community knew about the schism. Yet the letter is absolutely clear about one thing: To Clement and those Romans he represented, consensus and congregational solidarity were inviolable and depended on the orderly transfer of power.[30]

In Rome it must have been reassuring to recall, as Clement did, that the apostles had provided for the appointment of their successors and for all who followed them. Clement said that the apostles had anticipated that wolves would prey on their sheep for generations, spreading fear along with false doctrine. He said as well that the apostles had specifically expected communities would come unglued when contests for leadership prompted envy, discontent, and intrigue, which was why they had left rules for the selection of executives-in-residence. Clement revealed precious little about those rules, save that they existed, prescribed the participation of persons "in high repute," and required candidates to obtain "the consent of the whole church." In Corinth, however, those arrangements seemed insufficient. It looks as if intrigue was inescapable. Perhaps the professionalization of the residential leadership antagonized those Christians whose insurrection moved Clement to write. In Rome, however, professionalization must have worked quite well, for Clement gave no ground. He did not try to broker a truce, to negotiate a compromise in Corinth. He offered only one option: The rebels were to repent their defiance and reinstate the original executives, whose appointments, in form, had allegedly been endorsed by the apostles.[31]

The principal beneficiaries of Clement's attention, had the Corinthians accepted his and Rome's advice, would have been those elders or presbyters who had just lost their posts. Clement failed to name or count them. He gave no sense of the size of the presbyterial committee either before or after the insurrection. He referred to other church officials who may have participated in the presbyterial deliberations, explicitly mentioning bishops, but "bishop" may have been another name for "presbyter." Monoepiscopacy therefore seems to have been slow to develop in both Corinth and Rome. Clement's colleagues appear to have been persuaded that presbyterial government, of undescribed and perhaps unprescribed size, was apostolically approved and politically sound and adequately represented the interests of the majority and thus the community.[32]

Afterward, Christians did designate one elder to supervise the others as their bishop. Soter, whose term lasted until 175, seems to have been the first, although during the 180s someone compiled a catalog of bishops that stretched from Eleutherus, Soter's successor, back to Linus, who was said to have succeeded the apostle Peter. The name "Clement" was included, probably the Clement of the letter to Corinth, but we must not be misled. The letter itself yields no support for the catalog's contention that monoepiscopacy existed in Rome in the early second century.

Neither does *The Shepherd of Hermas,* the striking collection of visions, parables, and directives put together in the vicinity of the capital soon after Clement tried to assist the deposed elders of Corinth. The author of *The Shepherd* shared Clement's hatred for confusion and schism but did not stipulate that an arbiter with authority to impose consensus was the solution. The text referred to bishops, noting only their obligations to care for the poor, obligations later associated with the church's deacons. So notwithstanding the succession chronicled in the catalog, the verdict seems to stand: Throughout much of the second century Roman Christians were content with presbyterial government.[33]

It would be wonderful if we possessed enough information to fashion a perfectly manicured tale to take readers from Clement and *The Shepherd* to Soter, Eleutherus, and the list of bishops. Then we would know whether conflicts finally pushed Christians in Rome towards monoepiscopacy or kept them from it—one side or faction fearing domination by another. And then we could tell whether caring for the poor became more critical as the Christian community in Rome grew larger and more complex and whether the power to manage all church affairs was concentrated in the hands of those bishops mentioned in *The Shepherd* and ultimately, as Peter Lampe argued, deposited with one of them. But unfortunately that tale cannot be told. The late-century catalog of bishops reveals only that the concentration of executive authority we term "monoepiscopacy" was enthusiastically accepted and awarded a venerable past once conflict or complexity or consensus made that administrative change practicable and desirable.[34]

So Christians in Rome were still led by elders or presbyters when Ignatius of Antioch, calling himself "bishop of Syria," sent them greetings. He appears to have known little about Rome, save that the city had been the last stop on earth for the apostles Peter and Paul, the antechamber to their places in God's heavenly kingdom. Ignatius expected to follow them, first to Rome, then to heaven, for he wrote as a closely guarded prisoner, making his way from the Syrian city of Antioch, through Asia Minor, to his execution in the empire's capital. He wrote not only to Rome but also to the congregations of Christians in several cities he passed. The letters, neither long nor spectacularly weighty, nonetheless land with impressive effect when dropped into the history of the Christian traditions; they suggest that Ignatius was the earliest ideologue of episcopal government. Indeed, the letters show that while Roman Christians were still being governed by committee, their coreligionists in Syria and Asia Minor had beaten them to monoepiscopacy.[35]

Obviously, there had been some trouble in Antioch. Ignatius may have given himself up and gone off voluntarily to bring peace to his home church. He had not gone far, however, before learning that some reconciliation had been achieved. One reason he wrote his letters, pocket essays on church unity, was to encourage the Christians in other cities to congratulate Antioch and, by force of recognition, to put his church's reconciliation beyond recall. The Antiochene agreement was fresh and probably fragile; it could only be strengthened by the acclaim it attracted. The neighboring churches sent their bishops or one of their presbyters. Ignatius urged churches at greater distance to send a deacon or, at the very least, to compose letters. And he expressed the hope that Christians everywhere, by celebrating the consensus in Antioch, would discover how important it was to achieve unanimity and to preserve unity in their local churches, specifically to resist "the bait of false doctrine" that led some into schism.[36]

Ignatius described those baiting traps or hooks as "wolves." He was seldom more precise, but his creedal statements imply that the wolves were Docetists and Judaizers, whom we have already encountered. More to the point, here, however, is his instruction that the surest way to keep sheep safe from wolves was to insist they stay close to a steadfast, right-minded shepherd. "Where the shepherd is, there you, being sheep, must follow."[37]

> You must follow the bishop as Jesus Christ [followed] the Father and [follow] the presbytery as the apostles; respect the deacons as the commandment of God. Let no one do anything apart from the bishop that has to do with the church. Let that be regarded as a valid eucharist which is held under the bishop or whomever he trusts. Wherever the bishop appears, there let the congregation be; just as wherever Christ is, there is the whole church. It is not permissible apart from the bishop either to baptize or to celebrate the love feast; but whatever he approves is also pleasing to God, that everything you do may be sure and valid.[38]

Shepherds or bishops ought to be incorruptible; Ignatius said as much to Bishop Polycarp of Smyrna, the only executive whom he wrote directly. His letter, however, lavishes relatively little comment on episcopal conduct and turns quickly to his favorite point: To submit to the bishop was to conform to God's will, for the bishop's purpose was God's purpose. Nothing should be undertaken without the bishop's counsel, consent, and cooperation.[39]

The reason was obvious to Ignatius. Christians could not be Christians, he stipulated, unless they worshiped with "one mind, one hope, [and at] one altar," the altar being each Christian's "connection with the Passion," with the suffering but also with the promises of Jesus. Distance from the bishop meant that the dreaded gusts of false doctrine drove Christians farther from the altar and from the savior. "Take care," Ignatius warned, "to partake of one eucharist," and he returned frequently to the imagery of "one bread" and "one cup"—adding for the benefit of the Christians of Philadelphia, "just as there is one bishop."[40]

The Docetists stayed away from Ignatius's one altar as long as presiding officials spoke of the bread and cup as the flesh and blood of Jesus. They apparently arranged for separate celebrations of the eucharist during which they gave thanks for Jesus' exaltation but were subdued, if not grimly silent, about his incarnation. They were ardently interested in the kingdom to come but cared little, according to their critics, for the unity of the local church at hand.[41] Ignatius assumed that theological explanations of the incarnation could go only so far to retrieve the Docetists who had withdrawn from the one altar. Perhaps he anticipated that his words would lose their force once he had moved on to Rome and was forgotten, for he put his faith in the resident executive. He concluded that episcopal monarchy in each community could do as much as, and probably much more than, the most memorable phrases of the most persuasive itinerant to safeguard doctrinal unity, discipline, and liturgical correctness.[42]

During his visit to Philadelphia, several Christians there asked Ignatius to act as umpire. At first he was ready to give their grievances a fair hearing, he claimed, but while he sifted their complaints, he suddenly "cried out . . . with a loud voice, the voice of God: 'attend to the bishop and the presbytery and the deacons. . . . Do nothing without the bishop.'" That Ignatius had taxed the dissidents with their insubordination before all was made known to him fed suspicions that he had been coached by friends of the authorities or by the authorities themselves. Not so, he replied; "the spirit . . . made the proclamation." He was not about to deny his bias: He was "a man set on union," utterly convinced that submission to bishops and repentance were preconditions for divine pardon. He conceded that he was only partly and perhaps partisanly informed about the facts in Philadelphia, but he trusted that a more exhaustive account of the issues at stake would have made no difference. Ignatius believed God used him and his bias to frame a rejoinder to anyone contemplating or promoting disloyalty, disharmony, and division: Do nothing without the bishop.[43]

Reporting the episode in Philadelphia, Ignatius turned a rare trick in the history of the Christian traditions. He made the itinerant prophet and the resident church executive partners. But his statements about episcopal monarchy are like nothing else in the literature that survives from the first half of the second century. He seems to have been an apologist for a contested management strategy in

Syria and Asia Minor at that time, but were he and his correspondence the creations of cunning church executives who later tried their hand at inventing a venerable past for their preferred form of church leadership?

Robert Joly made one of the better cases for forgery. He did a superb job of deflating the pretension that an episcopal tradition of government extended back to the pontificate of Jesus' brother James in Jerusalem, but Joly's contention that Ignatius's isolation indicates subsequent and pseudonymous composition is ultimately unconvincing. Too little has been left us from the early second century, and utter isolation (*totalement isole*) in such sparsely populated territory hardly signals inauthenticity. To be sure, the letters of Ignatius are unique, yet the pastoral letters to Timothy and Titus, as I noted, hint at something like episcopal "rule," and they were probably written very soon after the bishop of Antioch completed his journey. Hence, it looks as if autocratic executives were proving their worth against wolves, certainly not everywhere in the Roman Empire but with enough success during the first decades of the second century in Ignatius's region to inspire "a man set on union" to stress the advantages of having one leader or chief executive in each city and to circulate an ideology for such episcopal government.[44]

Books for "a New Creation"

The advantages of well-defined congregational and regional leadership seemed to outweigh the disadvantages. And one of the heftier advantages was that persons who thought otherwise could be sent packing while they were still relatively harmless. The result for historians is that nothing is known about perceived disadvantages. We can only speculate about the arguments against professionalization registered, say, by dissidents in Corinth or about Docetists' alternatives, if any, to episcopal monarchy in Syria and Asia Minor. Committees of elders and bishops apparently were busy suppressing subversive ideas about their authority and evicting the subversives before whispers of sedition divided their churches.

Legend has it that several decades into the second century Bishop Polycarp of Smyrna chased Marcion from Asia Minor. Maybe bishops acted in concert and had sufficient muscle to force dissidents from the region, but the little we can ascertain from Ignatius is too little to credit the story. Polycarp must have hounded Marcion; his hostility is well attested. But it is just as likely that Marcion left of his own accord, realistically thinking that he and his ideas would fare better in Rome than at home.[45]

Had he not known before, Marcion must have learned on his journey that each Christian community derived its sense of the lessons, life, death, and resurrection of Jesus from a different jumble of oral traditions and texts or textual fragments. So to convey his distinctive ideas and to have them catch on, Marcion had to select and edit his sources. One biography of Jesus was enough for him; indications are that it closely resembled the gospel of Luke. But Marcion's interest in biography was limited. His gospel was merely a prologue for a larger project. He wanted to make the apostle Paul the foremost interpreter of the religion of Jesus. Marcion hoped to draw Christianity farther from Judaism, and he tried to minimize the intelligence and restrict the influence of the evangelists who seemed to him to demote the Christians' savior by associating him with the Jews' history of salvation.

We can only guess how Marcion handled Luke's tale of the tomb and of the postresurrection appearances, which perplexed Jesus' companions. Mary Magdalen, Mary, and Joanna were shocked that the tomb was empty until "men . . . in dazzling apparel" reminded them of Jesus' prediction ("and on the third day rise"). The women spoke of the miracle to the remaining disciples, who dismissed the "idle tale." Two of them subsequently failed to recognize Jesus, and all were astounded when he reappeared yet again. Presumably, Marcion exploited this incredulity to show how thickheaded the disciples were, yet he must have had to contend as well with the same chapter's suggestion that Jesus "opened their minds to understand the scriptures." Here was a passage that could very well have torpedoed Marcion's project: Marcion insisted that the father of Jesus was not the God of the law and prophets, whereas Luke's Jesus inclined disciples to see his ministry, passion, and resurrection as a grand revelation and sublime culmination of "everything written about me in the law of Moses and the prophets and the psalms."[46]

Critics complained that Marcion cut passages he could not reconcile with his position.[47] Indeed, in this instance he may have deleted Luke's recollection that Jesus thought the Hebrews' scriptures worth understanding. But what is particularly important here is that the letters of the apostle Paul placed Marcion under less of an obligation to cut and recompose. Marcion wanted to divorce Christianity from Judaism; Paul's displays of impatience with the circumcision party fit right into Marcion's plans.

Marcion's may have been the first collection of Paul's letters. But whether Marcion instigated a Pauline revival or steered one already in progress in a fresh direction, by the middle of the second century he was very busy promoting an ultra-Pauline Christianity. The apostle's letter to the Romans encouraged Marcion to contrast divine grace with Jewish law.[48] Paul's second letter to the Corinthians moved Marcion to cast Christianity as a brand new covenant and helped him disassociate the apostle from Judaizing rivals.[49] Marcion set Paul's letter to the Galatians at the head of the collection, perhaps because it emphatically announced that Christianity superseded the Hebrews' ceremonies and convictions: "Neither circumcision counts for anything, nor uncircumcision, but a new creation."[50] And Marcion was intent on stocking this new creation with sacred texts that purportedly explained and celebrated its novelty.

He was not alone in stressing novelty and spirituality. In the second century, Docetists reinforced their positions with a slew of texts and expositions. In scholarly literature, they are known now as Gnostics, and they, too, were drawn to the apostle Paul, particularly to his distinctions between flesh and spirit. Christians who opposed them and who hoped to cut the ground from under Marcion had a choice: They could either forsake Paul or rehabilitate and repossess him.[51]

Those favoring the second alternative were responsible for expanding the collection of Paul's letters. They were desperate to shove the Gnostics to the lunatic fringes of Christianity but eager to keep Paul, though not Marcion's Paul, at the center. The result of their reclamation is the apostle as he is now textually represented in the New Testament. The correspondence, in places, underscores religious individualism and marks differences between an old dispensation and a new creation. But conspicuously in the pastoral letters included—if not also composed—for this purpose, the "canonical Paul" endorses the authority of church executives-in-residence and the canonicity of the Jews' sacred literature. "All scripture is inspired by God."[52]

Marcion, then, compelled his opponents to reconceive Paul's legacy. Did he also force them to introduce a collection of texts that might reflect more comprehensively than his did the message and meaning of Jesus? Those who think so refer to a list discovered by Lodovico Muratori, an archivist in Milan and Modena in the eighteenth century. The Muratorian Fragment, apparently a Latin translation from a Greek original now lost, argued for four Gospels and showcased the canonical Paul, noting that the letters to Timothy and Titus were valued for their contributions to order and discipline. Last on the list of approved books, *The Shepherd of Hermas,* "composed very recently," enjoyed a peculiar status. It seems to have been hustled into the fund with some skepticism. The Fragment allows that this odd text should be read, but it was not to be classed with those of the evangelists, prophets, and apostles. As something of an odd man in, however, *The Shepherd* has become critical, for it inclines scholars to date Muratori's canon to the mid to late second century and to present it as a prompt response to Marcion.[53]

The telling phrase is "composed very recently in our times," which seems to signal that the list was compiled soon after *The Shepherd* had been written. But another translation is defensible. *Nuperrim[e]* can be rendered "most recently," alluding to the earlier composition of all the works preceding *The Shepherd* in the Fragment—the canonical gospels and the canonical Paul, among others. And it is not unreasonable to suggest that "in our times" connoted the Christian era rather than a generation or a span of several decades. So the Fragment could be pitched into a later period without scandalizing other scholars.

But where does all this uncertainty about the Fragment's date leave the question of Marcion's influence and the need for books for a new creation? What, in other words, can be learned about the composition of the Christians' sacred book? Muratori's document marked at least the beginning of the end of a period of transition from loose and laissez-faire to structured, restricted evaluations of religious literature.

Selective use of sacred writing was Christian practice from the start. The apostle Paul shrewdly deployed the Psalms and the prophets to illustrate the significance of Jesus' crucifixion and resurrection. Ignatius and Clement of Rome mined Paul's letters for their own purposes. During the later part of the second century, assorted apologists for Christianity followed suit to defend the faith against pagan and heretical critics. Maybe momentum alone would have driven the next generations of apologists to collect, authorize, and circulate their favorite texts. We will never know, but we may safely assume that they were more disciplined than their predecessors because the Gnostics were busy generating a literature of their own and because Marcion, who is frequently numbered among them, tampered with familiar and favorite texts. (The Muratorian Fragment ran down a Marcionite sampler of psalms and several Gnostic narratives.) Conflict, then, pressed one side to come to consensus about acceptable reading. So even though we cannot say that Marcion's influence was decisive, we may reasonably assume that he hastened changes that the Fragment finally recorded.[54]

The very best measure of Marcion's immediate influence is probably the multiplex campaign among Christians to defend the canonicity of the Hebrews' scriptures. Marcionites were eager to scuttle the Old Testament. Their adversaries' efforts to save the old were not unrelated to the compilation of the new.

Ptolemaeus was a Gnostic Christian, and as a Gnostic he was pretty much unconcerned with the prehistory of the Christian enlightenment. He was indifferent, that is, to all that preceded the revelations of Jesus. Nonetheless, Ptolemaeus did not reject the Hebrews' scriptures altogether, advising that readers of the law and prophets simply had to distinguish what was worth saving from what was not. He grasped that the Old Testament was the work of many hands—some inspired, some inept. Close attention to the sayings of Jesus, he said, helped Christians identify the right "hands" and set aside the rest.[55]

But this line of defense, a judgmental census of sorts, was unacceptable to Justin, a philosopher–turned–Christian apologist in Rome during the 150s. He did not trust Gnostics to make sound judgments, particularly because their sense of what Jesus had said was informed and shaped by their far-fetched interpretations of commonly accepted passages or by collections of secret sayings found exclusively in Gnostic gospels. Yet Justin also protested that the Gnostics forfeited the unitary character of revelation by vindicating only select portions of ancient scriptures. The very qualities that distinguished Christianity from philosophy and magic, he argued, were the singularity, antiquity, and continuity of its truth. If the Old Testament were packed with sets of "mere assertions," some better than others, it could not effectively be used to document that Jesus was a further, consistent, consummate revelation of God. And Jesus could end up as one purveyor among others of assertion, opinion, and magic.[56]

The problem in the second century, as Justin saw it, was that small-time sorcerers claimed to be apostles and eccentrics paraded as prophets—every freighter pretended to be a flagship. It was imperative, therefore, to underscore the distinctiveness of Jesus.[57] Only Jesus was the fulfillment of the promises made in the Hebrews' scriptures. The law, prophets, and Psalms were invaluable proof of his uniqueness and thus precious resources for Christian apologists who claimed that without Jesus the Old Testament was incomprehensible. On this count, Justin agreed with Ptolemaeus; Justin tried to persuade the Jewish critics of Christianity that their old law anticipated a new lawgiver and that their prophets predicted his fate. To the untrained eye, Isaiah appeared to refer to the disobedience and devastation of his own time, but training and then discernment, according to Justin, enabled Christians to see that the prophet Isaiah actually referred to the experiences of Jesus' disciples and persecutors. To enlighten trainees, the Gnostics appealed to mystifying oracles and elaborate expositions, Justin continued; he offered an alternative—namely, comparatively concise and straightforward reminiscences about Jesus' career.[58]

The reminiscences (*apomnemoneumata*) were indispensable. When the Jews insisted that Isaiah's anger ("woe to the wicked") applied only to days long gone, Justin referred them to tales of more recent treachery, to the Pharisees, for example, who were said to have responded with insult and injury when Jesus summoned them to repentance.[59] And when the Christians craved to learn how to cope with their neighbors' enduring hostility, he referred them to the reminiscences of Jesus' forbearance.[60] Justin was among the first Christian apologists to use material in the gospels extensively, yet he probably did not quote directly from the four as we know them in the New Testament. For most of the second century, they were not available in a four-gospel set. Matthew, Mark, Luke, and John, as well as the gospels ascribed to Thomas and Philip—along with the other texts that fell short of canonical status in due course—reached the Christian communities separately, sometimes in pairs, and occasionally as pieces in a patchwork. Some readers tried to combine accounts and harmonize reminiscences from the various early sources. Justin and his pupil from Syria, Tatian, did so, laboring perhaps on the understanding that a consensus was just around the corner if only their inclusive or composite gospels could make all others obsolete.[61]

A degree of conformity *within* most Christian communities was probably achieved by the end of the second century as executives exerted authority to set patterns for worship and indoctrination. One remaining challenge was to build consensus *among* communities, a rough coherence compassing some practices, ideas, rituals, and doctrines as Christian and branding deviations as something else, as something "other" and definitely un-Christian. Executives could do that effectively only in league with one another, and indeed bishops and their representatives would often meet through the next several centuries in regional councils, or synods. Their very convening would take officials a long stride toward meeting that challenge, yet Irenaeus of Lyons, following Justin and Tatian, supposed that consensus among congregations was unlikely as long as each Christian community possessed its idiosyncratic digest of sacred texts. If agreements on the fundamental doctrines were to be reached, Christians would have to credit the same set of gospels.[62]

Irenaeus started his career in Smyrna, where he was well acquainted with Bishop Polycarp. As Marcion before him, though under different circumstances, Irenaeus left for Rome, where he studied with Justin. In Gaul Irenaeus became bishop and directed his attention to, and his fire against, Gnostic Christians. A later Gnostic document accused church officials of strong-arm tactics, whereby, to achieve conformity within, they endeavored to push and pressure eccentrics out.[63] Irenaeus told a different story. Gnostic teachers, he said, could not resist the temptation to change or add to inherited doctrines. They meant to be innovators and masters, not disciples. The result was an abundance of secret sayings, gospels, and enigmatic revelations. On Irenaeus's reading of their record, the Gnostics were unhappy unless they were outsiders.[64]

Behind the Gnostic exodus, whether forced or freely willed, was the conviction that the critics of its masters' secrets and texts were caught in the coils of an inferior Christianity. And Irenaeus was outraged as much by the Gnostics' sense of superiority as by their ideas and scriptural expositions. Were they really wiser than the apostles, he asked? Did they have any grounds for presuming their doctrines superior to traditional teaching that passed through an official channel from generation to generation? For Irenaeus, that channel running through churches made them churches and made them one church. He would do all he could to deepen it.[65]

Irenaeus was emphatic: There was room in Christianity for only "one and the same way of salvation." It was the way charted by each of the four canonical gospels. Independently, and still more compellingly in concert, they presented the very ideas that offended the Gnostics: notably, the reality of the incarnation, the reality of judgment, and the reality of the resurrection of the body. That an incorruptible spirit should be associated with "mundane flesh"—either the flesh of Jesus or that of the souls restored by faith in the flesh of Jesus—seemed to the Gnostics, as it had to Docetists, patently absurd. That it had to be so seemed to Irenaeus self-evident and scriptural.[66]

The gospels gave the concrete details, but the Gnostics' interpretive acrobatics illustrated to Irenaeus how deceptive generalizations and conclusions could easily be drawn from the best evidence. So notwithstanding the apostle Paul's unenviable reputation among some apologists during the second century, the result largely of Marcion's ultra-Paulinism), Irenaeus appealed to Paul, recruiting him to transport Christians from the concrete to the conceptual—that is, from the life of Jesus to the meaning of Christ. Against Marcion, Irenaeus argued that Paul made no distinction between Jesus and Christ and that Gnostics were wrong to cast the latter, Christ or "savior" (*soter*), as a visitor to the former's flesh. What was more, the apostle relentlessly preached judgment and resurrection.[67]

Those who conserved Paul's doctrine were his successors. Those who risked changing it were unreliable. Yet congregational leadership attracted both kinds, so it was not nearly enough that someone ruled or taught decisively. Decisiveness might yield local agreement for a time, but to avoid confusion in the long run, authority in each congregation, according to Irenaeus, had to be awarded to executives whose doctrine and demeanor were consonant with Paul's. That channel through which the truths about Jesus, judgment, righteousness, and resurrection passed from the first through the second centuries, and then into and through the rest, cut straight from the apostle. Therefore, if scripture was to be interpreted "without danger," executives would have to hold their places in that line of succession from Paul to the present, an apostolic succession.[68]

All that Irenaeus said about the Gnostics need not be believed. Apologists notoriously played on the more preposterous ideas of their opponents, kidnapped remarks from their contexts, and made the strange seem stupid to reinforce counterarguments. Nevertheless, the most basic difference between the Gnostic orientation and that of their conservative critics is clear. Allowing for variation, Gilbert Vincent rightly concluded that the Gnostics indulged their "passion for the absolute" and subordinated the discourses their Christian critics cherished to their own desires for sublime knowledge and spiritual self-realization. Irenaeus defended what the Gnostics all but rejected; the associations that extended across time and space—from one generation to the next, from one region to another—and that subordinated private or sectarian philosophical reflection to church authority.[69]

If all else failed, if misleading literature was smuggled into the canon of some local church or if executives refused to subscribe to the apostles' doctrine, local religious conformity could be checked against the practice and policy of that "great, very ancient, and universally known church, found and organized at Rome by the two most glorious apostles, Peter and Paul."[70] Indeed, it was while elaborating this statement that Irenaeus introduced the aforementioned list of bishops to document antiquity and continuity and to feature Rome as the paladin against each congregation's isolation. Nonconformity could be checked simply by attention to the ways in which the executives of the Roman church preserved, interpreted, and applied the apostles' legacy. But the apologist who carried Irenaeus's argument into the next century, still contesting Marcionite and Gnostic notions, and who made the case for apostolic succession, the canon, and relatively restrained exegesis resided not in Rome but across the Mediterranean Sea. Tertullian lived most of his life in North Africa, in the Roman Empire's "second city," Carthage.

2

Tertullian

It is a shame we know so little about Tertullian, a man who wrote so much—a shame but not a shock, for had an enthusiastic and admiring biographer set to work fairly soon after Tertullian's death in the early third century, the manuscript would probably have been suppressed. Tertullian was, after all, a turncoat. He defended church executives against their heretical critics, but in the end "he was not a man of the church," as the scholarly Jerome said two hundred years afterward. Tertullian was a frighteningly bad apple, an apologist gone sour.[1]

Late in the second century, before Tertullian of Carthage turned "sour," he learned how to make passages from sacred texts bear the favorite themes of those church executives. We start the story there, having already watched as speculative and innovative Christians impelled their more conservative coreligionists to put the canon together. Tertullian continued their conservative work, making certain, against the Marcionites, that the Bible contained the Hebrews' scriptures as well as newer authoritative narratives and letters. Heresy remained useful, however, because once it had forced Christians to get the right book, its persistence gave them incentives to get the right book right, to build consensus around orthodox expositions, interpretations, and applications. And competition with heretics improved the ability of the church's interpreters to communicate to diverse sets of initiates what the sacred texts meant.

Carrying on the counteroffensive launched by Irenaeus, bishop of Lyons, Tertullian reassured Christians that the executives' standing in apostolic succession gave them, not the innovative Gnostics, final interpretive authority. The knowledge awarded to apostles, he said, had carefully been handed down in and through the churches over which the executives presided. This apostolic tradition and its executive custodians were trustworthy, whereas philosophical sophistication and heretics who possessed it were not. Heretical interpreters and those who listened to them were prey to philosophy, insolent, and irreverent. They trifled with the Bible and were contemptuous of the executives who had the right to interpret it—and the right interpretation of it.

On behalf of the churches' executives, Tertullian clawed at the Gnostics with rather unbecoming relish and criticized other philosophical interpreters of the sacred literature, whose only "crime" may have been the desire to make religion reasonable. He called their results sorcery and made himself and the churches' executives the champions of the historicity of Jesus' incarnation and resurrection. But Tertullian ultimately grew impatient with church executives in North Africa and finally turned against them. It seems that they liberally issued pardons to reintegrate wrongdoers into the churches at just the time he became obsessed with piety and purity. He berated bishops for having been drawn (and for drawing others) into the web of this world's corruption, for paying too steep a price for—of all things—companionship with known sinners. The executives' pardons for incest and adultery set off his protest, yet his about-face was far more than a response to excessive tolerance. Tertullian's alienation from executives was related to his former defense of them, and as we discover more about his defense and alienation, we see how rival kinds of authority—executive and prophetic authority—levered Latin Christianity into the history of Mediterranean civilization.

Useful Heresy

Late in the second century, a variety of Christianities kept competing for Christians' loyalties. Tertullian, just as Irenaeus before him, identified and tried to explain what he thought to be the genuine article, accusing the Gnostics of having carried the earliest and apostolic doctrines far beyond belief and of having exposed Christianity to ridicule. The Gnostic versions of Jesus' ministry and message were riddled with rambling secrets, he said, and made no secret of his scorn. Nevertheless, he also remembered that the apostle Paul had forewarned that there would always be heretical improvisation and mystification. Paul had offered some consolation. Unremitting competition between religious truth and heretical fantasy, he had suggested, ultimately benefits the former. Factions persist "in order that those who are genuine among you may be recognized."[2]

Apparently, then, God permitted heretics to circulate their odd interpretations of Jesus' incarnation and resurrection so the truth would be thrown into greater relief, so sober interpreters, Irenaeus and Tertullian among them, would intensify their efforts to elaborate, clarify, and authenticate what they had to say. It was a simple plan. Heresy was useful as a goad, but there was a catch: God not only supplied the heretics but also supplied them with sacred literature. Tertullian had some qualms about this arrangement. For the heretics then used cherished texts to defend their heresies, and, alas, their claims to have read the more complicated passages correctly could not always and easily be confuted.

Tertullian momentarily put texts and heretics together to explain God's strategy. Useful heresy depended on sacred texts; without them, he suggested, heretics would have had nothing of importance to misread. And without the contests over critical passages, there could be no winners, no losers—and therefore no heretics. God could not have given Christianity useful heretics without giving them, at least provisionally, the texts that made them heretics.

The difficulty, Tertullian said, was that heretics were the poorest of loser. They never conceded defeat. Long after a more commendable interpreter proved their propositions preposterous, heretics noisily reasserted them and tried to bully better Christians into accepting them. So Tertullian advised against attempting to take (or take back) texts passage by passage. Nothing was to be gained by that, save fatigue and frustration. There was only one way to get the best of heretics, whose persistence was not to be underestimated, and that was to deny them the right to appeal to sacred literature once their appeals had clearly distinguished them as heretics. It was true that scripture had been arranged for them, but only to enable them to be usefully heretical, "to give them enough rope," we might say. But once they twisted their texts into nooses, heretics should be left to hang by their wild speculations and extravagant expositions.[3]

The contests over critical passages taught heretics nothing. They lived in a fool's paradise where fantasy ushered them to the very strangest conclusions imaginable. Yet the contests did teach right-minded Christians something: to countenance only those expositions conforming to the prodigious tradition originating with Jesus and the apostles, who

> obtained the promised power of the Holy Ghost for the gift of miracles and of utterance, and after first bearing witness to the faith in Jesus Christ throughout Judaea and founding churches [they] next went forth into the world and preached the same doctrine of the same faith to the nations. They then, in like manner, founded churches in every city, from which all the other churches, one after another, derived the tradition of the faith and the seeds of doctrine, and are every day deriving them that they may become churches. Indeed it is on this account only that they will be able to deem themselves apostolic, as being the offspring of apostolic churches. Every sort of thing must necessarily revert to its original for classification. Therefore, the churches, although they are so many and so great, comprise but the one primitive church. . . . All are primitive and all are apostolic, whilst they are all proved to be one, in unity, by their peaceful communion.[4]

Cadres of heretics were not one, in unity with the authentic and apostolic churches. Hence, they had no legitimate claims to the legacy Jesus left his disciples and the disciples of his disciples. Heretics had no right to interpret the book.

The Bible belonged to Christians who traced their doctrines to those of the apostles. They alone "obtained the promised power of the Holy Ghost." As we learned in the last chapter, one great challenge for church leadership in the second century was to bridge the gap between the saved in each generation and the savior's first followers, a gap that predictably widened with the passing of time. Irenaeus, for example, greatly prized his acquaintance with the aged Polycarp of Smyrna, who repeated what he had been told directly by those who had heard Jesus. A succession of teachers, who happened to have been executives, preserved and "preached the same doctrine of the same faith to the nations." Some of them committed their instructions to writing. Perhaps for convenience, although quite possibly for liturgical purposes as well, several condensed their narratives and formulated rules of faith, following a precedent set by the apostle Paul, who composed a rule (*regula*) to recall Christians in Galatia when they strayed. Tertullian maintained that conformity with that rule and with others like it enabled executives to shepherd their flocks into the "one primitive church."[5]

Tertullian's several presentations of his rule, specifically the discrepancies in wording, suggest that he placed no premium on precise formulation. The discrepancy that most concerned him, however, was the one between his variously expressed rules of faith and the heretics' rules, opinions, and expositions. But Tertullian harbored hopes that what would seem to have been an irreconcilable difference, *dissensus,* would result in Christian consensus. Why else would God permit heretical speculation and contrive controversy and conflict if not to build and refortify consensus and to keep traditional, or "regular," Christianity on its proper course?[6]

To ears so many centuries removed from Christian antiquity, the case for the utility of heresy must seem uncharacteristically generous. To Tertullian, however, the case made eminent sense. Heretics alerted him to those places in sacred literature likely to trip up others, though he could not conceive that the special relationship between the progress of Christianity and the persistence of heresy afforded stubborn heretics any lasting advantage. The apostle Paul conceded there had to be heresies; nothing said or implied in the scriptures, however, suggested that the heresies would be anything but a backdrop. The heretics' factions and fictions merely provoked the development of sound scriptural exposition and accepted doctrine.

Actually the apostle merely said that heretics would enable "those who are genuine" to make themselves known. So Tertullian's apparent confidence in progress or development was something of an extrapolation. That confidence drove Tertullian to defend the authority of the Old Testament as well as that of the New and, having got the right book together, to insist on the role of tradition in interpreting and applying it correctly. That same confidence, moreover, finally set him against church executives, who saw the prospects for progress quite differently.[7]

Yet for now this much is certain: Tertullian was persuaded that heretics would inevitably and annoyingly lift passages from sacred literature to make their absurdly speculative ideas seem sensible and scriptural. He despaired of winning them over with counterexpositions. Nonetheless, he struck relentlessly at their interpretations, sparing no effort to make Christian revelation historically defensible and to discredit heretics' philosophical defenses and appropriations. He wrote volumes so that his fellow Christians might not be seduced by heretical expositions, so they would know what to make of the scriptural stories, promises, and consolations they frequently assembled to hear.

Prey to Philosophy

Little is known of those assemblies in Carthage, a city of as many as one hundred thousand people at the time, and it is the little Tertullian tells us. He never counted the assembled or said how many citizens of the city were Christians. Fifty years later, Bishop Cyprian complained that so many persons came daily for absolution ("thousands") that priests who absolved them could not adequately test for the sincerity of their repentance.[8] But Cyprian had some reason to exaggerate, as did Tertullian, inflating the influence of his new religion to show how imprudent outlawing it would be. The tax base would shrink appreciably, he claimed, should the Christians in Carthage be expelled. Moreover, he assured, Christians spent more in charity on the streets than pagans did in their temple offerings. And should Christians ever be tempted to avenge themselves on Carthage, their torches could do memorable damage.[9]

All this suggests a considerable presence, but confessional interests likely corrupted the estimates. Tertullian seems more reliable replying to pagan critics who complained that Christians were reclusive, secretive, and worse still, seditious. To set the record straight, he explained why Christians stayed away from public games and spectacles: Violence was inconsistent with their religion. The faithful took their pleasures less spectacularly but no less sociably. They met to pray, prayed often, and even prayed for the emperor (though not to him). And before and after prayer, they chanted Psalms and listened as the sacred texts were read. They thereby learned of divine censures that demonstrated their God was infinitely different from, and more compassionate than, those pagan gods presiding over bloodstained sports.[10]

Either at or immediately after some assemblies, peculiarly gifted members of the congregation volunteered impromptu, inspired expositions. Christians met to discuss them, to "probe" them, Tertullian advised, perhaps as soon as worship had adjourned. So it seems that many things were going on at or around the same time; something was likely to go wrong.[11]

Tertullian's reference to impromptu expositions may have reflected his experience among North African Montanists, who stressed the prophetic impulse in Christianity. Prophecy after public prayer and reading is not all that well attested, though Justin Martyr was sure that the gift or power of prophecy passed from Jews to Christians when the former refused to believe God's culminating self-revelation in Jesus. Ignatius, as we have heard, pronounced judgment near Philadelphia as the spirit's spokesman or oracle. During the 170s, not far from that town, Montanus and his close associates were regularly visited by a spirit relaying censures and instructions that the churches' executives found difficult to accept or endorse. The Montanists warned of history's imminent end. They frowned on marriage, forbade remarriage, and favored rigorous fasting.

But Christian authorities in Asia Minor had different standards and were unhappy at being overruled. They claimed to have caught the scent of a swindle.

They doubted the provenance of the Montanists' inspiration and ecstasies, denied the value of their utterances, and drove the new prophets from the churches. North Africa, however, seems to have been hospitable to ecstasies, prophecies, and puritanical Christianity because the controversy over special revelations had not yet reached crisis proportions when Tertullian was drawn to Montanism. So Montanism in and around Carthage cannot be called a separatist movement, although, as Paul Mattei concluded, Tertullian's notice of prophetic, impromptu exposition was a sign of schism waiting to happen.[12]

Tertullian was initially preoccupied with other matters. As valuable as concise rules of faith were for the indoctrination of initiates, recitations from the sacred book had to have marked the most uplifting moments during each congregation's corporate life and worship. Tertullian specifically mentioned readings from the evangelists and apostles as well as from the Old Testament's law, Psalms, and prophets. Circumstance, he said, dictated the choice. Then exposition and interpretation made it relevant to current practices.[13]

Christians, for example, had to understand that the warnings addressed to Israel were also addressed to them. The Old Testament did not explicitly prohibit attendance at public games and spectacles, but Tertullian said that the psalmist's blessing on "the man who walks not in the counsel of the wicked" directed Christians to avoid those events and the impious who were usually drawn to them.[14] To be sure, extracting fresh lessons from old literature was nothing new. The apostle Paul appropriated Hebrew Scriptures to censure misbehavior and correct misperceptions of God's will. So notwithstanding objections registered by Marcion and meaning to counter his insistence on the incongruity of Old and New Testaments, Tertullian argued that Paul eagerly raised precepts for a Christian morality from the "seeds" planted in the Hebrews' books.[15]

But Tertullian worried that the expositors and interpreters of his time, leaping from literature to life, would drop right into philosophy. True, lessons from the canonical gospels were relatively uncomplicated. Jesus' conduct was recounted clearly and was self-evidently exemplary. If we think only of how he entered Jerusalem and do so without much interpretive commentary, we have an excellent and unambiguous study in humility.[16] Yet it was also true that Jesus' teaching could be, and had been, misconstrued fairly easily. His parables all but invited missteps. Christians who gathered to pray, chant, and listen while passages from their sacred book were read and explained might find the wrong meanings and applications beguilingly, perhaps irresistibly, offered to them.

Tertullian was certain that philosophy was behind the lure and lunacy of heretical exposition. Heretics misappropriated the sacred texts, using them to corroborate favorite philosophical conjectures. Hermogenes, for one, thought the Stoics were infallible; under Zeno's spell, he dared to make matter coeternal with God. He clipped and rearranged countless passages from the Bible, and, Tertullian charged, he virtually changed Genesis into a Stoic manifesto.[17] The danger of turning faith into philosophy was great because generally imperceptible. Too few

Christians were equipped to see the distortions. Too few realized that Hermogenes and many other philosophically cultured heretics, although pretending they were at home in Judaea and Jerusalem, belonged in Athens with "unhappy Aristotle who invented . . . dialectics, the art of building up and pulling down, an art so evasive in its propositions, so far-fetched in its conjectures, so harsh in its arguments. . . . Away with all attempts to produce a mottled Christianity with Stoic, Platonic, and dialectic composition! We want no curious disputation after possessing Christ Jesus."[18]

Tertullian remembered that Paul had paired philosophy with treachery when warning the Colossians of "human traditions": "See to it," the apostle had advised, "that no one makes a prey of you by philosophy." Heretical predators, however, thought that caution was ill-advised. They imagined cautious Christians were innocents and simpletons. But it was better to be simpleminded, Tertullian answered, than to be wise, cunning, and perverse.[19] Simplicity in this instance was something of a virtue not far removed from humility, but late in his career Tertullian became intolerant of the unsophisticated, suggesting that all but a few Christians were fools, *idiotae.* Far too many of the faithful, he then alleged, were too stupid to comprehend the rule of faith and thus powerless to defend it and Christianity not only against predatory, philosophical interpreters but also against sinister church executives.[20]

Of course, philosophy repaid careful study. Knowledgeable Christian apologists need not surrender Plato to the pagans and polytheists; he could be saved for Christianity or at least made into contested territory. Those who knew philosophy could detect him edging toward monotheism, notably when he assessed Jupiter's superiority to other deities. And Tertullian did not think it pointless to declare how often he found Seneca on his and on Christianity's side of certain controversies.[21]

Christian apologists guessed that venerable philosophers of classical antiquity stole some ideas from the Hebrew scriptures but never really understood those sources. Sadder still, Tertullian put in, was philosophers' passing on their incomprehension to "their brood" of heretical interpreters of both the Old and New Testaments. Consequently, that literature became a place to prospect for insights and illustrations largely, and often wholly, unrelated to its purposes and most profound truths. Maybe the interpreters were only trying to make Christianity and its most sacred narratives philosophically respectable. But while making Christianity respectable and Christ reasonable, they made themselves heretics. They forgot the first and most fundamental of those profound truths: Jesus came to save the soul, not to speculate about its structure. None were guiltier of this forgetfulness than the Gnostics inspired by Valentinus, who taught in Alexandria around the middle of the second century.[22]

Disagreements kept Valentinians fighting among themselves, but a broad consensus about Jesus distinguished them (and other Gnostics) from Irenaeus, Tertullian, and like-minded apologists. The Gnostics refused to accept the reality of a suffering savior. They insisted that spiritual essences suffered neither change nor pain. The *soter,* or "savior," they maintained, descended on Jesus at his baptism and withdrew during his interview with Pilate, thus avoiding the cross. Tertullian declared this view utter nonsense. Had they tested their premises about spirituality and suffering against the accounts of Jesus' final days, the Valentinians would have learned that suffering and salvation were closely connected. Instead, they accommodated their philosophical assumptions, found some comfort in isolated passages, altered others, and forgot the plot of the canonical gospels.[23]

To Tertullian, the Valentinians' story line resembled that of the pagan poets whose gods were constantly commuting between heaven and earth. It amused him to point out how similar this *soter* seemed to the custodians pagans had appointed to preside over a host of human enterprises ranging from love to war and to watch over most stages of personal development. Strange to say, even the unborn had celestial protectors. One god attended conception, returning to heaven to make room for others who helped, in turn, with prenatal care, birth, and nursing. Another arrived to oversee the infant's first steps. Tertullian imagined that traffic down and up must have been horrendously heavy, but he wondered why no god descended to clean up the child's first filth.[24]

How credulous could Christians be? Or was there perhaps a conspiracy afoot? Had pagan philosophers duped Valentinus and company, along with the rest of "their brood," keeping them in the dark? The philosophers were adept at concealing the bluff and bunkum of poetry, which, according to Tertullian, lay beneath the surface of their pseudosophistication. Had the plan been all along to subject the sacred literature to ridicule and thus drive learned Christians to philosophy? As their witless accomplices among the faithful made over Christianity to look like a fable, did the philosophers expect to collect a cargo of converts? Tertullian's special countermeasure was to expose the pagan, poetic fictions and conceits at the foundation of philosophy, discrediting heretical Christian interpreters who admired it.[25]

The brood under attack, for its part, apparently claimed that philosophy helped make sense of puzzling passages in sacred literature. Philosophy relayed revelation, making the will of God intelligible to Christians who would otherwise have been stumped by the obscure references and allusions in the texts. Tertullian admitted that some passages presented problems; he also asserted that philosophy disposed those who used it to range far from the meaning of their Bible, thereby generating more interpretive difficulties than their speculative exercises could ever remove or resolve. Valentinians and the others excited by philosophy ended well beyond the pale of apostolic Christianity. They dragged biblical passages from their contexts, hauling hostage sentences along a backstairs route, as it were, through pagan schools or systems of philosophy, until they imagined they found the truths those passages figuratively expressed. For Tertullian, there were no backstairs routes from mystery to meaning. Everything that was necessary for interpretation was on view somewhere in the sacred texts. The enigmatic or obscure passages could be made plain and unproblematic once other, clearer, topically related statements were discovered, for God guaranteed that there could be no contradiction or inconsistency in scripture.[26]

To illustrate: Say an uncertain phrase snags a Christian's faith in the resurrection of the flesh. Could the old, burst, and discarded wineskins in one of Jesus' parables refer to the physical frames left behind when the faithful take their places in the afterlife? Did the apostle Paul say that spiritual or celestial bodies are utterly different from those we inhabit here? Not so, according to Tertullian, who urged the interpreters to assemble the many, incontestable, biblical references to Jesus' body and to Jesus' resurrection, along with God's promises to reward the faithful, body and soul. Unless other, incorrigibly heretical reviewers were ready to risk eradicating faith to stroke the intellect or acquire philosophical respectability, there would be no further problem. Undoubtedly, the resurrection of the flesh offended reason, but the best interpreters were indifferent to the offense. They busied themselves with the texts rather than with the fashionable ideas of their times, so they were familiar with the weight of textual evidence in favor of the resurrection and acquainted with the Bible's signifying conventions.

> When we read "Go, my people, enter into your closets for a little season, until my anger pass away," we have in the closets graves in which they will have to rest for a little while, who shall have at the end of the world departed this life in the last furious onset of the power of Antichrist. Why else did he use the expression "closets," in preference to some other receptacle, if it were not that the flesh is kept in these closets or cellars salted and reserved for use, to be drawn out thence on a suitable occasion? [Isaiah] shows that after that indignation the flesh will come forth from the sepulcher in which it had been deposited previous to the eruption of divine anger. Now out of the closets nothing else is brought than that which had been put into them, and after the extirpation of Antichrist the process of resurrection will be expeditiously transacted.[27]

I did not select this illustration arbitrarily. Tertullian thought the promise of resurrection central. There could be no fence-sitting; the resurrection was the continental divide of Christian theology. If Christians had no faith in that promise and in Jesus' resurrection, doubts eroded all their confidence in the virtues and rewards described by the church, its executives, and its sacred books. The mystery of resurrection, if "ambiguously announced," would seem more fiction than fact. Without intending to do so, heretical interpreters undermined Christianity, driving Christians to despair and, alas, to philosophy.[28]

And what consolation did philosophy offer? Tertullian could not fathom its appeal among the learned and was certain that the sensible of every stripe would soon reject it. There was nothing consoling in Seneca and Epicurus, for example; they thought that death was final. Some of their colleagues, doubting the prospect of resurrection, either suspended disembodied souls in ether or deposited them on the moon. Well, Tertullian intimated, so much for rationality!

Had philosophers and their brood only looked around, they could easily have learned from simple things, from the phenomenon of sleep, for instance. The soul is active while the body slumbers; its dreams and nightmares document restlessness. Until the body reawakens, however, the soul makes no impression on its environs. Tertullian argued that sleep and awakening are figures of death and resurrection, and he gratefully awarded the author and redeemer of the universe high marks for having made them so, for having instructed the faithful inside the sacred book and out. Those who carefully watched the way the world worked would "initiate faith, nourish hope, and learn both how to die and how to live." But those who listened to the philosophers and their brood would grow inconsolable.[29]

Even philosophers who conceded that immortal souls must have bodies rattled the faithful with such fantasies by denying that any body, once dead, could come alive. Tertullian could not abide the denial, which seemed baseless to him, but he thought a curious doctrine that had attached to it even more objectionable: Several philosophers implanted human souls in the bodies of dogs, mules, peacocks, and pigeons. Philosophy seemed to prefer reincarnation to resurrection, the truth attested by both sleep and scripture. Tertullian defiantly held that resurrection was far more defensible.[30]

Sorcery or History

When those explaining the passages in sacred texts flirted with philosophy, Christianity courted disaster. For Tertullian, philosophically inclined interpreters led the people astray. The consensus that the rules of faith had been formulated to create would easily be dismantled if, as often as not, Christians heard interpreters play down the incarnation, insist that Jesus' flesh was insubstantial, and declare against the resurrection of the body. Recoiling from the resurrection of Jesus as if it were sorcery, the philosophers among the flock, still calling themselves Christians, cast off the most critical part of Christianity. To Tertullian, they were "blind guides" guided by blind guides, for they had tailored their Christianity to fit the requirements for rationality and respectability shaped by pagan philosophers who would never have confirmed the new religion's principal propositions.[31]

Tertullian wanted to put three propositions beyond dispute: (1) Jesus was the savior promised by the Hebrew prophets; (2) he was son of David, seed of Abraham, very much in and of the flesh; (3) his resurrection was a pledge that the flesh of his faithful followers would be restored after their deaths. The statements, needless to say, were related, but the second seems to have been the opposition's favorite target. We already know that Docetists had grave reservations. Gnostics glossed or gave up entirely the passages that gave God flesh, overlooking the scriptural reports of Jesus' corporeality or understating their significance.[32]

The challenge was to emphasize the very passages and propositions that embarrassed the heretics. And so Tertullian relentlessly referred to stories proving that Jesus was no apparition, showing that his flesh and blood were not magicians' tricks. Jesus' flesh neither glowed nor gave way to the touch. It was not, as some insisted, phantom flesh. The gospels documented that Jesus hungered, thirsted, wept; Tertullian labored the point that the Christians' redeemer had taken humble, even contemptible form.

> His body did not reach even to human beauty, to say nothing of heavenly glory. Had the prophets given us no information whatever concerning his ignoble appearance, his very sufferings and the contempt he endured bespeak it all. The suffering attested his human flesh; the contempt proved its abject condition. Would any man have dared touch even with his little finger his body if it had been of an unusual nature, or to smear his face with spit, if it had not invited insult? Why talk of a heavenly flesh when you have no grounds to offer for such celestial theory?[33]

The contempt, humiliation, and suffering reported in sacred literature served a didactic purpose. They composed or enacted the drama of redemption that was then to be reenacted in the lives of all listeners, reducing the distance between savior and saved. The people who assembled to hear their sacred texts read and explained learned that God intended the weak to confound the strong, that a person had to die to the world to live eternally with God, be rejected by this world to be accepted in the next. Flesh and pain taught all this better than philosophy did.[34]

Jesus' flesh, pain, and impermanence on earth were solid evidence for the permanence of God's care for, and power over, history. The incarnation fulfilled old promises; the resurrection then made a new one.[35] The Old Testament predicted that the savior's suffering would precede acceptance and honor. Had Jesus initially come in glory, no one would have identified him as the redeemer mentioned in the Hebrews' sacred books. Marcion might then have cinched his case against the Old Testament. But as it happened, Jesus' contemptible appearance—superficially as incommensurate with his ministry and saving mission as could be imagined, yet directly related to them—forever bound Hebrew to Christian scriptures. The incarnation was neither sorcery nor illusion. According to Tertullian, it was history, a lasting monument in memory to God's fidelity and power. For who could deny that God had promised and delivered? History should have alerted Jews to the realization of their prophecies in the gospels: So much of what was predicted had occurred. And history should have thwarted the Marcionites' unconscionable efforts to get rid of the Old Testament as if it were the obsolete revelation of an inferior god. The continuity between promise and delivery confirmed the historical rationality of Christian revelation.[36]

Heretical interpreters made the flesh of Jesus disappear. Moreover, they upheld Christianity without a foundational faith in the resurrection. Now *that* was sorcery! History, as recorded in the sacred books, offered something more creditable. The Jews' prophecies, together with Jesus' ministry, advertised God's attention to detail and friendly intent: God promised and delivered.[37]

Tertullian complained that philosophers were stubbornly ahistorical, unconcerned with historical conditions affecting the formulations of their very own, purportedly timeless truths. They loved to draw insights from honorable

Socrates' last thoughts on the soul's origin and fate, for example, yet they assumed their hero at the time had been undistracted, clearheaded, and impartial. They badly miscalculated, and their miscalculation, in at least one ledger, cost them their credibility.

The very first sentences of Tertullian's treatise *De anima* recollect that Socrates was facing death when he spoke of the soul. That famous philosopher was badgered by sad and solicitous friends, alarmed by the prospect of leaving his wife widowed, his children orphaned. All his efforts to suppress sorrow, console friends, and maintain composure exhausted him. He barely had reserves to deprive his enemies of the satisfaction of seeing him disconsolate. According to Tertullian, Socrates' ideas on the immortality of the soul were contrived under conditions of such considerable stress that philosophical conviction was hardly a factor. Socrates wanted only to comfort his friends and disappoint his persecutors. Hence, to recycle and rely on his last thoughts without allowing for extenuating and debilitating circumstances were irresponsible, though such action was, Tertullian added, typically philosophical, namely, ahistorical and absurd.[38]

Heretical Christian interpreters of sacred literature were equally ahistorical, Tertullian charged. They managed to uncouple biblical statements that served their speculative interests from the contexts that gave those passages meaning. They drummed constantly, for example, on Jesus' apparent call for curiosity: Ask, seek, knock, and you will find. They used the injunction to justify inquiries that sacrificed the virtue of humility to intellectual games and virtuosity. The philosophically inclined multiplied interpretive possibilities and had the nerve to say that scripture licensed their license. Tertullian responded by specifying that the injunction had been addressed to the Jews. The Gentiles would not have known where to knock; they had not yet known there was a door. But the Jews, after stormy relationships with God, were just outside his favor, a door away from the meaning of divine revelation. And it made a world of difference that God's encouragement to ask, seek, and knock had been directed exclusively to them, for precisely that contextual detail set limits on interpretation and application.[39]

Seeking or knocking, then, had nothing whatsoever to do with philosophy. Matthew's gospel simply told Jews to look more deeply into and beyond Hebrew scripture. Tertullian argued, however, that the "beyond" was not boundless. Some sense of history and greater respect for the spirit as well as the letter of sacred literature should convince interpreters that the task before the Jews was to reflect on Jesus' part in God's revelation, in their salvation. That was a far cry from forcing the world's wisdom on them. They were instructed to seek, but not in the academies of this world and not perpetually. They were to seek but also to find— that is, to find in sacred literature an end to their seeking. Or as Tertullian finally paraphrased the passage, God urged the Jews and Christians as well to "let curious art give place to faith" (*cedat curiositas fidei*).[40]

"If only you look carefully at the contexts," Tertullian promised interpreters, misunderstandings of God's will and Jesus' ministry could be corrected. The conflicts over Jesus' divinity continued, he flatly asserted, alluding to Docetist and Gnostic resistance, because skeptics misconstrued the Old Testament's categorical declarations of God's unity. The context, however, showed that the prevalent concern at the time was competition from other gods. To say there were no other gods was not to say there would be no Jesus. Prohibitions against idolatry, in other words, were not early warnings against Christology.[41]

Interpreters who knew how closely content and context were related also knew that special circumstances prompted biblical directives, which could not be lifted from context and applied indiscriminantly. Therefore, not all directives were universal rules. On one occasion, Jesus had countenanced flight from persecution, but readers-turned-teachers erred when they echoed the statement to sanction cowardice, if not also apostasy. Tertullian counseled Christians to stay put, suffer martyrdom, and display their trust that God arranged all things, even their unhappy fate, for the good. The advice on flight, he said, had to be weighed against weightier biblical themes that transcended circumstance ("blessed are the persecuted") and appreciated in terms of the conditions of utterance. When Jesus had recommended flight, the Christian consensus had been in greater danger than it ever after was; the good news had been carried by too few to survive the death of any. For Tertullian, the lesson here had less to do with courage than with comprehension because to redeem contextual considerations was to render all isolated scriptural utterances more comprehensible and to curb deliberate, although reckless, heretical sprints from the specific to the general. It was also to solidify consensus among Christians and to protect the book from those interpreters only hunting for some specious verification of their peculiar ideas.[42]

Marcion was but one of the heretics in Tertullian's gallery of rogues, yet he was the one who drew most of Tertullian's fire. By arguing that the Old Testament represented the will and work of another, inferior god, Marcion all but proscribed efforts to ascertain continuities, so he posed a formidable threat to the historical rationality of revelation as Tertullian conceived it. Tertullian accused him of having dismissed contextual concerns to vindicate the master variable for his understanding of Jesus and Paul, the unbridgeable chasm between Judaism and Christianity.

What could it have meant that John the Baptist's followers fasted and Jesus' did not? To Marcion, it indicated that Judaism and Christianity were irreconcilable. Not so, replied Tertullian, who countered by supplying the context. No one would have thought twice about diet, he alleged, if the disciples of Jesus and those of John had been serious rivals. The very fact that such a minor discrepancy was noticed at all suggests that friends of John and friends of Jesus were friends of the same God. In Tertullian's hands, oppositions in context ceased to be oppositions of an extreme character.[43]

Tertullian denounced Marcion not only for overlooking historical context but also for altering it drastically by omitting passages or phrases that made his dualism untenable. Impartial interpreters would have no difficulty locating examples. Luke reported, for instance, that a lawyer had once asked Jesus about eternal life and had been directed to read the law. If "eternal" was permitted to stand in the lawyer's inquiry, Jesus' counsel could only substantiate the theological importance of the Old Testament and thus reduce to rubble Marcion's case against it. So Marcion doctored the translation, deleting "eternal"; his lawyer inquired merely about "the law of life." Tertullian appealed to context to save the text. Why would a lawyer have asked Jesus about the laws governing life on earth? *De lege vitae*—lawyers were experts. In all probability, Tertullian improvised, the lawyer had heard that Jesus was raising the dead. Intrigued by so miraculous a reprieve, he had wondered how he, too, could acquire life after death. Jesus' reply signaled that the laws of the Old Testament were indispensable. It was a reply Marcion hardly wanted to hear, but instead of tampering with the answer, he changed the question—and the context.[44]

Tertullian was persuaded late in his career that only the divine spirit's direct intervention assured intelligence about scriptural context, about what he termed "times and causes," or, as we would say, occasions and conditions. Tertullian insisted on stipulating times and causes in his earliest treatises to get the philosophical speculation out of scriptural interpretation. His expositions have been praised for "realism and restraint," applauded for their "down-to-earth view of the historical character of the Bible." Scholars are tempted to make Tertullian a pioneer of historical criticism because he hugged the coastline of sacred literature and seldom experimented with allegory, save for his relatively tame typological readings. He was content to find or insert indirect references to the Old Testament in the New, but he was reluctant to turn whatever he found or inserted into an emblem for, or glimpse of, some special secret. Nonetheless, the specimens already cited in this chapter suggest that Tertullian was by no means averse to cooking up historical contexts.[45]

Tertullian "cooked" or composed for his time as well as for his texts, which is to say that he tried to be both relevant and respectful of the text's authority. His sense of the historical rationality of revelation helped him balance past and present, for he was sure that faithful and informed exposition required not simply the affirmation of continuities between Hebrew and Christian scriptures but also the discovery of correspondences between the original aim of any given passage and its reappropriation in subsequent centuries.

Exposition, explanation, and then reappropriation completed revelation. The Old Testament could not be understood without the New and without interpreters contriving successfully to learn to whom and on what occasions statements were made. That contextual knowledge—and therefore a sense of the meanings of passages from both Testaments—depended on an interpreter's reflective and empathic involvement with the past, an involvement that fused the contexts (or horizons) of text and interpreter. But fusion required a sense of the meaning of the past for the present, for God altered ordinances to fit or address circumstances.[46]

To reconstitute the meaning of a sacred text, an interpreter had to know the historical context. But it was equally important to Tertullian that an interpreter had a fair picture of the present and knew both what the present required and what God required of it.

A Fair Picture of the Present

So much was riding on the interpretation of the sacred book. Interpreters addressed present predicaments and illustrated moral choices. They sifted biblical instructions, identifying the fixed principles and applying them to current crises. Obviously, interpreters needed help, and in the gospel of John Jesus promised that help was on the way—a comforter or Paraclete would tell Christians what Jesus had left unsaid, what they would want to know.[47] Tertullian stipulated that this comforting spirit would first instruct interpreters about Christian discipline. It would inspire and assist them to argue compellingly that Christianity-come-of-age required exemplary behavior of everyone professing the faith. Only then would the Paraclete help them draw their sacred book into that argument.

Critics could reply that the apostle Paul had not commended the strictest discipline when he explained the moral implications of Christianity, and Tertullian admitted that Paul had pulled his punches. But the best interpreters, discerning the context, knew why: Full disclosure would have intimidated new Christians, still weak in faith, and there had been few in Paul's day who had not been new. So unless the apostle had broken ground with concessions, Christianity might never have taken root. The time for concession, however, had passed.[48]

So knowing the times as well as the texts, inspired interpreters understood why Paul, much as Jesus, had deferred telling all, and such interpreters realized that what the savior and apostle had deferred telling—and what they would have to supply—would seem new in the late second and early third centuries. There was no avoiding the problems. The Gnostics had given novelty a bad name. Furthermore, what was new would be hard for Christians to hear—a set of moral standards far more exacting than anything yet developed from the sacred book. Novelty and severity made inspired interpretation unwelcome in some circles. Thoughtful interpreters, Tertullian advised, would anticipate inhospitality and try to reduce points of possible conflict, making sure, with the Paraclete's assistance, that all the perceived novelties were consistent with the rule of faith. They would make certain, therefore, that doctrines were not displaced while morality was improved. It was imperative to explain that novelty, such as it was early in the third century, was not discontinuity.[49]

Tertullian did not want Christians to shrink from occupying that higher moral ground to which the apostle had directed them. Concessions had been forced on Paul, he said, but the churches' executives lived in a very different world; they had no excuses. Inspired scriptural interpreters summarily dismissed executives' appeals to biblical concessions, for the rudiments of an austere discipline were not wanting. Set in sacred literature, lodging particularly in Paul's correspondence, those rudiments awaited prophets, outraged by immorality and counseled by the Paraclete about how Christians might best bear witness to the truth of their religion in a hostile world.[50]

Tertullian early in his career wrote favorably about the churches' executives. At that time, bishops and their deputies seemed to him the likeliest partners for the Paraclete. Yet the executives failed to see—as he came to—the need to assure that the church was uncontaminated by the ways of the world. He began to worry about indiscipline and to think he had been misled.[51] What gave executives away was their practice of pardoning what more puritanical Christians considered unpardonable, especially incest and adultery. Executives gave their pagan critics much to deride insofar as they pronounced against immorality only to absolve the immoral. Tertullian had no objection to clemency. After all, one of Christianity's distinctive and remarkable assertions was that God, constantly confronted with disobedience and ingratitude, had promised to pardon those who repented. But amnesty was not the new religion's only answer to every sin. Mercy did not abrogate divine justice. Church executives acted irresponsibly, Tertullian claimed, if they always spared the rod.[52]

Executives and their apologists drew from a reservoir of scriptural passages commemorating divine compassion and seeming to endorse the policy on penance that Tertullian deplored.

> They toss about much that eviscerates rather than strengthens discipline. Flattering God, they serve themselves. We are able to adduce in rebuttal just as much testimony that shows forth the threat of God's severity and exhibits our own constancy. For although God is good by nature, God is also just. As the case requires, God knows how to heal but also how to strike.[53]

How could interpreters have missed the connection in the apostle's correspondence between divine severity and Christian constancy? Despite his concessions, Paul had been the church's most outspoken censor. He had been a "pillar of discipline." He would never have sanctioned the penance epidemic, would never have endorsed practices that aimed at the correction of all, the repudiation of none. Tertullian admitted that the apostle had pardoned many things, but he had not pardoned everything. In first-century Corinth, incest had been unforgivable; incest centuries later in Carthage had to remain so. Had executives forgotten the apostle's calls for uncompromised conduct? Had they painted their "fair" picture of the present with such flattering pastels that they found no need to censure and condemn? Tertullian knew only that they and their retainers, uninspired interpreters of scripture, failed to turn up the apostle who had armed his heirs (and would have armed them) with a quiver of curses. What they found instead was an apostle of indulgence. Thus, they lost the chance to round off revelation, to conspire with God and to distinguish Christian virtue, the moral high ground, from moderation and the middle ground commended by philosophers.[54]

For Tertullian, biblical exposition and behavior were closely related. If the churches' executives went unopposed, Christianity would appear to condone the most serious sexual offenses.[55] The Paraclete's and prophet's proper role was to impart perspective, to illustrate predicaments facing disciplinarians, and to reform scriptural interpretation.[56] Executives were unlikely to give up the claims that Tertullian had once made for them. They were unlikely, that is, to forget that authority derived from their apostolic succession. The spirit or Paraclete was theirs; they alone were genuine successors of the apostles and prophets, who, they pointed out, had pardoned terrible crimes: Nathan, for instance, had forgiven King David's adultery and homicide. But Tertullian countered that the prophets occasionally had exonerated sinners because they usually and severely had condemned sins. Prophets had first earned reputations for reprimand and only then exhibited mercy. He could find nothing comparable to say about the executives of his time, for they were known to have pardoned promiscuously, with disastrous effect on the moral texture of church life.[57]

To the repeated assertion that church executives were the apostle Peter's executors and were entrusted with his authority to bind *and* to loose, Tertullian replied that powers and pardons were delivered to Peter, *personaliter*. The spirit that had empowered Peter did not settle on institutions or offices; it settled on persons who understood the indispensability, but also the limits, of penance and pardon. And those "spiritual persons" were seldom executives of the established churches. Very early in the third century, it became clear to Tertullian that most executives of his time, in his church, were poor candidates for Peter's vast powers.[58]

Tertullian's former insistence on apostolic tradition was undercut by his subsequent emphasis on prevailing indiscipline, which he put in the foreground of his professedly fair picture of the present. He heaved the ugliest facts of corporate life at his former ideals. The taboos and toughness of an earlier time seemed to have no place in the churches of the early third century. How, then, could continuities be discerned? Where Tertullian once had seen orderly succession, he now saw confusion. The practices and traditions in one city or region contradicted those in others. Time often honored, and local traditions enshrined, error and compromise; the customs of each church were founded on opinion. Recourse to scripture was one remedy. But when overly indulgent executives and their apologists monopolized the interpretation of sacred literature, real remedy would arrive only with a prophet's fair picture of the present, a sound perspective on discipline, and the Paraclete that bestowed both.[59]

Custom founded on opinion left too much to choice and to chance; the Paraclete refined Christians' sense of righteousness, empowering them to "set truth before custom." For the Paraclete was assumed to have been the very same spirit that instructed prophets and apostles.[60] Tertullian asserted that the content and import of their truths were ordinarily understated by church executives and understood only by those prophetic and inspired interpreters whom he defended. Only they could be certain that they perceived what God and the authors of sacred texts meant. Only they had a fair picture of the present. They judged that theirs was no time for concessions to human weakness, no time for polite censorship—the moderately unchaste could no longer to be considered chaste. God would soon call the church to account.[61]

The Paraclete favored the pure and puritanical with its presence, enabling them to bring God's revelation to completion with every inspired application of biblical directives to current crises.[62] The churches' executives failed to enforce the highest standards for discipline; their pet and partisan interpreters of scripture justified this failure by misappropriating passages from the faith's literary treasures. Tertullian held that interpreters who were hostage to the executives' interests did as much damage to the meanings of sacred narratives as did any philosophically inclined heretic. The apologists for executive authority and the philosophers forced divine oracles to conform to, even to ratify, present practices and ideas when they should have been urging all who were listening to refashion understanding and human will to conform to the divine will. Who, then, should interpret and rule? Almost certainly, a caste of puritans and prophets with striking interpretive skills—perhaps, as historian Peter Brown plausibly insinuated, "a spirit-filled gerontocracy"—but Tertullian never specified.[63]

Possibly Tertullian contemplated spiritual leadership when he composed his *De praescriptione* against heretics. His chief purpose was to confirm truth's passage from Jesus through disciples and apostles to recent executives, but Tertullian was also interested in direct inspiration. His first rule of faith stipulated that the spirit conscientiously governed the church: To dismiss heretics' suspicions that there had been miscommunication and uncertainty at the start, he recalled that the Paraclete had visited the disciples soon after Judas was replaced and while they were preparing to circulate word of Jesus' ministry and message around Judaea. Part of that "word," Tertullian determined, was the assurance that the Paraclete would oversee religious instruction in every church. The heretics doubted spiritual superintendence, but Tertullian argued that the unanimity achieved by nearly all Christian congregations attested spiritual vigilance.[64]

Unquestionably in his later work, Tertullian amplified the Paraclete's part while mapping an alternative course to the institutional one advanced in *De praescriptione*. The succession of teaching offices in the church meant less to him as he became frustrated with indiscipline and grew intolerant of partisan and less-than-penetrating scriptural interpretation, to which church executives appealed. The executives had been the hands-on keepers of Christian tradition. Then Tertullian changed his mind, and the Paraclete was "the only prelate because [it] alone succeed[ed] Christ."[65] The executives' picture of the present, he said, was irredeemably out of focus and unfair. They resisted and resented the Montanist prophets, treating them as if they were clowns or, worse, crooks.[66]

Nevertheless, it seemed as if the prophets were on the verge of a breakthrough when the bishop of Rome withdrew his support. Tertullian blamed Praxeas, a heretic, he claimed, with faith in philosophy and with no sense of the Paraclete's powers. Praxeas was unduly influential, and Tertullian believed that the bishop's susceptibility signaled the general unwillingness of executives everywhere to take spiritual counsel. They all liked to listen to learned Christians who pandered to the intellectually curious and morally compromised. Executives feared the spirit; they were trying to halt the progress of revelation.[67]

Tertullian grew confident that the Paraclete disclosed to the Montanist prophets what their times required and the sacred texts relayed. It showed them what provisions and prescriptions completed divine revelation and made for a more robust and a morally textured Christianity. During the first decade of the third century, either slowly or suddenly, it dawned on Tertullian that the inspired interpreters knew something that executives and their friends had forgotten: *Nemo proficiens erubiscit*—there is no shame in making progress.[68]

Making Progress

God could have put a stop to heresy had it not been useful to have heretics circling as hawks to keep their prey alert and resourceful.[69] And as we have seen, heresy *was* useful. It was, for Tertullian, part of an ideal interpretive context: Conflict and crisis edged Christians closer to a consensus and to a more perfect righteousness. Heresy was responsible in some measure for the apologists' earliest extensions of biblical truths—that is, for the churches' first rules of faith. Tertullian introduced his initial formulation by indicting philosophically inclined interpreters. He accused them of parading curiosity as a virtue to capitalize on a consequent eagerness for inquiry and to promote their heresies. The way to counter that contemptible marketing strategy, he argued, was to keep curiosity within proper bounds and to stay alert and articulate against disapproved doctrine.[70]

The churches' executives posed a different challenge for right-minded interpreters and for Christianity. If Tertullian's later polemic can be trusted, bishops prized custom more than they cared for perfection; they attacked inspired interpreters bent on remedying indiscipline, rehabilitating revelation, and perfecting the religion. God could have silenced attackers had their opposition not contributed to an advantageous interpretive context, had the Montanist prophets not needed executives and adversity as well as the Paraclete to spur them to make progress.

The objective was always to clarify, amplify, and advance the good news in Christianity's sacred texts and to elaborate implications for personal righteousness and church discipline. The apostle Paul knew the storyline: Opposition arose, he said, so that "those who are genuine among you may be recognized," so that a Christianity faithful to its texts and fruitful for its times might be all the more conspicuous. That view was central for Tertullian's work. Of course, there was a risk that dreadful doctrine would acquire notoriety and perhaps an unintended appeal while apologists labored to confute it. Executives, too, might achieve a certain celebrity while Montanist prophets arraigned their practices. But Tertullian expected that controversy, no matter what the short-term effects, cumulatively built consensus around three ultimately incontestable propositions and pivots of Christian doctrine: the corporeality of Jesus, the historicity of the resurrection, and the historical rationality of revelation.

Tertullian gave over much of his largest canvas, the treatise against Marcion, to his opponent's special pleading, reproducing Marcion's interpretations of biblical passages to dismantle his argument for two gods and for the irreconcilability of the two Testaments. The advantage was that Marcion's otherwise worthless, though treacherous, seductive ideas drove Tertullian to declare ever more compellingly that New Testament revelations called believers into a new age, yet not into the service of some new god. Could the historical rationality of God's revelations have been articulated as forcefully without the heretic?[71]

Episcopal critics of the new prophecy also provided precious provocation. Their alleged indifference to strict discipline and especially their contempt for Montanist prophets helped the more astute and discerning prophetic reformers understand empathically the apostle Paul's predicaments and indignation. In other words, hostile church executives made it easier for the prophets to reconstruct the contexts of their favorite texts. The Montanists experienced what Paul had experienced: antagonism, skepticism, arrogance. Much greater assistance undeniably came with and from the Paraclete, the spirit the Montanists shared with the apostle as they developed their apostolic perspective on, and impatience with, current Christian practice. The later Tertullian certainly thought that Montanists were Paul's authentic descendants; their prophets were so unlike the executives whom he and they accused of being more eager to issue furloughs than enforce discipline.

From Tertullian's perch, church executives seemed to have comprehended their times and texts no better than philosophers who soared above contexts and deployed scriptural passages to endorse and ennoble unscriptural ideas. But if we survey the prospects from the executives' loft, times, texts, and contexts look quite different. For from that perspective, progress amounted to growth, and, simply put, growth generally required the extension of penitential discipline, an extension that occasionally necessitated the renegotiation, and even the relaxation, of penalties. The executives looked for room to maneuver; the next chapter was, and is, theirs.[72]

3

Leadership: Bishops, Councils, and Emperors

Rome was crowded with ideas. People arrived from all over the empire to exchange goods, services, favors, and theories. Marcion was not the first to come to the city during the second century to hawk some special brand of Christianity; nor was he the last. By the end of the century, Valentinians, Marcionites, Montantists, adoptionists, and monarchians had divided the Christian community into camps, and several of the church's more prominent executives were straining against the diversity, straining, that is, to articulate orthodoxy, a singularly authoritative way to understand revelation, resurrection, repentance, and morality.

Perhaps their predecessors had decided to appease all factions rather than to favor one and anger others because adoptionists were startled, they said, when authorities in Rome pronounced against them. Adoptionists were sure God appointed or adopted Jesus, "a mere man," to convey divine truths, and they had no recollection that the church's executives in Rome had ever insisted on an alternative interpretation, no memory that the church had ever endorsed propositions that favored the preexistence and divinity of Jesus.[1] But precedent or none, from 186 to the 220s Bishops Victor, Zephyrinus, and Callixtus were intent on reaching some consensus on Christology. The adoptionists were heard disputing the divinity of Jesus and were shown the door.

That was not the end of it. Christology generated plenty of controversy early in the third century. Some complained that the adoptionists' enemies compromised divine unity, exaggerating the distinctiveness of Jesus' preexistent divinity. Bishop Callixtus had an answer; he said that father and son were the same reality yet were different manifestations of the divine spirit. Both the manifestations existed, although not as distinct deities, before God created the material world, thus before the incarnation. But the bishop's answer failed to impress the outspoken theorists of preexistence. They preferred to personalize father and son (or logos). Hippolytus, speaking for them, could neither find nor fathom any different features where there were no distinctions. Callixtus, he charged, was running from adoptionists right into the camp of monarchians, who alleged God was father *and then* son, identical with the son, whose incarnation was God's creation of himself as a separate mode of divinity.[2]

Callixtus expelled Sabellius, the leading monarchian, but that did not satisfy the defenders of a preexistent logos. They were angry with the bishop for having turned a deaf ear to their appeals. Hippolytus was also upset because Callixtus had acquired a large following. He accused Callixtus of deliberately trading doctrine and discipline for popularity and thus put a sinister spin on the policy that historian Manlio Simonetti called "comprehensivist" and "centrist." In all, Hippolytus denied the wisdom of steering a course between extremes, between distinctive, preexistent divinity and the absolute identity of father and son.[3]

Growth invited diversity, diversity often led to conflict, and conflict, to say the least, complicated efforts to achieve unanimity among members of growing congregations. The churches' executives, therefore, would have been hard-pressed to reconcile their objectives, growth and consensus, had they not discovered that their hard line against diversity actually favored both.

Greek and Roman religions had long offered initiates a dazzling variety of mysteries and rituals. Nevertheless, "you could pile one religious insurance on another yet not feel safe," if E. R. Dodds judged correctly. Dodds thought tolerance and diversity undermined religious security in late antiquity, and he claimed that the new Christian religion's popularity and its "victory" over paganism resulted from its "exclusiveness." Christianity all but "lifted the burden of freedom from the shoulders of the individual," he continued; "one choice, one irrevocable choice, and the road to salvation was clear"—clearer still, of course, were it not posted with rival Christologies. So while Christianity made "a clean sweep" of the pagans' alternative mysteries (Dodds again), the churches' executives swept their own quarters and created a more or less single-minded religion, which enjoyed decisive advantages over a polymorphic paganism. Pagan cults simply could not compete with Christian congregations "in an age of anxiety."[4]

Anxiety in the third century was not simply a consequence of the burden of freedom and the vast supply of religions; social disorientation, military setbacks, and political disintegration contributed to the uneasiness in the empire. In 200, Tertullian could still assert that the government kept barbarians at bay, that Rome could rightly claim credit for peace and prosperity along the North African coast. But a half century later, Cyprian of Carthage was worried about widespread corruption, anarchy, and demoralization. Raids across the empire's frontiers decimated some communities, distressed others. Affluent Antioch nearly fell to the Persians in 242. Peasant insurgency complicated and then compromised the defense of Gaul. Only one of the twenty-six reigning emperors escaped violent death during the third century. Charles Cochrane's conclusions complement those offered by Dodds: "Such miserable records as survive," Cochrane declared, "point to an intensification of anxiety as the empire plunged into more and more hopeless confusion . . . [and as] men began to anticipate the end of the world." Yet in that end, if one could count on the predictions of the prophet Isaiah, "the house of the Lord will be established and all nations will flow to it." Bishop Firmilian of Caesarea in Cappadocia wrote to Cyprian in 256, reminding him of that consolation and assuring that Christians were fortunate indeed to share that "house" in such desperate times.[5]

The church was seen as something of a way station where hope for the next world flourished, presumably because this world appeared to be hostile and hopeless. During the third century, Christianity often came under attack; this world's hostility, however, only confirmed Christians' convictions about its approaching end and made for much greater congregational and cultic solidarity. The faithful were happy to have secure points of reference in, as well as refuge from, their patchwork empire, which seemed just then to be coming apart. Bishops and priests were regarded as parents in their extended families, indeed, as far more influential than parents. For natural parents only gave their children life, John Chrysostom later observed, but priests gave Christians eternal life, interceding for them to avert God's anger. As churches emphasized priestly paternity and sacramental intercession, the priests' cultic functions gained even greater prominence. But long before Chrysostom explained how priests, as parents, protected their "children," those parents were offering sacrifices, recapitulating Jesus' sacrifice and presenting it as a eucharist both to God (as a gift from their people) and to the people (as a gift from God).[6]

Third-century lists of church offices and cultic functions document what has been called a *hierarchisation* of church leadership. Bishops were atop the hierarchy. They presided over sacrifice and sacrament as priests. They learned from those who preceded them and from sacred texts; then as teachers they groomed others to impart the meaning of Christianity. Naturally, bishops were organizers as well. They appointed elders and watched over their deliberations; they tried to manage conflict and struggled to shape consensus. Disputes over discipline and doctrine made for generations of constant crisis, but in the third century episcopal monarchy was the norm or rule.[7]

Persecution and Pardon: Cyprian of Carthage

Cyprian, the leading third-century theorist of episcopal and conciliar authority, was elected bishop of Carthage, possibly the busiest port on the Mediterranean Sea, in 249, late in the reign of Emperor Philip. Philip seems to have been relatively friendly to Christians—not openly and officially antagonistic. A century later, it was rumored that had the bishop of Antioch dropped a demand for full public disclosure of the emperor's sins, Philip would have professed his faith and participated in eucharistic celebrations. Eusebius of Caesarea was the chef-chronicler who cooked up the tale to give political history a somewhat milder flavor, but even he did not hide the fact that violence against Christians could erupt at any time, regardless of the emperor's friendship. Too many pagans blamed Christianity for too much of their misfortune. During Philip's last year, an unnamed scoundrel incited a mob in Alexandria to stampede through the streets, loot Christians' homes, and murder those residents who refused to make scandalous charges against their faith. Then came the official persecution, soon after Philip was killed in Verona by Decius, who resented whomever his predecessor had favored. Decius's edict against Christianity arrived in Alexandria early in 250; its purpose, to compel Christians to give up monotheism and worship government-approved gods. The new emperor and his deputies gathered that the best way to overcome any resistance was to go after the churches' leaders. Bishop Dionysius of Alexandria was immediately hunted down. Cyprian fled from Carthage and was able to stay hidden.[8]

Bishops should withdraw, he said, if prudence recommended and circumstance permitted. Nonetheless, they should remain in communication with less conspicuous colleagues in the ministry whose relative obscurity in the city enabled them to carry on more freely. Cyprian noted that the churches' chief executives were easy targets; running for cover was a responsible, not a cowardly, response to the crisis. Life on the run, far from the city, was no picnic. Episcopal refugees had no leisure. Thieves and wild animals constantly preyed on the fugitives, whose daily battles against hunger, thirst, climate, and loneliness added to their ordeals.[9]

Presbyters in Rome recoiled when they heard about Cyprian's "retirement." Their bishop, Fabian, had been martyred soon after Decius declared war on Christianity, and they saw persecution as a test of faith, martyrdom as the prize for victory. Fabian won; Cyprian had not, and lasting shame attached to the faint heart. The church authorities in Rome pointed out to their counterparts in Carthage that executives who were less than courageous greatly complicated the work of those left behind. It was up to them to steel the nerves of the confessors held in prison as well as monitor the remorse and penance of the lapsed, those who had caved under pressure and wanted pardon and readmission. Clerical superiors in hiding could hardly be cited as models.[10]

Cyprian did not respond promptly to his critics. He was preoccupied with and troubled by his presbyters' unauthorized readmission and reintegration of the lapsed, some of whom had rushed to the pagans to avoid the slightest inconvenience. Of course, others had submitted under considerable duress. Then there were those who purchased certificates attesting sacrifices they had never made to the pagans' gods, purchases thought to have been the equivalent of apostasy, a desertion of the faith. But what is surprising is that so many of the lapsed were anxious to participate again in their churches' eucharist and worship before the persecution had run its course. Many who had the certificates as a result of their sacrifices or bribes sought another kind of document; they approached the confessors in prison and asked for letters of recommendation. Did they figure that the presbyters would find it difficult to refuse recommendations and requests from the local heroes of the faith? Perhaps they anticipated that support from the confessors would eliminate the need for extended periods of penance, public confession, and the ceremonial act of reconciliation and readmission. The church expected all that from the remorseful, but all that, the public disclosure of remorse, was dangerous in those extraordinary times.

The presbyters in Carthage thought that extraordinary times called for extraordinary measures. They honored the confessors' petitions and welcomed back the lapsed, suspending traditional penitential practices. Cyprian believed that crisis called for consistency rather than change. Secure points of reference were all the more precious, he asserted, when all else was uncertain. Furthermore, to suspend fundamental rules for reintegration was to jeopardize the salvation of the very persons whom suspensions and shortcuts were devised to serve. Premature reconciliation did not fortify the faithful against further temptations. A quick fix was no fix at all. It could not bring genuine consolation, and it sent the wrong signal to those who persevered in righteousness. Cyprian urged everyone in the city—presbyters, confessors, and lapsed—to await his return from exile. When peace was restored, there would be time to examine the conditions under which each penitent had lapsed, to take account of the confessors' clemency, and to assign the appropriate penances.[11]

The bishop wished that the confessors had been more discerning and selective when issuing letters for the lapsed. He regretted and protested that the confessors' kindness had given presbyters in Carthage an occasion to suspend disciplinary procedures, yet he was understandably reluctant to blame those who had suffered for their faith. He assumed the confessors agreed with him that reconciliation should follow normalization, if only because he was uncomfortable frowning at them. Instead, he slapped at his presbyters, the executives still in residence who were acting against

> the law of the gospel. They conspicuously offer sacrifice for the lapsed and admit them to the eucharist before having them do penance, confess their grave and horrible sin, and receive reconciliation from the bishop and clergy. Presbyters dare to profane the sacred body of the Lord, although it is written, "whoever therefore eats the bread or drinks the cup of the Lord in an unworthy manner will be guilty of profaning the body and blood of the Lord." True, the lapsed may be forgiven for this; who would not rush to be revived after defecting and dying to God? But the job of the appointed leaders is to instruct the hasty and the uninformed. Otherwise, pastors become butchers of their sheep. For to forgive those as yet unreformed is to deceive them. No lapsed person is made upright by such deception. On the contrary, because God is offended, the lapsed [and too hastily absolved] are driven much faster to ruin. Therefore, let the presbyters, who ought to have been your teachers, learn from you [confessors], and let them hold your requests for the bishop.[12]

It seemed wise to make an exception, and Cyprian allowed that persons who had acquired confessors' recommendations and who were fatally ill ought to be readmitted without delay after making their confessions. For the healthy who could not wait, however, there was a time-honored route to salvation that no bishop would block: Lapsed Christians could simply screw their courage to the sticking place, making themselves confessors and martyrs.[13]

Cyprian could only have been half serious; apostasy, after all, demonstrated a temperament not quite made for martyrdom. It was not unthinkable, only improbable, that the lapsed would have hastened to pay for their sins with their lives. Haste, however, seemed to Cyprian to be his church's primary problem. He did not trust the lapsed who were frantic for redemption. He was unhappy that the confessors and presbyters were so quick to oblige. They were accomplices in undermining order, not just the church order and discipline over which the bishop should preside but the very order of salvation. Cyprian thought his presbyters guiltiest of the lot. They ought to have been educating confessors and lapsed alike, dramatizing the danger of relying on the interventions of their peers: "Cursed is the man who trusts in man." Haste based on the goodwill of the worthiest intermediaries availed nothing. The confessors could not give sinners their righteousness. Prayers, appeals, and recommendations from the faithful in prison and on the threshold of martyrdom were valuable, but righteousness was required of the lapsed—and its discernment and measure, of the bishop.[14] From Cyprian's perspective, only bishops stood between impulsive penitents and their ruin and, in Carthage, between the reckless presbyters and the ruin of the church. That was exactly what a good pastor or father was supposed to do, which surely was why God set bishops atop the hierarchy and set them against the haste and hocus-pocus that promised penitents a prompt and painless reprieve.[15]

When Decius was killed campaigning against the Goths in 251, official persecution ceased for a time, and Cyprian came home to manage the church's affairs. He summoned his episcopal colleagues to a meeting to discuss procedures and penance. Presumably to a sympathetic audience, he declared it the bishop's prerogative to inquire into the conditions under which each apostate had lapsed. Confessors might advise them, but only bishops set the terms for reconciliation. Should the terms of any bishop seem frivolous or extreme, conferences of bishops—councils and synods—would then ascertain the circumstances and come to some judgment about his discretion and conduct.[16]

Rigorists were wary. They thought some bishops too lenient, and they expected Cyprian to agree. Not long before, he had resisted his presbyters' efforts to suspend penitential discipline. But after returning to Carthage, he concluded that his church's interests were better served by compassion.[17] Rigorists contended that amnesty after one persecution weakened resistance to the next. Cyprian replied that Christians' virtues were not dependent on their executives' punishment of vices. Forgiven, or even uncensured, sins did not automatically imperil virtue. Had pardons for promiscuity made chastity obsolete? Obviously not. And martyrdom would never have failed to attract decisive Christians, he continued, because it was the way to acquire rewards for faith in an instant. The bishop's kindness might shorten the route to reconciliation for the luckiest among the lapsed, yet it could not allay anxieties about salvation. It did not offer the lapsed the kind of assurance and relief enjoyed by the confessors and martyrs. For reconciled sinners could never be sure that God would put through the pardons their churches had issued. Everything remained unsure until the day of judgment.[18]

Cyprian conceded that bishops made mistakes. But what were the alternatives? If grief got sinners back to churches, should the bishops always turn sinners away? Even if executives proved to be too generous and councils too complacent to correct them, God would make the proper determinations in due time. Reconciliation did not automatically and infallibly signal redemption. Cyprian suspected that rigorists wanted their bishops to preempt divine judgments. To him, they seemed smugly certain that they knew what God required. Seceding from more moderate executives, they wrecked chances for a much-needed churchwide consensus on readmission. The rigorists might someday die as martyrs, Cyprian said—their unyielding spirit made martyrdom a pretty safe bet—but their severity and inflexibility doubtlessly would bar them from heaven. They would spend eternity elsewhere because they lacked charity.[19]

Novatian, an esteemed presbyter in Rome, was so disturbed by the appointment of the mild and moderate Cornelius as bishop that he set up an independent altar. Novatian's secession was well known around the Mediterranean, particularly after he dispatched delegates to win support. But Cyprian's North African colleagues were slow to take sides. Cornelius's record was exemplary; he had risen through the ranks at a respectable rate. Novatian, however, appealed to instincts—once Cyprian's—and urged caution in the readmission of the lapsed. In North Africa, if not also in Rome, what finally tipped the scales was Novatian's insolence. He dared to disobey his bishop. He tried to unseat an incumbent, to depose God's deputy, and, failing that, to promote schism and overturn God's order.[20]

Cyprian appealed to the vast compass of that divine order when he wrote Cornelius to explain why the North African church took some time to endorse his election. The delay, Cyprian said, was God's doing. Novatianists pressed for rearrangements not just in Rome but elsewhere. They found allies among rigorists in nearly every district or diocese. To achieve the unanimity that would enable Cornelius, Cyprian, and moderate colleagues to prevail against Novatianists and their allies, God gave the bishops in North Africa time to get rid of the doubts and suspicions that the rigorists had planted, to hear from investigators sent to Rome, and to approve Cornelius without exception or dissent.[21]

The investigators probably inquired about the character of the rival candidates in Rome. They would have had no difficulty determining the priority of Cornelius's appointment; Novatian's was quite clearly a reaction. Cyprian placed enormous value on proper electoral procedure, so we may infer that he asked the investigators to check on the rituals of clerical and popular consent. To prove that Cornelius's election was divinely sanctioned, they would have had to audit the community's response and certify that his candidacy had been widely acclaimed.

Community participation and acclamation normally resembled more a public hearing than a popular vote. There were practical reasons to prefer crowds and publicity to backroom negotiations and deliberations, the results of which could easily be influenced by fees and fraud. Cyprian noted that rituals of consent and acclaim afforded opportunities to assess candidates' virtues and identify their vices. That was why the apostle Peter had assembled a crowd to discuss Judas's replacement, Cyprian argued, conveniently forgetting that instead of sifting qualifications, onlookers watched while the candidates cast lots. A principal reason for popular acclaim, viewed from Cyprian's seat, was that it expressed God's judgment or choice (*Dei judicium*). The voice of the people, not the luck of the draw, was the voice of God.[22]

The obvious implication is that outstanding choices were the rule, although Cyprian knew there were exceptions. When it became clear to episcopal colleagues that a mistake had been made, they had to remedy it, he advised, depose the incumbent, and nominate a replacement. Bishops in conference possessed that authority, but a bishop's rivals and subordinates on site did not. Novatian, for instance, had no standing whatsoever against Cornelius. Much the same was true of a deacon who challenged the aged Numidian Bishop Rogatianus in the late 240s. Cyprian reminded the challenger that Jesus had exhibited respect to the high priests; therefore, those who were called to imitate Jesus' humility were all the more bound to obey executives, who unlike those priests, held their commissions from God. Apostles and bishops were named by God. They then named deacons to help them. To mutiny against the maker was monstrous disloyalty, whether the deacons turned on bishops or the bishops turned on God.[23]

We might infer that Bishop Stephen of Rome tried to apply Cyprian's principles when, knowing no episcopal judgment against Basilides, he ordered the Spanish bishop reinstated. Cyprian saw the situation differently and wrote on behalf of the congregation that had deposed Basilides. Rome's reversal of its decision was quite inconsistent with local autonomy, but autonomy was established, if at all, in custom, not in law, and the prestige of the old capital attracted petitioners as well as pilgrims to its churches for many years. Basilides, however, seems to have been the first bishop outside Italy to have placed a case before the bishop of Rome. Cyprian did not appear to consider the fact or form of an appeal outrageous or objectionable, but he did think Rome made the wrong call. He was careful not to blame Stephen, assuming that his colleague was misinformed, that Stephen had not been told about his petitioner's discreditable behavior during the most recent persecution.[24] By bribes or sacrifices, Basilides obtained the certificate from pagan authorities that saved him from prison. After the persecution, he was pardoned, readmitted to the church, and laicized, which is to say he was deprived of his clerical status. He was no longer eligible for an episcopal appointment. He could not be bishop if he were not a priest; no council was needed to determine that much. Moreover, as Cyprian reported, the election of his successor had gone without a hitch. Episcopal consent and popular acclaim made Sabinus bishop, *de Dei judicio*. Basilides came out of this rather badly. He violated the terms of his penance and pardon, misrepresented the circumstances that led to his laicization and deposition, and, on the strength of Stephen's orders, shamelessly pressed several Spanish bishops to countenance his reinstatement and thus divide the church.[25]

We know nothing about this episode's outcome, but Cyprian's correspondence tells us a bit about how the claims for, and the resistance to, episcopal, conciliar, and Roman jurisdiction were tested in the middle of the third century. His insistence on the laicization of failed leadership makes him seem an enemy of the permissive practices condemned by Hippolytus and Tertullian, yet he disagreed with those critics, defended the bishop's right to dictate the terms for penance, and doubted that rigorists had an adequate vision of the church's functions and future. But the pull of his position drew Cyprian to close ranks with rigorists and to demand that episcopal councils assure that each bishop be beyond reproach. The reason seemed self-evident to him, and he sounded genuinely surprised when the occasional executive balked at relinquishing a post and forced him to labor the obvious: Bishops who lapsed would forever be registers of human weakness, certainly not indices of church strength.[26]

Cyprian later extended the penalty of laicization to those executives who wished to return to their churches after having experimented with heresy. In 256, again lecturing Stephen, Cyprian summarized the findings of the council he had assembled in Carthage to approve the extension:

> Dear brother, we add something more about which we have reached a consensus. Presbyters, deacons, and others are ordained in the Catholic church and then defect and stand against us. . . . Should any of these officials return to the church, they ought to be received as laymen. They should attend the communion as laymen, and it should be enough that they are welcome at all. . . . Can there be a greater crime than to have fought furiously for discord and against the concord and consensus of the people of God? Even if these officals return to the church, they cannot restore others seduced by them who perished outside the church without enjoying its peace and communion.

Executives who lapsed compromised the dignity of their church, and executives who flirted with heresy compromised its unity. Neither set could be trusted again with the prerogatives and privileges of office. Furthermore, the reinstatement of those compromising—and thus compromised—officials left episcopal colleagues with little to say to Christians who never lapsed, never withdrew, to the *non recedentes*. What can we tell the innocent, Cyprian asked Stephen, if we typically and richly reward the guilty?[27]

The bout between Basilides and Sabinus was not the only contest to bring the bishops of Rome and Carthage to ringside, although the next time we find Stephen and Cyprian corresponding about extra-Italian matters, they are in the same corner. Cyprian was urging Stephen to intervene in Gaul, where there was no prepotent Gallic bishop to umpire disputes and as yet no significant regional synod activity.

Bishop Faustus of Lyons had written to Cyprian for counsel and cooperation when a neighbor and colleague appeased rigorists and shut his church to many local penitents. Bishop Marcianus of Arles, just as Novatian, thus became "an enemy of God's mercy." Probably because Carthage was so far from the crisis, Cyprian turned the problem over to Rome, expecting Stephen to take two analogies seriously and act appropriately. When harbors became hazardous, helmsmen look for other refuge from rough seas, so it is smart as well as responsible for those along the coast to post warnings and direct them to safer ports. And if it is too risky to approach a particular inn, provident proprietors designate or furnish alternative shelter for travelers. Cyprian wanted Bishop Stephen to have Marcianus deposed, to close down his "harbor" and "inn" to prevent the wreck or ruin of those Christians who sought fellowship with the rigorists at Arles. Why the job fell to Rome is not altogether clear, although Cyprian may have supposed that Stephen was somehow bound to champion the comprehensivist policy of his predecessor, Callixtus.[28]

The trail left by Cyprian is hard to follow. His comments on the controversy in Arles appear to head toward an endorsement of Roman jurisdictional supremacy, yet how could he conceivably have had much confidence in Stephen's management? Stephen accommodated Basilides, unwittingly (to give Stephen the benefit of the doubt) but decisively helping split the Spanish church. Rome reinstated a disreputable bishop; Spain sped into schism. Moreover, Stephen had been slow to commit himself against the rigorists, needing thick lenses from North Africa to see the problems in Gaul. Cyprian was irritated, and his irritation developed into outright opposition when Stephen objected to the rebaptism of heretics returning to the church. For rebaptism was the custom in Carthage.[29]

Cyprian admitted that the apostle Peter was the "rock" on which the church was built and that the bishops of Rome, as his heirs, acquired a certain celebrity status. Peter, however, was not infallible; the apostle Paul reprimanded him with just cause, according to Cyprian's reading of the account given in the Acts of the Apostles. Besides, celebrity was not the same as and did not necessarily imply supremacy.[30] The questions of appellate jurisdiction and supreme authority in church affairs were not yet answered definitively. There is little evidence they were raised systematically. The third century, as Enzio Gallicet observed, was still some distance from producing "a general theory of the church." Cyprian composed pronouncements on discipline and organization to resolve specific conflicts; he was, as I said at the start, the leading theorist of episcopal authority and—calling on North African bishops to exercize collective oversight—of conciliar authority as well, but he had no chance to refine theories and piece everything together.[31]

Another persecution drove Cyprian from his see in 258. This time, however, he was apprehended and executed. His final letters and the last year of his life memorably associate leadership with martyrdom, for he suggested that the churches' executives had to be guides along the steep, rugged path from adversity through death to eternal life.[32] A decade earlier, during and immediately after Decius's short reign and the brief, yet intense persecution of the church, confessors and rigorists so jostled some of the churches' chief executives that Cyprian's tributes to the confessors' courage were accompanied by his demands for their obedience to the bishops. Yet the bishop of Carthage exited with unfeigned and unqualified admiration for the martyrs, among whom he was numbered after 259. Administrative difficulties created by persecution and pardon were left for others to resolve, but the resolution came long after the government grew much friendlier to Christianity.

Persecution and Patronage

Gallienus became emperor in 260 and showed no interest in persecuting Christians. For the next forty years, they were only intermittently hectored and harassed. Emperor Aurelian thought of circulating an edict against them in 275, but nothing came of the idea. Eusebius of Caesarea looked on the long calm as something of a miracle. He sensed that God let there be peace so that bishops could repair old and vandalized churches, build several new ones, and journey unmolested to regional and faraway councils to repair or build consensus on critical issues. No doubt at the meetings church executives heard complaints like those lodged against the comprehensivists at midcentury, for Novatian had done more than raise objections to a particular bishop; he had tapped into a stream of discontent with institutional policy that fed the frenzy for purity animating many Christians. His partisans multiplied, yet it took another round of persecution and pardon—another ordeal and advantageous outcome for the new religion—to rekindle the strident opposition to moderate church administrators.[33]

It is said that victory over the Persians during the 290s "gave a new force to the ideals of Roman discipline and Roman god-given glory" and that "the last great persecution [of the Christians] was born from [that] success."[34] Emperor Diocletian presided over the heroics on the eastern frontier, the nostalgia for old ideals, and the increasing enmity against the new faith. He particularly disliked the kind of Christianity advocated by the devotees of Mani, probably because Manichaeanism originated in Persia (though its Docetic Christology and severe dualism were known as far west as Carthage and Rome). But Diocletian was also incited against Christianity by pagan priests who said that they could not retrieve oracles and omens from their gods as long as the emperor hospitably received Christians of any stripe at court or accepted them into his armies.

More than a decade later, when the edicts of persecution were rescinded, a government official remembered that popular pressure had played a large part in getting emperor, priests, and lesser lights to persecute the Christians. He maintained that citizens, alarmed by the phenomenal growth of the new religion and the corresponding neglect of the traditional cults, compelled authorities to pull the Christian juggernaut to the curb.[35] That claim, however, was presumably a result of the rush to exonerate and exaggerate—perhaps to exonerate a single claimant but almost certainly to exaggerate the new religion's influence—and we should greet it now with great suspicion. But whereas the causes of "the last great persecution" are conjectural, consequences are well attested. The Christians were expelled from the army in 299. Four years later, the first edict was posted in Nicomedia, the emperor's headquarters in the eastern empire. Christians were forbidden to worship their God. Their sacred texts would soon be confiscated and burned, their churches leveled. And when Diocletian retired in 305, two rabidly intolerant caesars, Galerius and Maximinus, shared power in the east, hounded Christian executives, and herded them to prison.

Egypt, it seems, was hardest hit. Dozens were brutally put to death in a single day. Mourners were dragged to Palestine to work in the mines. Eusebius specified that the Thebaid in upper Egypt experienced especially intense persecution, yet the Nile delta knew no peace for eight years.[36] What brought Melitius of Lycopolis hundreds of miles downriver to the Nile delta is still a mystery. Perhaps he was one of several rigorists sent to inform Bishop Peter of Alexandria about the hardships in the hinterland. Perhaps he braved the long journey to have Peter consecrate him as successor to Bishop Apollonius, who had capitulated to government authorities.

We hear much more about why Melitius stayed than about why he came, for his stay was controversial. Melitius found the delta churches without their bishops. They said from prison that they had made provisions for the welfare of their communities, for preaching, teaching, liturgy, and aid to the destitute, but Melitius thought otherwise. He stepped in to provide essential services and to appoint deputies to replace the bishops' agents. For their part, the imprisoned executives rejected the idea that Melitius was only a conscientious colleague responding to the emergency. They believed he was a cunning opportunist turning their absence to his advantage and to the advantage of their enemies, whom he illicitly promoted to serve and lead their churches.[37]

In any event, the effects of Melitius's meddling show how persecution and schism often went together. Government hostility intensified rivalries within the delta churches. When Melitius disposed of Peter's agents in Alexandria and then favored their critics, he stirred stored-up animosities and generated new ones. Conflict and schism spread quickly and existed conspicuously for the next fifty years in the Thebaid, where the Melitian bishops courted support from monks. What started in the delta during the last great persecution could be stopped only much later, long after Emperor Constantine had become personally and politically interested in Christianity and thought it inexcusable that the new religion, which he expected to unite his empire, was itself deeply divided.

Constantine spent years of his youth at Diocletian's court, so he must have been aware of the government's measures against the Christians. But his father had no stomach for persecution and never fully implemented those measures in the northwest quarter of the empire he was left to govern when Diocletian retired. In 306, Constantine rejoined his father, who died soon thereafter. The troops demanded that son replace father, and Diocletian's other successors had no choice but to accede.[38]

At first, Constantine seemed indifferent to religion and concentrated on consolidating his power in Gaul and Britain. He tripped up opposition within his territories and twice crossed the eastern frontier to confront intruders in theirs. In only a few years, he proved himself a competent commander in the field, a caesar worthy of his partisans' loyalties. Meanwhile, Galerius, Diocletian's principal heir, was far less fortunate. He alienated his subjects in Rome and in the rest of peninsular Italy, taxing them as if they were provincials. He marched the praetorian guard from the capital and into his field army, planing the prestige of both the guard and the city.

Maxentius, his son-in-law, was eager to capitalize on the discontent. He killed Galerius's chief agent in the region and grabbed control over Italy and North Africa. He decimated one army sent to overrun his new share of the empire and exhausted another. But defense was extremely costly. It cost Maxentius his popularity; he had to tax and spend if he expected his troops to help him preserve his authority. In 308, his North African subjects protested and stopped supplying grain to Rome. Hunger and rage in the capital led to riots, which Maxentius had savagely suppressed. City streets littered with lifeless bodies hardly recommended him to those left standing. His inveterate enemy, Galerius, was dying, but Maxentius's days were numbered.

The chance to be the beneficiary of Maxentius's unpopularity drew Constantine from his quadrant. He understood that he had to move quickly to beat Galerius's successor to Italy and sensed he could use, and should arrange for, divine support. While contemplating his campaign, he had a vision and either seized on or acquiesced in the interpretation that he had been invited to conquer in the name of Jesus. Maxentius was not a ruthless persecutor; quite the contrary, he was curiously kind to Christians. But Constantine was a Christian, or very nearly so, when he arrived before Rome. The fact that Maxentius proceeded to lose everything, his territory and his life, so suddenly and dramatically made God's purpose crystal clear, possibly to Constantine, unquestionably to his eulogists. From the range of options available to the besieged, Maxentius selected what turned out to be the worst imaginable. The usurper left the city, crossed the Tiber, and readied his forces for the fight. Before long, disaster struck; the enemy fell on him, and he could not manage to retreat to the safety of the city. Immediately after the rout, Constantine entered the capital, the North Africans resumed their shipments of grain, and the Romans were spared the effects of a difficult winter. The events and outcome of 312 seemed divinely orchestrated. Constantine's victory was complete and impressive, scored by the Christians' God, so to speak, to make emphatic and, some said, irreversible the deliverance of their religion.[39]

Constantine was extravagantly grateful. He lavished gifts, privileges, and immunities on the churches' chief executives. He subsidized the restoration of their churches and larded imperial law with ordinances favoring their faith. The new emperor may not have suppressed pagan opposition as quickly as and to the extent that the Christians wanted (I am guessing), but cordial relations soon developed between statesmen and bishops, much indeed to the material advantage of the latter. Incontestably, Christianity had surged forward. Its leadership now had to learn to adapt and come creatively to terms with a brand new problem, their dependence on the government's goodwill.[40]

The rigorists were least likely to learn. Their overtures to Constantine exhibited the intransigence that probably contributed to their failure to get desired results. It all started in North Africa when seventy bishops objected to the election of Caecilian as bishop of Carthage. He was unfit, they charged, because he and his friends in episcopal office had acted badly during the last years of persecution. Conceivably, Caecilian's only crime may have been his reluctance to defer to confessors, but the seventy repudiated him and chose a bishop more in sympathy with their views on the laicization of lapsed leadership and more enthusiastic about the cults associated with the region's recent martyrs. The rigorists then sent a dossier with a summary of their deliberations, through the proconsul, to Constantine.

The new emperor referred the dispute to Bishop Miltiades of Rome, who summoned colleagues to a council in the capital in 313. Three bishops from Gaul joined fifteen from Italy. They conferred and acquitted Caecilian. However, the rigorists from North Africa persevered, underscoring their allegation that one of the bishops who had consecrated Caecilian had capitulated to government authorities during the persecution. (Later the rigorists accused Miltiades of collaboration.) But a second council, that of Arles, echoed the verdict of the first in 314, and Constantine reiterated it the following year, responding to yet another rigorist protest. The rigorists in North Africa were still arguing their case against Caecilian a century later before bishops and imperial officals, but their early complaints as well as their impolitic persistence bear watching now inasmuch as they suggest why the rigorists failed and the moderates succeeded with the government.

Moderates in North Africa had long maintained that the rigorists were pressing for a retrial after the verdict for Caecilian and against them in Rome. It served the moderates' polemical purposes to hold that their tireless opponents pursued due process, got it, and then condemned the procedure that condemned them. The rigorists, for their part, passionately denied that the Caecilian case had ever been submitted for government, or additional episcopal, arbitration. Their point was that the council of seventy, which was on the spot, knew far better what had happened in North Africa than any sovereign or synod across the Mediterranean. Rigorists sought confirmation, not reconsideration of their council's decision. Their delegates pestered Constantine in Rome, Trier, and finally Milan, but not to convene more tribunals or listen to more evidence. They were after independence. They came to have their authority recognized, not to acknowledge the authority of others. Their persistence and near defiance drove the emperor to lash out at their audacity and arrogance. And his response did not augur well for rigorist leaders who refused to follow.[41]

Caecilian's accusers collided with Constantine while the new relationship between the church and government was still being negotiated. They tried to muscle the man whose political conviction and religious conversion were probably based on his intuition that Christianity would reunify his realm. The accusers made the wrong moves at the wrong time. The future belonged to moderate church officials who knew when to keep silent and, above all, when and how to conspire with the political authorities to build both regional and Roman religious consensus.[42]

But consensus seemed a remote prospect. Reunification of the vast realm under one emperor was nearly complete by 324, but despite his desires, Constantine could not make the empire's new faith one faith. The dispute in North Africa was ongoing when another, equally intractable and intense disagreement urgently came to the emperor's attention. Church executives were deeply disturbed by colleagues who reportedly equivocated about Jesus' full divinity. Executives alleged that when these equivocators stated Jesus was God, the title had about as much significance as—and clearly no more than—the promise made to Moses to allay his fear that he was too unimportant and unimpressive to convey God's word in Egypt: "I make you as God to Pharaoh."[43]

The bishops who initially prevailed with Constantine argued that Jesus was of one substance with God the Father and was not as Moses had been, a man made formidable by God. It surprised no one when the emperor summoned church executives to Nicaea in 325 to settle the issue. Emperors in the past had been energetic overseers of official cults, and by then regional councils were expected to deal with both doctrine and discipline. But Nicaea was unthinkable before the conversion of the government. While Constantine watched, bishops from nearly every region he ruled debated competing Christological formulations and then drafted their summary of the council's final position on full divinity. The executives who refused to subscribe were deprived of their positions. Among them, a presbyter from Alexandria named Arius was singled out for criticism and sent into exile. Thereafter, equivocators were known to their enemies as Arians.[44]

Some Arians quickly came to regret their opposition to the council. The emperor was pleased with their second thoughts and urged bishops of the Nicene party to welcome them back. Regrets, however, were greeted with suspicion. Bishop Eustathius of Antioch did not trust the erstwhile equivocators. Despite Constantine's wishes and instructions, Eustathius kept those Arians from communion; impatient with disobedience, the emperor deposed and exiled the Antiochene executive in 327. Ten years later, Bishop Marcellus of Ancyra was told that Arius had been readmitted and was so upset by the news that he declined to make some strategic public appearances, forfeiting the emperor's goodwill. The Nicene party steadily lost the ground it had occupied at Nicaea, lost favor, that is, with the authorities. Polemical literature at the time insisted that Arius and his more outspoken allies made concerted, effective attacks on the Nicene, or orthodox, position, yet that position eroded under considerably less pressure from its critics. Nicene bishops seem to have turned on the government, which then turned against them.

The Nicene party blamed impressionable counselors at the court of Constantius, Constantine's son and heir to the eastern portion of the empire in 337 and to the whole of it in 353. A cry went up against deception and corruption at the very center of government and against injustice wherever the Arian revival resulted in embarrassments and losses for the local Nicene executives.[45]

Was official abandonment of Nicaea—Constantine's grand council and the definitive, consubstantialist, Christological position on Jesus' identity with God that was formulated there—a case of theological seduction or political reshuffling? To propose and defend an explanation would be to digress, yet we must not leave the government's switch from Nicene to anti-Nicene partisanship unattended. We have to find some route through the story rather than around it if we want to learn how authority was distributed within the church. For Emperor Constantius made remarkable use of the churches' councils in the west. His pursuit of unity has been described as "obsessive." Needless to say, he shared his father's objectives and was disappointed with the Nicenes' resistance to reconciliation. But whatever the prompting, quite soon after his accession in the east in 337 Constantius decided that the Arians, or subordinationists, as I call them, had the better chance to end the quarrels and reunify the church.[46]

The Nicene bishops could not convince the court to the contrary. Eusebius, bishop of Nicomedia and then Constantinople, influentially opposed them soon after Nicaea adjourned in 325 and with increasing effectiveness as time went on. Subordinationists compellingly claimed the run of scripture. Consubstantialists, they argued, could find neither their vocabulary nor Christology in sacred literature, where Jesus declared that God the father was greater (*major me est*). Therefore, despite the accusations of equivocation the Nicene party was hurling at the subordinationists, it seemed guiltier than the opposition of wobbly reasoning and forced interpretation when it tried to dismiss the "greater" in Jesus' statement as an exemplary yet empty gesture.[47]

The subordinationists agreed on Jesus' inferiority, yet the longtime allies became rivals for the emperor's endorsement when they discussed exactly what *major* meant. Some bishops in the east insisted on utter dissimilarity; for them the "greater" opened a huge gap between father and son. But numbers of their colleagues shaded toward a compromise with the Nicene consubstantialists, conceding Jesus was similar to God, although stipulating that similarity in no way suggested identity. The feuding heirs of Arius would probably have discouraged an emperor set on unity had he not had good cause to stay the subordinationist course and had his brother Constans not ruled the west and preferred the Nicene solution. It is possible and perilous to give sibling rivalry too large a significance, of course, yet there is no denying that the arrangement that divided the realm among Constantine's three sons seems to have been forced on Constantius, who had grounds to think himself his father's favorite. Moreover, after having eliminated the other brother, Constans meddled in the religious affairs of Constantius's territory on behalf of the leading Nicene theorist, Bishop Athanasius of Alexandria. The result in the east, I have little doubt, was resentment as well as a degree of instinctive contrariness.[48]

Constantius was obliged to come west when the usurper Magnentius murdered Constans in 350. Although Constantius was generally preoccupied with the Persian frontier, he could not overlook injuries to the dynasty and let his brother go unavenged. At Mursa in 353, he prayed alongside Bishop Valens while his army thrashed Magnentius's troops. Valens, an ardent subordinationist, exploited the victory, asserting that an angel had relayed the news to him and interpreting both the vision and the victory as God's reward for Constantius's opposition to the Nicene party. And the emperor generously attributed his success to the merits of his clerical advisers, Valens and other Danubian executives, notably Ursacius of Singidunum and Germinius of Sirmium, who thenceforth engineered the successive setbacks for the Nicene bishops in the west during the 350s.[49]

The bishops were asked to subscribe to charges filed against Athanasius, whose long career had dominated the formative phases of a consubstantialist Christology. Constantius had earlier assured Athanasius that he would be left in peace, even after Constans died, although Valens and his associates wanted to depose their old enemy. To persuade the emperor, subordinationists close to court picked over, maybe manufactured, evidence of Athanasius's disloyalty. He was accused of having incited Constans against his brother and of having encouraged the usurper Magnentius. Athanasius categorically denied the charges, comparing himself to Naboth the Jezreelite in sacred literature, who was slandered and then slain on Jezebel's orders, and fleeing Alexandria to avoid capture.[50]

Constantius was prepared to believe the worst. His defeat of Magnentius greatly increased his territory but left him less secure. Gallus, whom he deputized to manage affairs in the east, proved himself a rogue and had to be removed. In Gaul, Silvanus rose against the regime. Insurrection could crop up just about anywhere, and Danubian subordinationist bishops apparently played on Constantius's fears to portray their Nicene adversaries as politically subversive. Valens and several friends were commissioned to ferret out the religious opposition. They convened councils at Arles (353), Milan (355), and Béziers (356) to condemn Athanasius and, it seems, to require western consent to some creedal formula, which was, if not overtly subordinationist, at least "patient of an Arian interpretation."[51]

Athanasius alleged that his episcopal colleagues in the west had been forced to comply and conform, that the emperor, present at Arles and Milan, ordered the executions of those who opposed the Danubians but settled for their exile to the east. Bishop Paulinus of Trier was sent packing from Arles; Dionysius of Milan, Eusebius of Vercelli, and Lucifer of Calaris, from a council in Milan. Hilary of Poitiers was exiled at Béziers; Liberius of Rome, soon thereafter, without "benefit" of council.[52]

The three leading Danubian bishops met in Sirmium in 357, after the episcopal dissidents had been disgraced and chased from their sees in the west. The emperor was there as well. He was closer than ever before to solidifying a confessional basis for unity.[53] He summoned two councils, much larger than the others, to ratify the creed his clerical advisers had formulated. Several hundred bishops from the west assembled at Rimini on the Adriatic coast of Italy in 359. The majority implored the emperor to hold fast to the phrases approved at Nicaea and to let them return to their churches, but to no avail. The Nicene delegates from Rimini were denied a hearing at court.[54]

By contrast, the subordinationist delegates sent from Rimini by the minority were well received, and Constantius demanded that the majority conform or stay at the conference site indefinitely. Sulpicius Severus reported that the ultimatum caused considerable commotion (*perturbatio*), but several decades later Bishop Ambrose of Milan, laying slabs of insults in his commentary on the gospel of Luke, suggested that the episcopal conferees had given up too easily: "While trying to stay in [Constantius's] good graces," he said, "they lost the grace of God."[55] The government was unrelenting; any resistance was likely to have been compromised sooner rather than later. Although it is unfair to suppose that the majority succumbed overnight, the next mission from the council of Rimini to Sirmium was able to report episcopal acquiescence in the west. When Constantius's council in the east subsequently endorsed the subordinationist position, the Danubians could legitimately claim complete success for their Christology and for their conciliarist strategy. On paper, they achieved confessional unanimity. In the principal episcopal cities—Alexandria, Antioch, Constantinople, Sirmium, Rome, Milan, and Arles—they placed likeminded bishops. To all appearances, they had snapped the spinal column of Nicene dissent. Constantius and Valens had their unity by 360, "a unity of impiety," according to Hilary of Poitiers.[56]

Milan: Hilary, Auxentius, and the Election of Ambrose

Hilary probably did not think the imperial, conciliarist, subordinationist victories of the late 350s could rapidly be reversed. He was startled to hear that Nicene orthodoxy *intra Gallias* was making a quick comeback by 360. He was in exile when the letter arrived from his episcopal colleagues saying they had already met in council to condemn "all the blasphemies you have exposed." Their council also condemned Valens and his principal Gallic collaborator, Bishop Saturninus of Arles. Hilary may well have been the ringleader of the nascent Nicene resistance before Saturninus engineered his exile at Béziers. If so, Hilary's friends' long silence—they had not written for three years—must have dismayed him, but he was delighted when word came that they could report progress. They said as well that they were preparing to pass ordinances to laicize the clerics who would not relinquish positions articulated at Béziers and Rimini. And they appear to have promised Hilary that their confederacy and councils would overrule those meetings called by Constantius, conducted under duress, and choreographed by Valens, the Danubians, and their client bishops in the west.[57]

Recovering ground from the subordinationists would be a high-maintenance initiative, and Hilary was asked to enlist the support of episcopal colleagues in the east and perhaps appeal for government reconsideration. The court had moved from Sirmium to Constantinople, where Hilary found and flattered Constantius. The overture was extremely deferential. He harped on the emperor's piety and nobility, accusing the Danubian subordinationists of having misled the court. It was almost as if the exiled bishop of Poitiers were offering to replace Valens and to place the confessional unity of the empire, east and west, on a more secure, Nicene footing. His petition may be reduced to one simple, partisan observation: The council of Nicaea had rendered all subsequent Christological deliberations superfluous. Whatever difficulties others had identified in the wording or substance of the Nicene consensus attested their incomprehension, not the incomprehensibility or inadequacy of the old formula. The proliferation of creeds during the 340s and 350s proved only the ignorance of their authors and redactors. If the emperor wanted confessional solidarity and religious harmony, he need simply turn to the exquisite tools that Constantine and his great council had supplied—and turn to those church executives intelligent enough to use them.[58]

But Constantius was having none of this. Perhaps, as one contemporary proposed, the subordinationists at court prevailed on the emperor to send Hilary home, fearing that he had become a real threat in the east, a *perturbator Orientis*, who day by day found ways around their censorship.[59] More likely, Hilary just became a nuisance. In any event, he and other exiles were soon free to go west. His parting shot, publicized only later, again cited the proliferation of councils and creeds but this time in a snide description of imperial patronage. He accused Constantius of having sponsored a series of councils and a confusion of creeds to conceal his opposition to Christianity. Danubians were lackeys, Hilary now said; they had been set to work by their emperor to undermine all that Constantine and Nicaea had made possible.[60]

The returning exiles echoed this accusation to reawaken discontent. Bishop Liberius of Rome, one of the last to leave, was the first to return. He had little trouble ousting Felix, Constantius's appointee, who appears to have considered himself nothing more than an interim arrangement. Liberius resettled in the old capital and proclaimed himself an "antidote" to poisons the Danubians and their imperial overseer imported and injected into the western churches. But recovery in some regions was not as prompt as it was in Rome. The subordinationists in Milan dug in and held out. For one thing, Bishop Dionysius died in exile. For another, his replacement, Auxentius, unlike Felix, had the time and ambition to give the Rimini consensus an appearance of finality and to fortify his pontificate against the Nicene resurgence.[61]

Hilary and Eusebius of Vercelli ranged over north-central Italy in 364. Hilary aimed to discredit and unseat Auxentius. The government of the empire by then had changed hands several times: Constantius had given way to Julian, Julian to Jovian, and Jovian to the partnership between Valens in the east and Valentinian in the west. Valentinian happened to be residing in Milan, ready to accommodate bishops of either party who could maintain municipal order. Auxentius played to that prejudice, branding his opponents as outside agitators, who were "everywhere" dividing churches and creating chaos. But the emperor permitted Hilary to confront the incumbent, and the confrontation suggested that Auxentius had not put the subordinationist position beyond recall.[62]

"I never got to know Arius; I did not learn his doctrine," Auxentius publicly insisted in reply to Hilary. Auxentius appealed to the agreement reached at Rimini: Subordinationist Christology held up because the latest grand council had upheld it. He thus restarted a guiding bureaucratic assumption that the councils of the church, the culmination of imperial patronage, generated authoritative pronouncements.[63]

Hilary could have returned to the argument he had tried before (and against) Constantius, to the duels between councils, as he composed them—Nicaea versus Rimini, Nicaea versus all comers. Instead, he attacked Auxentius for hypocrisy and suggested that the right to hold executive office in the church depended on a candidate's or incumbent's enthusiasm for "the truth of divinity." Hilary charged that the current bishop of Milan was toying with words rather than touting the truth. Hilary complained that Auxentius was evasive, relied on circumlocutions, and tried "diabolical cunning" where straight talk would convict him. The straight talk of scripture, according to Hilary, certified that father and son were consubstantial; regrettably, he said, a war of words perpetuated by more or less throwaway councils obscured that talk. Of course, he did not abandon Nicaea, but the council itself ceased to be central to Hilary's argument.[64]

In his closing remarks, Hilary dared Auxentius to summon additional councils and have him declared a heretic, a dare that could be taken to document the bishop's ability to marshal local episcopal support. But I am inclined to interpret the dare as a taunt, signaling, if anything more important than Hilary's hot temper, the bishop of Milan's inability to organize conciliarist counteroffensives. All we know about neighboring bishops is that the executives in Trent and Aquileia soon stood against Auxentius and that the bishop of Brescia promoted the Nicene resistance in Milan. We hear nothing of, or from, Auxentius's friends. Be that as it may, at Valentinian's court, where municipal order was preferred to confusion, the visiting dissident was no match for an ostensibly irenic, resident church executive. Hilary was asked to move on.[65]

He left Milan admitting Auxentius was the better diplomat but recalling a time when Christianity had survived without diplomacy and official patronage. The administration of the current bishop "boasts that it is loved by the world," Hilary exaggerated, while adding that the Christian church "cannot be of Christ unless the world despises it."[66] Nostalgia for persecution, however, was curiously out of place. It served the self-image of troubadour executives wandering through Italy, as did Hilary and probably Eusebius, trying to drum up support, but government officials ordinarily were cooperating with their bishops, removing pagans' statues, for example, to inconspicuous corners of the cities. Moreover, a caste of energetic, dedicated, and respected characters chose to advance their careers in the church rather than at court. The tide turned in favor of Christianity. Nevertheless, Hilary idealized his mission and ministry, recuperating his faith's underdog status to encourage the Nicene network in Milan. "The apostles," he wrote, "came together in secret." So elements of the Nicene resistance could surely survive Auxentius, endure relative obscurity for a time, mingle with the opposition at public worship, yet receive the sacraments privately and with priests and Christological propositions more to their liking.[67]

Auxentius's death in 374 brought the Nicene resistance above ground. The election of his successor seemed deadlocked when the provincial governor agreed first to intervene and then to become bishop. Unfortunately, the accounts that exist are untrustworthy, but we know that Ambrose had recently been sent from Sirmium to Milan to administer justice in the Ligurian provinces. We know that he was raised in Rome and that his family had been on good terms with Bishop Liberius. We suspect that he had influential friends at court, notably Petronius Probus, who was, after the emperor himself, the most powerful patron in Illyricum and Rome. The disputed election in Milan may have been the first and last great crisis of Ambrose's civil administration. His biographer Paulinus implied that the partisans were inches from a pitched battle when a child's voice pronounced "Ambrose bishop." Or did both of the deadlocked sides determine in concert and without a divine sign that their would-be arbiter would make an excellent, impartial, compromise candidate? If so, subordinationists were quickly chagrined, for Ambrose insisted on being baptized by a Nicene cleric. He later proved to be, from the Auxentian perspective, the worst possible choice.[68]

Yet one of the most perplexing parts of that story is the Auxentian perspective—to be precise, the silence that shrouds it. If Neil McLynn is right, if Ambrose actually cultivated or catered to the Nicene resistance before the episcopal election, that strange Auxentian silence is even more baffling. McLynn's new study deflates the myth of preelection neutrality while allowing that the governor was not sub rosa seeking church office. Nonetheless, "if he did not seek out the [Nicene] opposition group," remarked McLynn, "he can hardly have escaped [its] attention," and he became a "creature of [the] party," plausibly only pretending to mediate. Through it all, the Auxentians were quiet, even after Ambrose showed himself less the creature than the re-creator and redeemer of the Nicene faction. McLynn imagined that a "public relations campaign" put one over on the subordinationists and then, more realistically, that the Auxentians were awed and intimidated by Ambrose's good friends at court, by his "connections," we would say. Yet both hunches presuppose a coherent and dominant Auxentian party in Milan and in the vicinity when a failure to mobilize may more simply be explained by a failure to materialize.[69]

The contested election of 374 documents the Auxentians' existence, if also their disorientation. Their coherence and dominance, however, are sheer speculation.

Did Auxentius ordain fiercely partisan priests in Milan or consecrate loyal episcopal colleagues in Lombardy? Paulinus heard nothing from them. (Or did he
suppress information about them?) The Christians in Milan, if Paulinus can be
trusted, were excited by the prospect of having Ambrose as bishop and would not
be denied. So when he reputedly, repeatedly refused and tried to disqualify himself, ordering the torture of political prisoners and associating with prostitutes,
the crowd argued his eligibility: "Let your sins be on us." One shred of evidence
that might help us understand the clerical silence and popular desperation suggests that the Milanese Christian community may have experienced a sense of isolation after Bishop Damasus of Rome assembled nearly one hundred episcopal
colleagues in 370 or 371 to censure Auxentius and Rimini. Basically, bishops at
the conference looked on Milan as an outpost of the Illyrican confederacy of
church executives who still held out for the faith defined by the Danubians. The
council stopped short of deposing Auxentius but not, it seems, because he could
muster political or peer support. The bishops sounded as if nothing were left for
them to do, as if his cause were already lost. After his election, Ambrose did what
he could to make sure that it was.[70]

Ambrose of Milan

Ambrose at first was apparently not troubled much by the Auxentians in northern Italy. His chief critics were in Illyricum, as was Emperor Gratian, who, almost
certainly at their bidding, asked him to explain his faith. Ambrose replied at great
length, fastening a lawyer's homespun analogy to his scriptural arguments for the
full divinity of Jesus. The easiest way to an unfavorable verdict in the courts, he
ventured, was to insult the presiding judge. He knew from experience that justices
were alert to the slightest show of contempt and mockery. All humans were sinners, he went on; all awaited God's judgment and hoped for acquittal or, at the
very least, amnesty. When Christians equivocated about Jesus' divinity, they with-
eld honor from God. Offending their judge, they prejudiced their cases.[71]

Equivocation also exhibited a startling disrespect for the sacred texts, according to Ambrose. He instructed Gratian that the thrice repeated "holy" nesting in
Isaiah's prophecy ("holy, holy, holy is the Lord of hosts") signaled the unity,
equality, and divinity of the three "persons" of the trinity. The repetition suggested to him that divinity was divided among them without diminution, and he
argued that the creedal consensus at Nicaea had done no more than elaborate this
fact. Should the equivocators find it impossible to reconcile the consubstantialist
position articulated at Nicaea with Jesus' humble appearance, they ought to dwell
on the manger rather than the man. Those humble circumstances of the savior's
birth had not deterred the wisest of visitors to Bethlehem from honoring the divinity in the infant.[72]

For over half a century, doubts about that divinity had proved extremely con-
tagious, so Ambrose vented his frustration with the subordinationists, hoping
that it, too, would catch at court. How could "Rimini-first" proponents gloss over

the thrice-repeated "holy" and the three wise men at the manger yet claim there was insufficient evidence in scripture for the Nicene formulation of full divinity? How could they turn a deaf ear to God, whose voice was heard from the clouds proclaiming, "This is my son . . . listen to him"? Ambrose admitted sonship was susceptible to a subordinationist interpretation; sons, for a time, were inferior to their fathers. The command to listen to Jesus, however, was incontestable, and Jesus said plainly and conclusively, "All that the father has is mine." Unless the subordinationists presumed that Christians had been enjoined to listen but allowed to disregard what they heard, equivocators had no excuse for equivocating. Unless they stopped preaching a vague and partial divinity, Ambrose warned, they would surely lose that fraction of faith they still had, and worse still, they would end up sabotaging the salvation of the Christians who were listening to them rather than to Jesus.[73]

Ambrose later declared that the equivocators were grubs or worms, eating at the church from the inside. No wonder, then, he refused when Gratian's stepmother Justina asked that a church be reserved for them in Milan. The emperor sent her and her young son to the city in 378 when Sirmium seemed unsafe. He could hardly overlook her request and the bishop's reply, so he sequestered the church in question. Neither Justina nor Ambrose was the clear winner of this first struggle for a basilica, although the latter was able to deny the equivocators a pulpit and, for a time, to keep worms in his precincts working underground.[74]

To defy the royal will was to risk the kind of displeasure that often had grave consequences in late antiquity. So Ambrose was more than a little surprised, he confided, when the emperor suddenly returned the church he had impounded. The government so swiftly changed from neutral to Nicene, possibly because Gratian was influenced by Theodosius, the Spanish field commander whom he had appointed to rule the east in the wake of the imperial defeat at Adrianople in 378. Theodosius promptly turned over the church in Constantinople to the Nicene party, directing that all Christians subscribe to Christological propositions prescribed by the Nicene bishops of Rome and Alexandria. This occurred in 380; Gratian returned the basilica to Ambrose within the year.[75]

The good fortune of the Nicene party may have galvanized the subordinationists in Milan, who elected their own bishop, a second Auxentius, and appealed again to Justina in 385. By then, she was better able to assist them. No longer ruled and overruled by her stepson, Gratian, who had died shortly before, she all but ruled her son and emperor, Valentinian II, and she had his court designate the Portian basilica for subordinationist worship. Ambrose would not yield it. Moreover, he refused to discuss his refusal at the palace. Crafting a convenient consensus without having convened a council, he claimed that his episcopal colleagues did not condone any public discussion with heretics in which the court ultimately planned to determine doctrine.[76]

But the court was not about to cave. Emperors and their kin restored, built, and gave churches to the church; they could take them away just as well. Troops seized one of Ambrose's basilicas and surrounded the others to discourage his partisans.

From the pulpit, he transformed Psalm 79 into his anthem: "The heathen have come into thy inheritance; they have defiled thy holy temple." Psalms, sermons, prayers (perhaps) and a slice of good fortune (definitely) saved the Nicene resistance to Justina and her friends. For at that very moment, Magnus Maximus, who governed the northwest quadrant of the empire, was posing as a defender of Nicene orthodoxy and was threatening to attack and dislodge Valentinian II, his mother, and their army from northern Italy. A strong stand against Ambrose virtually invited invasion. It would also have provided Maximus with a batallion of Milanese collaborators eager to see that his intervention was successful.

So before Justina altogether compromised the region's security, cooler heads at court bowed to the bishop, recalled the troops, and restored his church. Ambrose, anxious to circulate a glowing account of Nicene courage and conquest, publicly must have been more conciliatory than smug; he was a statesman. Later, however, he described the result as a harvest, suggesting that the heirs of Arius had finally fallen to the mowing and had been bundled back into the correct faith and its churches. Nevertheless, at the time, he was incapable of letting the vindication of episcopal leadership go unremarked. Privately to his sister, he offered his view of the settlement: Emperors henceforth would manage their palaces, while the churches' chief executives managed their churches.[77]

Late in the fourth century, there was a growing number of churches to manage, thanks to the industry of Ambrose and his episcopal colleagues. To this day, archaeologists continue to stumble across the remains of their vast construction program. Their stated purpose was to make the profound mysteries of the faith intelligible and meaningful to as many as possible. When artfully, compellingly conveyed, Ambrose advised, those mysteries burned the stubble of sin and doubt from the Christians' hearts. The Deuteronomist claimed that God was "a devouring fire." Luke said that Jesus came "to cast fire upon the earth." Fire burning in old and new churches, Ambrose elaborated, did not just consume illicit passions and stubborn skepticism; it also warmed or consoled the faithful once the stubble had been cleared to make room for faith.[78] He called faith "a planting"; virtue was the crop. The church, therefore, was a field; the bishop, a field hand, the *operarius,* whose managerial and pastoral duties were legion. Field hands, Ambrose said, should maintain "an appropriate splendor" to attract elite, affluent parishioners and to interest them in funding the construction of new churches. Yet field hands must guard against extravagance and waste, making sure that the material needs of their fields' less fortunate were met by the selfless goodwill of all.[79]

All the while, of course, episcopal field hands had to keep rival faiths from their fields. Ambrose remembered the council at Rimini in 359, where the equivocators and the emperor had pressured a majority of the bishops in attendance to ratify the wrong creed. He thus insisted that when field hands assembled to reflect on their faith, they come avowedly and resolutely to enforce their Nicene consensus. They should be ready to end quarrels, not to air them.[80]

Ambrose presided at a council in Aquileia, two hundred miles or so east of Milan, in 381, about five years before his decisive confrontation with the subordinationists in north-central Italy. He came east to discipline, not to discuss. Bishop Palladius of Ratiaria came west to defend the doctrine that Nicene bishops, more than twenty of them, maybe as many as forty, were keen to suppress. The council had barely started when Ambrose, producing an old letter from Arius, challenged Palladius to condemn what it proposed or face conciliar censure. The procedure was inexcusable, irregular, and unfair, Palladius said, coming close to depicting Aquileia as a cartoon council, a kangaroo court. Ambrose, he asserted, had no authority to issue the ultimatum. *In concilio pleno,* in a full, more representative council, he assured the bishops from Italy and Gaul, he would be ready and prompt with an answer. But in a council so stacked against him, he would have nothing further to say.

Ambrose, however, was relentless. His battery of accusations and questions finally elicited more expansive replies. Palladius ventured into the conversation and made one critical mistake: He garbled the passage in which Jesus described the father as *major,* as greater (*major me est*), and gave Ambrose an advantage that he hardly expected. Palladius tried again to harp on his procedural objections, but Ambrose and his allies were not going to let him off the hook ("today we have demonstrated that you falsify sacred scriptures"), and they appealed for the emperor's endorsement of Aquileia's consensus, which, they said, was Constantine's Nicene consensus. The government should want but one faith in all its bishops' fields and ought to support the diligent executive field hands who were ruthless with Nicaea's and Aquileia's critics.[81]

So much for the imagined interest of the government. But was it all that glaringly apparent that government support was in the church's best interests? Most of the material effects of official patronage seemed to argue so, though Ambrose often suggested that the council of Rimini had shown how government favors, concerns, and coaxing worked to the church's disadvantage. Its partnership with politicians compromised the church, if only because the practice of politics in late antiquity was obviously incompatible with the foremost Christian virtues. Anger ought to be suppressed "at all times," and "wrath destroyed wisdom," Ambrose intoned. Yet political authorities could not disarm their troops and remain authorities. Sword and wrath belonged together, but only the most rigorous of rigorists dared to exclude emperors and soldiers from the church. The upshot was that friendship with government officials put Christians, disavowing anger, uncomfortably at the hilt end of the sword. Ambrose urged caution and repentance. Theodosius, at his best, was an excellent model. His sword (and good sense) preserved some semblance of order after Adrianople. He reunited the empire after manhandling Maximus. And from the start, he was a sincere Nicene Christian. Once, "after seeing the enemy dead on a battlefield, he abstained from celebrating the sacraments until the arrival of his sons signaled [that he had not lost] God's grace."[82]

The reported battlefield remorse calls to mind the episode in Ambrose's criticism and courtship of the court that has gained the greatest notoriety, the emperor's repentance for the massacre at Thessalonica. In 390, a popular athlete in that city was taken into custody. During riots that followed, Butheric, the commander of the garrison, was killed, a casualty of such distinction that Theodosius either planned or permitted revenge on a grand scale. Legend has it that the emperor sent orders for the indiscriminate slaughter of citizens, realized his wrath had got the better of his wisdom, and dispatched a second messenger, who could not overtake the first with a stay of execution. The garrison might have been equally, maybe more, to blame for the magnitude of the retribution, but in any event the dreadful consequences seemed to shove Ambrose into a lose-lose situation. He could not ignore the tragedy; other bishops who happened to have been meeting in Milan when news of the atrocity arrived condemned the government and scolded him for his special friendship with the emperor. Yet if he denounced Theodosius to appease his episcopal colleagues, he was likely to forfeit whatever influence over the regime he had acquired.[83]

Two years earlier during worship, Ambrose had seemed ready to stop the service, to withhold the eucharist, because Theodosius had ordered Mesopotamian Christians to rebuild a synagogue they had destroyed. The pause had embarrassed the emperor, who had agreed finally to rescind the order. Nonetheless, the memory of the sovereign's prickly response probably chastened Ambrose when he was again confronted with the prospect of correcting the court.[84]

So he wrote a "confidential" letter to Theodosius. Ambrose made no display of his indignation; the story that he barred the door to the church against the emperor is untrue. His discreet letter alluded to King David's humility and detailed the instructions Ambrose had received in a dream telling him not to administer the eucharistic sacrifice in Theodosius's presence unless the Christians' emperor imitated the Hebrews' king and begged God's forgiveness. Late in 390, the court returned from its short visit to Verona, the emperor publicly professed his sorrow, and the bishop gladly announced his pardon and reconciliation on Christmas day.[85]

The churches' executives, reconciling their patrons, retained influence over them. The rigorists turned this simple fact into a stinging accusation, impugning moderates' motives. Ambrose warned Novatianists, whose party survived into the fourth century, that God was more likely to disapprove of the severity of executives pretending to be agents of a full-dress divine retribution than to disassociate himself from the compassion and clemency of the moderate leadership. For the prime beneficiary of the rigorists' retribution, he said, was satan. Rigorists who expelled sinners killed off hope, and hopeless souls ceased to beg for God's forgiveness. The devil hated the begging and savored the silence because begging, by anticipation, attested God's power over sin and silence sustained the illusion that diabolical forces found or improvised a way to frustrate God's mercy. Ambrose concluded that the illusion also subverted morality and order by making the government's service far more complicated and satan's successes still sweeter. Citizens who were convinced that God either could not or would not pardon and reconcile them tended to disregard law and wreak havoc and hell on earth.[86]

For Ambrose, prospects for pardon kept the peace. For his friend Bishop Chromatius of Aquileia, that stately beatitude "Blessed are the peacemakers" applied to the clerical estate, especially to the higher reaches of the hierarchy. He was not referring to squabbles over doctrine, discipline, and property settled by the churches' chief executives. Chromatius gave pride of place to the bishops' "more sublime peacemaking," which quelled the disturbances within each Christian's soul and reconciled and reintegrated penitents. In theory, that pastoral work assured the peace and harmony of the churches.[87] But in fact it locked rigorists and moderates in conflict during the third and fourth centuries, and it seldom stopped the quarreling between Nicene executives and subordinationists after 325. Yet for all the quarrels, Christianity at this stage in its evolution in the west was capable of growth and regional consensus, a result of imperial intervention, conciliar deliberation, episcopal leadership, and various combinations of the three.

❦ 4 ❦

Augustine

Augustine came to Milan in 384, most likely to attract attention. He taught rhetoric in Carthage, then in Rome, but opportunities for advancement seemed greater in the bustling north Italian city where much government business was transacted in the late fourth century. A fine orator could go far.

His mother was an ardent Christian; her son, something of a skeptic. Christians had yet to persuade him that the ostensibly preposterous stories of the Old Testament yielded important lessons for life if read allegorically. And Christians had yet to persuade him that the seemingly simple wisdom of the New Testament was so much more telling than the secret wisdom highly valued by his Manichaean friends. Augustine nevertheless went to hear Ambrose preach because the bishop of Milan had such a splendid reputation for pulpitability. As expected, Augustine admired Ambrose's rhetorical skills but also discovered that this preacher teased sensible observations and advice from sacred literature's curious passages, improbable plots, and deceptively simple parables.[1]

It would be hard to overstate Ambrose's profound influence on Augustine, who all but acknowledged that the bishop made him more receptive to Christianity. The most important aspect of that influence might have been the general trajectory of Ambrose's career. In Milan Augustine was busy accumulating students, cultivating powerful friends, and arranging a "proper" marriage, all of which would have eventually landed him a political appointment, a provincial governorship, he dared to hope. This was precisely the position Ambrose resigned more than ten years before to assume the leadership of Milan's community of Christians. Then Augustine, too, changed course.[2]

The Calling

The standard line is that Ambrose's influence was primarily intellectual and only indirectly vocational, that the Platonic cast of his Christianity appealed to Augustine, who guessed it would have appealed as well to Plato. In the absence of the infallible intelligence for which philosophers had yearned, Christianity was able to promote the very virtues that antiquity's best philosophers had counte-

nanced. In other words, faith did just what was wanted of philosophical knowledge: It loosened disciples' attachments to the things of this world and retired, to
an appreciable extent, "the ambition of this world." But for all that, Augustine was
slow to give up his ambition, and both the ambition and the slowness bothered
him.[3]

In 385, he was preparing to deliver an important speech, one very likely to gain
him great and enviable notoriety. Quite understandably, he was nervous, yet he
found that anticipation and stage fright were only partly responsible for his jit-
ters. Augustine discovered that he was harboring serious doubts about his profession and intentions. He met a beggar on the streets of Milan and at the time
saw some similarity between his own "begging" for the government's patronage
and the indigent's appeals for a few coins. The main difference was that he, the
more refined and learned man, cut a far more miserable and reprehensible figure.
He and the beggar were looking for security, yet he alone was ready and eager to
purchase it with his dignity, ready to flatter and eager to please rather than to instruct. Thus, he displeased both himself and God.[4]

Ambrose apparently took no direct interest in Augustine's self-incrimination.
A mutual friend, however, told the troubled orator the story of Victorinus, the
renowned rhetorician in Rome, who had eloquently defended paganism until
God had changed his mind and friends had prevailed on him to declare the conversion publicly. He had done so with "the splendid assurance" that Augustine by
then desperately desired for himself.[5] As he remembered it later, God soon
obliged, supplying him both the conviction and the courage. A child's voice sent
Augustine to the Bible and urged him to "take up and read." His gaze fell instantly
on the apostle's injunction to forsake profane ways and "put on the Lord Jesus
Christ." Suddenly Augustine found the will to do it and declare it. He was won
over.[6]

In some circles today, people might say he had been called, although from the
evidence available it is difficult to argue that he as yet had a calling. He informed
his students that they could no longer count on his services. Then he retreated a
few hours' journey from Milan to Cassiciacum to consider what to do with the en-
ergies he had once poured into framing and fulfilling his worldly ambitions. Once
vacated, his former ambitions seemed to him flat and pathetic. The desire that replaced those for wealth, honor, and influence was simple, spare, yet pregnant with
possibilities. *Tui juris esse cupio:* Augustine longed to be under God's sway.[7]

He was baptized by Ambrose in 387. At the age of thirty-three or so, Augustine
felt reborn. The yoke of guilt for his sins had been lifted, he said, and he was awakened to "the extraordinary sweetness" of the divine counsels concerning salvation.[8] He was anxious to learn, read, and talk more about those counsels. With
two like-minded Thagastan friends, his teenage son, and his mother (who died en
route), he started back to North Africa, his small company having resolved to stay
and study together in seclusion at his family estate. But three years of that had not
prepared him for what happened while he was visiting a coastal town sixty miles

away, where he was accosted by Christians who had heard of his remarkable abilities and were determined to keep him among them as their priest. They presented him for ordination to Bishop Valerius, who probably sold Augustine on the prospects of church service and leadership. These prospects must have occurred to him after meeting Ambrose, yet Augustine seems not to have taken them too seriously at Thagaste. He asked Valerius only for some time to study how to make himself useful. He was supremely confident in his faith, he remarked, though he wondered and worried whether he was fit to confirm the faith of others, implying that the reading practices of a working priest were hardly sufficient to transform him into a serviceable executive.[9] This appeal for time may also suggest that he was loathe to give up his former contemplative, communal life. But his appointment and change of career turned out very well indeed. Within a year, he was a celebrated preacher. In 393, his colleagues asked him to deliver the keynote sermon at a council in Carthage. And three years later, Augustine succeeded Valerius as bishop of Hippo.

Reclusive contemplatives had choices. They measured exactly how much of the world, if any, they might take into their thought and decided what commerce with society, if any, they would either permit or promote from its margins. By contrast, the churches' executives had very little choice. Willy-nilly, they brushed against those with political authority while carrying on their business close to society's centers of wealth and power. They umpired disputes, provided for the poor, ransomed captives, and pronounced on morality. The world's calamities and crises flooded over them and filled their thoughts.

Augustine tried to control the flow. He asked priests to surrender their properties and to live communally. He commended study and reflection, although not the kind he had undertaken at Cassiciacum or Thagaste. Inquiries that had intrigued him a few years before seemed immaterial. So many philosophical problems seemed simply, finally, to defy solution and to frustrate the limited intellects of even the most intelligent. Augustine had too little time in Hippo to chase shadows. He still felt it critical to ponder those counsels concerning salvation, but certainly not to "scrute" the inscrutable reasons for election and reprobation, to find out why some were saved and others damned. He probed and pondered to ascertain "the path of faith," to hold to it, and then to help others persevere in a like manner.[10]

Nearly a dozen men "graduated" from Augustine's community of priests in Hippo to become bishops elsewhere, including those two Thagastan friends who had accompanied him from Milan: Alypius and Evodius. They all traded whatever leisure remained to them for some supervision over that "sublime peacemaking" commended by Chromatius and memorably represented in their mentor's colorful *Confessiones* by the image of a dutiful, cheerful shepherd bearing a wayward lamb on his shoulders back to the flock.[11]

Augustine's *Confessiones* was composed soon after his election and consecration as bishop of Hippo. It is the chief source for much of what has been reported here. Maybe it started as a stocktaking or as an answer to accusations that his past indiscretions disqualified him from holding episcopal office.[12] Be that as it may, the *Confessiones* also suggested what lay ahead—namely, the disquiet and dis-ease that Augustine remembered, anticipated, and featured as hallmarks of an authentic Christian's pilgrimage through time: "Until finding rest in God, our heart is restless," *inquietum*.[13]

Inquietum, Augustine's term, described his early experiments with Manichaeanism, philosophy, even Christianity. Generally, in confessional narratives description tends to overtake and shape experience. Autobiography has justly been called the last refuge, and an ideal reserve, for the wildest imaginations. But Augustine revealed his restlessness elsewhere as well. Other works show how he grew disenchanted with the Manichaeans and why he found them to be, quite simply, wrong. He also became disillusioned with philosophy because without Jesus' counsels, it was impoverished and, more grievously, misleading. And even after he converted to Christianity, Augustine was *inquietus*, raising restlessness to a new level, settling on it as a goal for the spiritual person, who should be active, even agitated, in this world but never of this world. He insisted that genuine Christians enjoyed (*frui*) only God, retired their worldly ambitions, yet looked ceaselessly for ways to use (*uti*) what God had given them.[14]

Highest Expectations

Occasionally during the fourth century, and sometimes apprehensively, bishops used the empire to legislate religious conformity, protect their churches' properties, and assure their episcopal prerogatives. Augustine thought that God also made use of government officials to tell the faithful a hard truth about their faith. Had each Christian emperor enjoyed a long and happy term in office, fewer subjects would have dared to question the superiority of Christianity to other cults, but then many would have converted for the wrong reasons, having associated faith with worldly success. The hard truth was that Christians would often fall short of the material returns they expected on their cultic investments. Harder still, however, was the hint that God deliberately arranged the shortfalls, disappointments, and even disorienting adversities to devalue ambitions, which had no place in Christianity.[15]

By the time Augustine had his say about the bad things that happened to good emperors, Rome itself had "fallen." The city was sacked in 410 by the Goths, and that humiliation prompted despair and speculation that the usable Christian empire was used up. Had God carried the lesson about faith and material success too far? Would the fifth century dawn with and then buckle under the weight of uncertainties about the compatibility between Christian faith and material survival?

Historians were once bent on blaming fourth-century emperors for the disintegration of the western empire. Tribes from beyond the frontiers had long before raided border colonies but usually returned swiftly to their own territories, often enough with the Roman militia in hot pursuit. Increasingly, however, the

Germans, Goths, Assyrians, Armenians, and others were invited to settle in the empire and recruited into its armies. Incursions of the Quadi in the region of the Rhine River, for example, baffled the troops under Julian's command until their commander was convinced that it would take thieves to catch thieves. He welcomed the Frankish tribesmen called the Salii into his forces, defeated the Quadi, and then made squadrons of both the Salii and Quadi regular parts of his units.[16] Entire divisions came to be composed of peoples from beyond the pale; their leaders gained greater and greater leverage with the governments they served. Stilicho and the infamous Alaric, something of a loose Gothic cannon, were principal players in the drama leading to the shock in 410.

In the late 390s, Stilicho made himself indispensable to Honorius, Theodosius's son and eventually Stilicho's son-in-law, who ruled the western empire. At the time, Alaric enjoyed much less influence in the east. Pressing for better terms for the mercenaries under his command, he ran afoul of the regime in Constantinople, which twice borrowed Stilicho (in 395 and 397), hoping to bridle Alaric's troops. But what most unnerved Alaric in his favorite theater of operation, Macedonia and Thrace, was the conflict between other Gothic warriors, Fravitta and Gainas, fighting, respectively, for and against the eastern emperor. Their struggle left fewer spoils for Alaric's army, so he went west and next confronted Stilicho in Italy.

Alaric reached Milan early in 402. Stilicho was recalled from campaigning in Gaul and struck decisively near Verona in late summer of that same year, driving the Goths back to the Balkans. But the enemies soon became allies, largely because Stilicho and Honorius had designs on the eastern empire and wanted to use Alaric against Constantinople. Alaric's Goths, however, were kept waiting; for years they camped in Illyricum, expecting reinforcements and orders. Their new allies in Italy, meanwhile, were distracted, at first by another Gothic invader, Radagaisus, and then by an insurgent who set up an independent Gallic empire and governed it from Arles as Constantine III. These were by no means negligible challenges; Stilicho and Honorius could ill afford their eastern adventure while so pressed in the west.

While assessing the complications in Gaul and reconsidering the delayed eastern offensive, Stilicho was murdered in 408, the victim of a faction dedicated to reducing barbarian influence in imperial politics. Alaric was left in an awkward, yet advantageous position. The ranks of his army swelled with Stilicho's soldiers who feared sharing their general's fate, so he had finally got the promised reinforcements for an expedition east, although not quite as planned. But there were better reasons to go west. The empire there was especially vulnerable; the Goths would not have to contend with Stilicho. Alaric therefore chose to try Italy again, and this time he and his troops moved at will into and down the peninsula.[17]

When Rome surrendered and Honorius refused to negotiate with Alaric from Ravenna, he simply named a new western emperor. When his puppet proved unmanageable, Alaric deposed him. Alaric was master of most that he surveyed; his soldiers were all but unopposed in the field. Only inclement weather deterred them from realizing his schemes for the consecutive conquests of Sicily and North Africa. But for all his swagger and success, Alaric enters and swiftly exits many interpretations of the empire's humiliation, little more than a cipher, an occasion. Most historians concede that the Goths hastened the inevitable "decline and fall," but Edward Gibbon, the closest we come to an official coroner, put the cause of death elsewhere. "Immoderate greatness," he judged, ran its course, got flabby, and finally collapsed—death by "exhaustion."[18]

That fatal fatigue was blamed on Christianity. Gibbon himself sniped at the Christians of late antiquity for having despised the very virtues and ambitions—what Augustine called the "lust for domination"—that formerly motivated conquest and effective defense. But Gibbon's autopsy was only advancing a line of argument drawn in countless earlier assessments. Fifth-century critics regularly attributed the decadence, decline, and fall to Christianity's contempt for Rome's ancient religions. The pagans' gods, they said, had been trustworthy guardians of character and conquest until Constantine, beguiled by his new cult, exchanged their patronage for the lightweight protection of a jealous new God. The Christians' God had proven unreliable. After 410, then, the churches' executives and apologists faced an accusation that often came as a question: If theirs was the true religion and if their God was really singularly authentic and supremely powerful, why had Rome fallen in "Christian times"?

Augustine crafted one reply for both critics and Christians. The empire's misfortune afforded him an excellent opportunity to explain history and Christianity to the former and to reorient the expectations of the latter. Neither the times nor even the churches, he said, were genuinely Christian, for Christians were paganizing Christianity. They frequented sorcerers and consulted astrologers. Sometimes they stooped to seeking cures from the oracles of the old gods.[19] All this made them easy prey for a new breed of scoundrels, who cleverly used language customarily heard in churches to dignify superstitions, who proffered their "poison and add[ed] honey to disguise the taste." Augustine claimed that this ruse and others related to it took a heavier toll than had previous persecutions, drawing Christians into an orbit utterly alien to their faith, making them new pagans, neopagans. He wrote as if he had encountered the rogues whose remedies and prophecies were "poison," he said, because they led to a kind of death. They started their victims down the slope from deceit to defection. At first, those seduced deceived only themselves. As their trips to seers and healers became known, however, they covered their shame with excuses and lied to others. The lies and excuses soon came to seem perfectly logical to them. The neopagans would say, for example, that they still trusted their souls and salvation to the Christians' God and that they brought only their aches and pains and harmless curiosity to the altars and agents of lesser gods. Augustine, however, assumed that only fools practiced in their foolishness would not have seen the offense to one God in their flirting with others. Furthermore, only fools could witness that flirtation, listen to the lies, and nonetheless refer seriously to Christian times.[20]

Augustine bristled at the neopagans' rationalizations, for they showed just how little understanding of—and faith in—God's sovereignty circulated among Christians. That was painfully clear to him when he contemplated the arguments that evolved from their excuses. For neopagans apparently assumed that divine rule and retribution would roughly correspond to their slender sense of justice. Certainly, they said, if they were so evil, God would not let them live. That they lived, therefore, was proof that nothing had come undone that could not eventually be put right. Augustine might have let that by had neopagans not resisted the suggestion that their repentance was the precondition for putting things right. But, alas, they were pleased with themselves rather than sincerely and urgently penitent.[21]

So, according to Augustine, all the talk of Christian times was gibberish. Pagan critics had invented and repeated characterizations of that kind principally to press their case that Christianity's rise occasioned Rome's fall. The times were definitely not Christian. Indeed, he insinuated, paganism had so taken revenge on the new religion that Christianity was no longer Christian. In plain words, repentance had given way to arrogance among some of the faithful and to superstition and self-pity among others.

Augustine's sermons assailed critics' inflated opinions of Christianity's efficiency in converting the times and complained about the churches' inefficiency in monitoring Christians' conversions and removing the residue of paganism. He associated that residue with skepticism about divine sovereignty, with superstition, and with shabby behavior. His favorite places to look for neopaganism were the once solemn Christian festivals that drunkenness, dancing, and disgraceful pranks had turned into unruly parties. He believed that the poor, unlearned, and newly converted were largely responsible for the pandemonium, yet he also blamed neopaganism on churches that failed to censure and stop the sacrilege.[22] Above all, Augustine's indictment concentrated on what has lately been described as neopaganism's "spiritual narrowness." Worship should structure each Christian's desires, he said, yet worship was increasingly structured around—and pandering to—the neopagans' desires for spectacle and pleasure. Perhaps reversals such as this are more easily imagined—as are preferences for easy answers from seers and quick fixes from healers—if we try to imagine the decadence of a declining empire, but for Augustine decadence was a matter of experience, not imagination.[23]

At the very least, able church administrators should have assured orderly religious observances. This seems the injunction informing Augustine's criticisms, although he was also known to have excused the permissiveness of his fellow executives. Yet there is no mistaking his concern and alarm that various church anniversaries had become embarrassments. When he preached about the martyrs in whose honor those anniversaries were celebrated, he recalled that they were revered precisely for their "hatred" of self-indulgence. He had no doubt they would have stridently disapproved of the revelry at their tombs and shrines.[24]

Sermons and moral suasion alone were unlikely to produce the results he wanted, so Augustine prevailed on church councils in Carthage in 392, 397, and 401 to prohibit grave site dancing and drinking. From that repetition and from his recurring complaints, however, I infer that the goals of sobriety and decorum receded as he struggled ahead. Moreover, his advance was not as relentless as he sometimes made it seem. Quite often he rehearsed the horrors of paganization, yet he explicitly allowed that pagans, on adopting Christianity, could not be expected to abandon their pleasures and habits as quickly as their illusions. The completion of conversion required executives' patience, diplomacy, tolerance. If, without fail and without compromise, the boozy behavior had been proscribed and promptly punished, the martyrs' honor and the church's commemorations would have been more adequately defended, but at what cost to Christianity in the currency of new converts?[25]

Augustine tried to shame, intimidate, legislate, and conciliate. He was also interested in getting to the source of the problem, the "spiritual narrowness" of so many Christians, and thus in prying those neopagans from their worldly pleasures. Rome's fate in 410 figured prominently in his reformulation of Christianity's criticisms of paganism and in his formulation of alternatives to the neopagans' pretensions and expectations.

At first blush, the pagans were the big losers in 410. Their old capital was in ruins. Their prized poet, Virgil, all but lost credibility, for he had promised that the gods would forever protect it. We have already heard the pagans' explanation: Conversions to Christianity, they said, angered the gods. Nevertheless, explanations of that sort hardly diminished the demoralization occasioned by the ease of Alaric's conquest. To be sure, the shock and aftershocks affected Christians as well, maybe more so, because they imagined that Rome was protected by the apostles. Augustine was surprised that the faithful saw nothing unusual in transferring custodial responsibility from the pagans' gods to Peter, Paul, and other martyrs interred in and around the city. Few more obvious and outrageous examples of neopaganism could have been cited or conjured, and the transfer occurred without much dissent.

Augustine twice visited Rome during the 380s, displeased both times by what he found. But he could scarcely deny that the Christian community there was prospering. In those happier times, the city was filled with tombs, crowded with visitors to its impressive basilicas, baptistries, and shrines. The prefect Prudentius wrote home to Spain to encourage prospective pilgrims. He raved about the new construction financed by Bishop Damasus and about the spectacles, the commemorative festivals. Residents of the city were fortunate, blessed, he said; they could worship daily at the graves of the church's most venerable heroes. They need not await anniversaries or travel far to see magnificent and inspiring monuments dedicated to Peter and Paul, their city's stalwart protectors.[26]

Meanwhile, the Manichaeans ridiculed Christians who flocked to tombs. How infantile to think ghosts hovered above graves waiting to be fed, honored, appeased! Augustine hardly could draw down the blinds to prevent the Manichaeans' willful misunderstanding; it was better to correct those whose disdain for Christian credulity he had once shared. So he explained to them that worshipers did not leave gifts for ghosts to buy influence. Christians came to the grave sites to honor the God whom martyrs had honored, to offer their thanks to God where the martyrs had offered up their lives. But that explanation was not quite right, and he knew it. Augustine knew the Manichaeans had a point, for the neopagans among the faithful did try to curry favor. They headed to tombs and shrines looking for an advantage.[27]

We might say they were looking for a lift, as was the widow in Nola who believed that proximity to a martyr's bones would get her dead son to heaven. She petitioned to have his remains buried in the basilica of Felix the Confessor. Her bishop, Paulinus, had often extolled Felix's powers and welcomed her request, though he wrote Augustine for a second opinion. The reply lectured both the bishop and the bereaved. Augustine asserted that it mattered what was done *in* the body, not *to* the body postmortem. Animals devoured the corpses of some martyrs; the bodies of others were left to rot. Nonetheless, angels would find and assist the souls of the righteous, wherever their bodies were deposited. Certainly no disadvantage followed from being buried far from the graves of the famous. And there was absolutely no room in Christianity for pagans' superstitions about the fate of the unburied. Excessive concern for burial savored of paganism.[28]

Yet Augustine realized that cherished practice could not be set aside summarily without the innocent being confused. In this instance, he wrote to enlighten executive and innocent alike, reconceiving, rather than directly challenging, their devotion:

> When one thinks of where a dear friend is buried and when the place of burial is associated with the name of an esteemed martyr, one affectionately commends the soul of the departed to that martyr in one's thoughts and prayers. And when the piety of their dear and faithful friends is shown them, the deceased doubtlessly benefit, to be precise, those deceased who, while they lived, merited that such should benefit them after this life.[29]

Benefit or comfort after death depended on a person's having lived well. But mourners could not tell for sure whether friend or kin had been reprobate or righteous—righteousness resided in hidden dispositions as well as in deeds. The upright were well advised, therefore, to make arrangements that might console those laid low, for it was smarter by far, Augustine said, to do what could be unavailing than to omit anything at all that would comfort or console the righteous.

That was the view of a tactful administrator, a tough critic of neopaganism who as a pastor was not unmindful of a mourner's grief and consolation. Augustine admitted that specific grave site locations might make sorrow more bearable, yet something vastly more important was at stake as well. While visiting the remains of friends and family members, commemorating anniversaries of their deaths, or commending in prayers the souls of the dead to the martyrs, the bereaved were reminded of the resurrection. Ideally, they would recall the martyrs' contempt for this world and their desire for the next. Instructed by church executives, the bereaved would recall that heaven and earth pass away, that they themselves were citizens of an eternal kingdom, heirs to the promise inscribed in the resurrection of Jesus. Mourners would learn, in other words, that the faithful and righteous would rise as the martyrs had. Augustine wrote and preached to lock learning such as that into place, a sturdy brace for Christians' highest expectations.[30]

If heaven and earth were to pass away, how could Rome remain undisturbed, invincible, eternal? We will probably never know how many Christians half believed that the apostles protected the old capital. For Augustine, however, the capital's humiliation in 410 was proof of its passing importance; he composed his compendious *De civitate Dei* to assure that the shards of all the expectations for Rome's glory (and for the radiant destiny of a Christian empire) were swept into the rest of the debris left by Alaric and then broomed away. He saw no sign God had ever promised to preserve buildings, monuments, cities, estates, and empires—no word or sign either that God had promised to redeem the Christians who let material interests and objects shape their worship, take over their lives, fill their expectations. They put faith in facts, in *facta,* the things they made, the things their ancestors had achieved. They had too much faith in the stamina of their civilizations. In all, they were at home in this world rather than pilgrims passing through a world that would pass away. Augustine argued that those so attached to the world would pass with it into oblivion, never having taken to heart the promises made in their sacred texts, mediated by their church, explained by its executives.[31]

Rome fell because it was a monument to human achievement. It generated pride and spawned great, yet fatally flawed, expectations. It fell, moreover, because the churches' executives there had gone soft on neopaganism. They tolerated disorder, indecency, and excess, and their tolerance was often cited to get executives elsewhere to lower their standards. Augustine excused the bishops of Rome; after all, everyone knew that the city was just too big to police effectively. It was an administrator's nightmare. Its population was made ever more diverse and unmanageable by waves of visitors and tides of refugees from all parts of the empire. Rome played host to a bewildering variety of customs and pieties. Extenuating circumstances aside, however, Christians in the old capital were insulting their martyrs and their God. They turned worship into farce and carnival. The city itself had become an insult. Its fall was an indictment, or, to be precise, Augustine brokered its fall, fashioning an indictment to call attention to the egregious narrowness of the citizens' spirituality and to remind Christians of the one place it was safe to "build" and "store up treasures."[32]

Neopagans looked for a painless way around or out of their troubles. They were disenchanted with the God who presided over their hardship. Augustine bid them to refocus or reorient their expectations. He urged all Christians to use mishaps and crises on earth to reassess what they lived and hoped for. His *De civitate Dei* transformed tragedy into an occasion for piety, and piety, in this context meant trust in divine providence and desire for eternal life, both of which should have shown conspicuously well in Christians' perseverance.[33] That Augustine was distressed by a poor showing is not surprising. Nor should it surprise us that he sifted recent history and biblical texts for incontrovertible proof that God orchestrated crisis and hardship just to frustrate narrowly materialistic expectations. Augustine strained to get neopagans to see the true colors of this world's rewards. Without hope for the resurrection, this world's glitter was dull and drab and "miserable." With that hope or expectation, even the rubble and stumps of this grim world—images used rhetorically to stir insight, modesty, and mutual affection among Christians—enabled passage to the next, passage from the grim to the glorious.[34]

That hope or expectation constituted a pilgrim city of God. Neopagans were not in it. Although they might stay in the church, their instinctive reactions to crisis and adversity gave them away. These were not the reactions of pilgrims, who had learned that misery here was a summons to blessedness hereafter. Pilgrims "sighed" for repatriation, Augustine said; they sighed, that is, for the peace of their eternal, "natural" home (*patria*). Their sighing (*suspirantes*) was a sign that they accepted their alien or pilgrim status, lived restlessly with their failures as well as with those of society, and ever revived their hopes for the happiness promised them in the resurrection. They accepted that the greatest "tranquillity" available here and now was sighing for there and later.[35]

Augustine was frank about how little peace an individual could hope for here, but he believed a foretaste of the peace that surpassed that of the kingdoms of this world was possible. That foretaste was the tranquillity found in the highest expectations nurtured by the church. Falls and failures deflated all others. Such tranquillity was cut from the same cloth as the *inquietum* described in his *Confessiones,* agitated, yet calm. This feeling came to him after he had groped for answers to his philosophical inquiries, the strength to conform to God's will, and a more intense faith in God's purpose and promises. By 410, twenty-five years after he was baptized and fifteen after he became bishop, he saw history in the light shed by the cross and resurrection. The paradox of a supremely good and powerful God who created and governed a cruel, wicked world ceased to trouble him. His troubles, immediately apparent to anyone who reads what he wrote from 400 to his death in 430, were with Christians who misconceived God's sovereignty and seemed to underestimate human wickedness.

Donatist Churches and Augustine's Universal Church

For centuries, *De civitate Dei* served as the characteristic Christian explanation and consolation for misfortune, arguing that Christians were not responsible for Rome's fall—certainly not in the way pagan critics claimed—but allowing that their God was. The *De civitate* showed that God could keep faith with the faithful, yet arrange for, even accelerate, the passing of their world. And Augustine's book made the silences in sacred literature speak: No passage in the Old or the New Testament suggested Christians would enjoy uninterrupted prosperity in Constantine's shadow; none enjoined them to "build" on earth; none prophesied a last-second reprieve from the Goths. The narratives gave no support to the neo-pagans' narrowly materialistic expectations. The Bible was a book about the ordeals of the elect, the captivities of Israel and the passion of Jesus.

Yet Augustine knew that neither the Bible nor his book could disabuse Christians of their hopes for this tumbledown world. If they were to understand the relevance to their redemption of all that had been written about impermanence, the right church would have to instruct them. And the problem in North Africa was that there were so many wrong churches. For the Donatists had not quietly fallen back in line when the verdicts at Rome (313) and at Arles (314) went against them. Instead, they vilified executives who sided with Caecilian. They seceded and worshiped separately, leaving the "Caecilianists" to their fate.

During the 320s and for decades thereafter, Caecilian's chief rival in Carthage proved to be a genius at organization; Donatus managed to set a congregation alongside, and opposed to, nearly every church frequented by the Caecilianists in city and countryside. By midcentury, Donatists outnumbered their rivals in several regions of North Africa. By 400, they had achieved a "massive superiority" in the important province of Numidia, Serge Lancel said, suggesting that Christians loyal to Caecilian lacked comparably aggressive leadership. It would seem that Donatus also exploited another "deficit": North Africans tended to have little or no respect for Rome, emperors, absentee Italian landlords, and European church councils. Indictments of Caecilian and his allies across the Mediterranean Sea tapped North African nativism, which erupted as insurrection just often enough to signal its existence.[36]

Augustine admired what many of his North African neighbors resented. He was excellently schooled in Roman culture. He had once hoped for appointment to a high government post in Europe. All this made the Donatists especially suspicious, as did the fact that he had been converted and baptized in Italy. As Caecilianist bishop of Hippo, Augustine was irritated that so many Christians preferred to worship with his closest Donatist competitor. Later, he insisted that numbers counted for little, that the Donatists' numerical superiority did not automatically turn them into the moral majority. And numbers, he averred, afforded the Donatists no legal standing.[37] Yet the statistics did alarm him at the time, and the challenge of catching up lay claim to his best efforts, first to convert and then to suppress his rivals. The Caecilianists "have always disturbed our peace and made things difficult for us," a Donatist bishop complained in the early fifth century. "Always" quite likely reached as far back as the conciliar verdicts at Rome and Arles, but from the late 390s on, Augustine stepped up the campaign against Donatism, made things manifestly more difficult than before, and defined the church more influentially, I think, than anyone either before or after him.[38]

The Donatists said they had developed their definition of the church from instructions in the sacred texts. They gathered that when Jeremiah asked what straw and wheat had in common, he implied that they were best kept apart—straw and wheat, the sinful and the sinless. And could anything be clearer than Ezekiel's bullhorn censure of priests who "made no distinction between the holy and the common . . . the unclean and the clean"? Moses also put cleanliness next to godliness; combined with the prophets' warnings against integration, his "divine statutes" permanently quarantined the unclean. According to the Donatists, the apostle Paul picked up the theme and ordered Christians not to associate with the immoral: "Drive out the wicked person from among you." But the churches had not been listening. Their executives failed to drive Caecilian and his friends from their communities in the early fourth century, and the failure had terrible repercussions: Caecilianists throughout the next hundred years were contaminated by the wickedness they tolerated and excused.[39]

Augustine countered that the Donatists' favorite passages from the sacred book, once they were reset in the contexts from which Donatus and his descendants dragged them, had no bearing whatsoever on the question of secession. Moses, Jeremiah, and Ezekiel addressed concerns peculiar to their times. And Paul's injunctions had limited application. Augustine concluded that puritanical Christians had neither historical cause nor biblical justification for leaving the church in the early fourth century and for remaining outside it in the early fifth. Nothing in the sacred narratives suggested that Christianity could or should be utterly antiseptic. Responsible church executives were never far from the gritty, sorry, sordid facts of life. They ought not to be. Every day, bishops scolded adulterers and other cheats, bridled contentious Christians, and mended, as best they could, broken vows and broken lives. Augustine occasionally mentioned his daily rounds: the lawsuits he umpired in the mornings, the penitential discipline he enforced at all hours. Large-scale sifting of the good from the evil was not his business. It was beyond all powers of discernment and discipline, save God's. Yet the Donatists, he said, were intent on preempting divine judgment. They should know better. They should rejoin the church and mend rather than cast off or drive out what seemed broken. And they should wait for God to separate straw from wheat, the wicked from the good.[40]

But the Donatists could not wait and were anxious to tell why. They usually started by reiterating their objections to the consecration of Caecilian. One of the consecrators, they charged, had been guilty of collaboration. He had surrendered sacred texts to the persecutors and thereby forfeited sacramental powers. Thus, he had had nothing to give Caecilian, who therefore gave nothing to the priests he ordained and the bishops he consecrated. As a consequence, all were imposters. The sacraments they administered were worthless. The ordinations and consecrations they performed were unavailing. Caecilian, moreover, was an active metropolitan, so the invalidity of his consecration infected all congregations, save those of the secessionists, within a few decades. So if the Donatists rejoined Augustine and his colleagues and waited beside them patiently for God to separate good from evil, it would soon be impossible to say with any certainty at all whose sins were effectively absolved. Everyone would be waiting in the wrong chamber, where Caecilianist imposters, "dead men," spread death. And within two or three generations, no one would be able to preside confidently over rebirth and regeneration.[41]

Had the Donatists really remained pure while an infection spread among their adversaries? Augustine made fun of the idea and went combing for scandals. "Take that case of Rusticianus," he said to Macrobius, the Donatist bishop of Hippo after 409,

> a case that compels me to write with great sorrow and distress. Rusticanus was expelled by his priest for bad habits and reprehensible conduct. Moreover, he had run up many debts, and the protection he sought from debts and discipline was rebaptism. He expected his creditors to clean the slate as [easily as] the Donatists had cleansed him of his sins. Your predecessor [Proculeianus] similarly rebaptized one of our deacons and made him a Donatist deacon though he had been expelled by us. Soon thereafter he took up with crooks, as he had planned all along. During a spree of robbery and arson, he was killed by those who were coming to the aid of his intended victims. Such are the fruits of this schism.[42]

Possibly this other fugitive was Primus, one of several European church officials who crossed to North Africa to escape disgrace. But word traveled fast, and refugees arrived only shortly ahead of the information about their misconduct. Caecilianists shunned them, proving to Augustine's satisfaction that his allies cared more than their rivals for church order and discipline. For the Donatists were said to have welcomed the discreditable from any and every quarter, despite their churches' claims to a superior righteousness.[43]

On second thought, however, this Primus was not a promising candidate for "one of our deacons," inasmuch as Augustine noted that Primus arrived from Spain with two of the many nuns he had seduced there. He did end up among the local Donatists, but all that he seems to have had in common with the second fugitive featured in the letter to Macrobius, apart from the hospitality of Bishop Proculeianus, was his unfortunate association with the hooligans known at the time as Circumcellions.[44]

When historians finish with Augustine's graphic stories of those hooligans—most of which are unverifiable—they look a bit like angry itinerant farmworkers periodically assaulting persons of property and authority. Augustine was persuaded that they were the Donatists' militant wing. He acknowledged the misgivings of the moderates among his rivals who cringed at the violence. But if we trust him, we have to assume that this loose confederacy between church and criminal showed how comic and unconvincing it was for the Donatists to boast of their discernment, discipline, and purity.[45]

Augustine bundled an assortment of crimes into his inventory of Circumcellion mischief. The ruffians' very existence, he said, terrorized the decent people of North Africa, who all the more avoided antagonizing their neighbors, employees, and servants for fear that the offended parties would summon Circumcellion retribution. An evicted tenant could conceivably bring down an entire estate. Landlords were humiliated or slain; officers of the courts, intimidated; tax collectors, stopped in their tracks. As Augustine dramatized Circumcellion depredation, stockpiling episodes to embarrass moderate Donatists, he was also appealing for imperial intervention.[46]

The misadventures of Optatus, Donatist bishop of Thamugadi, were splendid specimens, tailor-made to humiliate the moderates and to worry the government. Optatus's first pontifical project, the suppression of opposition within the Donatist network, led him to solicit Circumcellion support. Then he conspired with insurgents to assert North African independence. This led him into heaps of trouble when the insurrection was put down in 397. He died in prison the next year. If the Donatists were serious about "driv[ing] out the wicked person," why, Augustine inquired, had they not expelled their enterprising, yet defiant and ruthless colleague?[47]

To Augustine's feigned astonishment, the leading Donatists lionized Optatus while he lived and afterward treasured him as a martyr. Even the moderates seemed to forget the bullying and the bloodshed. Forgotten as well, Augustine insisted, was Jeremiah's injunction "Cursed is the man who trusts in man," for Optatus and his accomplices were expected to deliver Donatists from the imperial officials who intermittently harassed them and from the Caecilianists who constantly badgered them. The Donatists scowled at Caecilianists for having been indulgent when they should have been indignant, but they themselves indulged Optatus and thereby signaled conspicuously that no faction enjoyed a monopoly on wickedness.[48]

Yet we do well to remember that Optatus, the Circumcellions, Primus, and others were introduced into the argument to dispose of a striking claim made *for* the Donatists rather than *by* them. From their criticisms of Caecilian and their impatience with the Caecilianists, Augustine developed a Donatist perfectionism that he could rather easily confute. Donatists said they were holier than their rivals. Augustine inflated the claim so the noise would be louder when he punctured it.

In some measure, then, Donatism was created as it was being confuted. Today we might say that the Donatists were "set up," although it is hard to detect just where their "holier than thou" stopped and Augustine's exaggerations started. This interpretive difficulty should not obscure a central issue to which the rival Christianities in North Africa invariably returned. The Donatists insisted they represented the religion of the sacred book better than the Caecilianists did because they seceded from executives who collaborated with persecutors, whereas the Caecilianists did not. The Donatists said that they were uncontaminated (unstained by that one sin of cowardice and capitulation, not necessarily free from all other sins) and that their relative purity or holiness made their church "catholic."[49]

Augustine countered that catholic meant something very different. It described a church's reach, not its rigor. His Catholic Christian church reached back to Jesus. Caecilian was not its "father," not its founder, but a "brother," one Christian among a world full of others. For the Catholic, or universal, church reached across the known world as well as back in time. Reach, of course, was not wholly incompatible with rigor. Within a Catholic Christian church, the executive ought to stand up for, and stand out for, purity and holiness. Under no circumstances, however, should any executive withdraw and stand outside.[50]

Augustine stressed sacred literature's high regard for unity and universality. In Matthew's gospel, Jesus said that "many will come from east and west"; from "the ends of the earth," promised the psalmist, and "all nations" would serve God. The implication for Augustine was that all the faithful would serve and worship in one church. He argued that the unity of the universal church was prefigured by Jesus' tightly woven tunic. At the crucifixion, soldiers had cast lots for that seamless garment—they had not ripped it and divided the pieces. How irreverent, then, the Donatists were! What pagans had spared, they dared to tear.[51]

The Donatists were therefore the real traitors. They called the Caecilianists "accomplices" (*traditores*) for having handed over the sacred texts to persecutors and in subsequent generations reviled them for having shrugged or winked at the betrayal. But Augustine cautioned that secession was a higher treason and that stubbornly to remain outside the church was heresy:

> Not only were you [Donatists] unable to prove us traitors, but your ancestors were unable to prove that ours were. And even if our ancestors had been convicted, they were not, strictly speaking, our "fathers," as you assert, for we have not followed in their footsteps. Surely, we have not been torn from the fellowship and unity [of the church], from the seed of Abraham in which all Christians are blessed. . . . According to the apostle, "let each carry his own burden." If one among you is a a thief, you are all not thieves. If one of us happens to be a traitor, we are not all traitors. We are Catholics on this count: we do not forsake unity. You truly are heretics. You do not wish to stay with Abraham's seed because of some real or imagined transgression.[52]

Augustine asserted that the best response to transgression, whether incidental or habitual, was to correct and transform the transgressors. To secede from them was to leave the situation unresolved and to create new problems, specifically schism and an enduring enmity. The church had once been a sprinkling of small clusters of saintly souls but was not meant to remain so. The church was meant to grow—and it had grown—into "a large school for sinners."[53]

A School for Sinners

Augustine's arraignment of the Donatists featured, as we just heard, the observation that their secessionist strongholds never effectively barred the door to sinners. Their claims to a superior righteousness therefore appeared to Augustine to be fantastic and fraudulent, much as their idea that some strange infection sickened the rest of Christendom in North Africa. His case against secession, however, crested at another level, and there we find that his large school for sinners begins to take shape. A single decade of gangsterism proved to him that Donatists *did not* exclude the likes of Primus, Optatus, and the criminous Circumcellions. Four centuries of the church's history, its faith, and the intuitions that patterned every executive's experience convinced Augustine that bishops *should not* and *could not* exclude the wicked—should not, because pastors were supposed to welcome stray sheep. Jesus' parables about prodigals and lost lambs established the drill, yet the Donatists were known to drive visitors from their churches. They nastily interrogated the curious and ostracized the feeble. "They look after their own interests, not those of Jesus," Augustine complained, applying to Donatist intolerance the apostle Paul's indictment of the delinquent pastors at Philippi.[54]

Maybe stray, curious, frail sheep deserved the sympathy and hospitality Augustine recommended, but certainly Donatists were justified in raging against wicked shepherds! Surely there was nothing to say against spurning impious, irresponsible pastors! It seemed eminently sensible to staff a school for sinners with sinless schoolmasters and to transform transgressors by example. But Augustine thought otherwise and stretched one of the apostle Paul's metaphors to make the point.

"Neither he who plants nor he who waters is anything, but only God gives growth." Augustine elaborated: God furnished the seed, prepared the soil, and fashioned the right climate; seed, soil, climate, and God went about their business irrespective of the planter's sanctity as long as the crops were tended—while the sacraments were administered—in God's name.[55] The character of the planter or priest was irrelevant. To claim that wicked planters infected crops or that wicked priests infected Christians whom they baptized was to limit God's sovereignty, and limitations suggest, if I may switch metaphors, that an infinitely powerful God could not possibly use blunt instruments to create desired and flawlessly crafted results. Besides, if the character of priests left indelible marks on their parishioners, then the Donatists permanently scarred the Christians in their camp with their ludicrous passions for perfection, their intolerance, and their combativeness.[56]

Augustine never tired of insisting that the sacraments did not belong to the priests who administered them. Nor, he argued, did they belong exclusively to either of the rival churches in North Africa. The sacraments were God's.[57] And they were only effectively administered where the climate was right—that is, where congregants' faith, hope, and charity sustained the results of initiation and the remission of sins. So the right church made a great difference. Even if he could have been persuaded that the Donatists had faith in more than their holiness, that they hoped for something other than its (and their) just reward, Augustine was unalterably convinced that they lacked charity. They had too little compassion. They vilified and shunned the Caecilianists. They divided the church, whereas love unified. So much, then, for "should not"; the Donatists should not have culled lost lambs and lax pastors from their flocks. Having done so, they destroyed any basis for their claim to be a Christian church. They misperceived the Bible as a manual for perfection. They would not see that it was essentially an elegant and urgent manifesto for patience and humility. They trusted their "planters" and their own virtues. They trusted man, Augustine said again and again, rather than God.[58]

Segregating good from evil in this world preempted divine judgment. But what if the situation were different? What if wicked sheep and unprincipled pastors might be sent off without offending God? What if the Donatists were right to fear contamination and right again to think they *should* toss the rotten to protect the ripe? Augustine was emphatic and unequivocal: They simply *could not* do so. They could not sift the clean from the unclean, the wheat from the chaff because, regardless of how insightful they were, sifters were only human and thus could not probe the caverns of others' souls. Sin was easy to hide. In fact, it was everywhere, inescapable. And sifters themselves were sinners.

On the first point, the ease with which sin could sometimes be concealed, the Donatist scholar Cresconius tended to agree. Planters could well be artful dodgers. How might parishioners expose a priest who was a cunning and conscientious dissembler? Odds were against trusting laypersons, so Cresconius depended on what his church's executives were able to learn and free to tell him. He relied, in other words, on priests' reputations. Among the Donatists, priests were as good as their reputations.

Augustine pounced on this curious concession. He remembered how the Donatists had converged on the supposed, secret shame of the Caecilianists, challenging them to tunnel into their executives' pasts and prove pedigrees by tracking a series of ordinations and consecrations through generations. An impossible stunt, it would seem, but the alternative, they said, was for Caecilianists to live with insecurity and face the prospect that their officials were imposters, their sacraments ineffective, their many sins unpardoned, and their souls unsaved. Yet here was the Donatist Cresconius content, although his priest's piety might well be hypocrisy. Reputations, after all, often were unexpectedly but deservedly shattered. How comfortable could he be assuming the best until some fresh disclosure or indiscretion showed up the worst?[59]

In Augustine's opinion, it was senseless to assume the best and to confirm or disqualify on the basis of reputation. It was only reasonable and realistic to acknowledge that sin was as common as flesh. He allowed that most Donatists could justifiably utter the standard disclaimers, "I burn incense for no god" and "I commit neither adultery nor murder." But Augustine could not imagine he would ever meet anyone who dared to say, or even dared to think, "I am not a sinner." For just a moment, then, and for the sake of his argument for the pervasive character of sin, he altered his caricature of the severe, unself-critical Donatist Scrooge. Augustine nearly always pictured the perfectionists propped up on every side by their invincible arrogance. Here, however, he professed that no one could be so self-satisfied as to be unmoved by the impulse to pray, "Forgive us our tres-passes."[60]

Sin was pervasive, but Augustine was not about to put up with it (although ru-mors to that effect circulated, thanks to Donatist critics). No, Augustine pressed bishops to punish as well as warn offenders. He wanted church councils to repri-mand and discipline irresponsible executives. He feared contamination and con-tagion much less intensely than did the Donatists. Nevertheless, winking at scan-dal was never an option for him, so there was a stretch of common ground to be staked and settled. He wrote to Donatist moderates, looking for opportunities for discussion and debate. For several years after his ordination and consecration, he believed he could lead them back to the church if he could get them out to talk and, of course, to listen.[61]

But they seldom came out to talk and listen on Augustine's terms. Had they forgotten the apostle Peter's injunction "Be prepared to make a defense to anyone who calls you to account"? Had they forgotten it or misconstrued it deliberately, Augustine asked? Did they prefer to "make a defense" with clubs rather than con-versation? Augustine played up the Circumcellions' assaults to make all Donatists appear dangerous as well as intractable, and predictably the emperor's agents re-sponded to the sensationalism, increasingly so, after Optatus participated in the insurrection of 397.[62] Imperial edicts prohibited the Donatists' worship and pro-vided for the confiscation of their properties. The bishop of Hippo endorsed the measures, admitting in effect that proposed conversations, when they occurred, were not working; that his words persuaded too few; and that coercion, though regrettable, was necessary. The situation had deteriorated. The time had come for the persecutors *of* Christianity to become persecutors *for* Christianity. It was time, he announced, to force the issue of reunion (*cogunt ad unitatem*).[63] Sometimes cruelty was kindness, as when God struck the apostle Paul from his horse and blinded him so he might come to his senses. If the Donatists had to be wrestled to safety, so be it; better by far to bruise the body than lose the soul.[64]

Augustine's apology for coercive Christianity required two delicate maneuvers. First, he had to embrace an empire that most everywhere was falling apart. Second, he had to distinguish the hard times he and government authorities pre-pared for the Donatists from those hardships endured by the pilgrim city of God. He did not want to associate North African secessionists with the select, privileged company he was just then assembling in his *De civitate*, so he stressed that Jesus only blessed Christians persecuted for the sake of righteousness. The Donatists, he said, were persecuted because they had divided the church and then plotted against the more faithful part. Not every cross carried a martyr. Undeniably, Donatists suffered, but so did the thieves posted alongside Jesus on Calvary, and no one mistook them for heroes of the faith.[65]

The Donatist bishop of Cartenna was shocked by Augustine's consent to coer-cion, but his shock and protests in 408 elicited only an energetic defense. Even if

Augustine had been moved to reconsider, however, the Donatist position would have continued to erode. Imperial edicts and envoys were making it hard for the secessionists to suppress the subschisms that revived after Optatus's death and harder still to close ranks against the Caecilianists.[66]

Was it desperation, or just possibly exhaustion, that brought Donatists to the conference table in 411? Possibly they perceived the emperor's invitation to lock horns with their old enemies as an excellent opportunity to regroup, for pending the outcome of the proceedings, the government suspended all action against the bishops who agreed to come to a council in Carthage. Maybe the Donatists trusted the emperor's designated arbiter, Marcellinus, when he promised impartiality. But Augustine was never in doubt that officials had prejudged the affair. The government had given no hint it would reverse standing policy, so he "generously" offered to submit to whatever Marcellinus and the council decided.[67]

Apparently, the Donatists hoped to influence authorities with a display of their numerical superiority. They entered the city impressively. During the first session, they insisted on a roll call, which showed that the last decade of efforts to close them down had actually buoyed them up. For nearly every Catholic bishop there was a Donatist from the same village anxious to name his rival "persecutor."[68]

Scribes kept a record of the exchanges that followed, and precautions were taken to assure accuracy. Monitors from both camps regularly checked transcripts. Marcellinus periodically replaced weary with fresh squads of secretaries, who swept long and serpentine speeches as well as curt replies and unflattering remarks into verbatim accounts. But Augustine complained of one omission: He was only sorry that the scribes had found no way to include the laughter occasioned, he said, by the idiocy of his adversaries' arguments.[69] His more serious and solemn complaint, however, was that Donatists delayed. They fussed over who first accused whom of what. "So much is said and done, so that nothing will get done." At issue, Augustine pressed, was the nature of the church, whether the Catholic Church was a regional, North African network of self-declared saints or a school for sinners and a universal communion.[70]

Augustine stiffened his and Catholic Christian resistance. He argued that the regional character of the Donatist church told against its claims, though the Donatists could not see why. Their disaffection seemed no less real or righteous to them because it was regional. Were they suspect for having failed to turn every church in the Mediterranean basin against Caecilian? Augustine might have said so; he would have faulted them for having been unable to win the universal church had the history of the long conflict not afforded him a related, though better, argument. The Donatists had not just failed to win; they had lost. The councils of Rome and Arles had acquitted Caecilian, finding blameless the bishop who had consecrated him. And the Donatists had not just lost; they had left.

The Donatists' answer (and excuse): The councils and their acquittals had been rigged. Miltiades of Rome, they said, had been a patron of *traditores,* an accomplice of the very type of traitors from whom their ancestors had seceded to save

the church. Their character sketch elicited criticism from Augustine, who determined that their brushwork betrayed haste and improvisation. Their case against
Miltiades, he bellowed, was atrociously unfair. If there had ever been evidence, it
had vanished. Donatists' front-page, unsubstantiated accusations were worse than
back-page gossip. Then with Bishop Miltiades in the clear and Caecilian in the
church, just as the fourth-century councils had ruled, Augustine packed up all the
events of those early years in the Catholics' corner of the great debate in Carthage.
He summed up spiritedly: Jesus had come and had died to reconcile "the world"
to God; at Rome and at Arles that world rejected the secessionists and their
claims.[71]

I should add before adjourning that the world Jesus reconciled to God yielded
strikingly different interpretations. Bishop Petilian argued in 411 that it referred
to Christians whom God wished to redeem. It was a small world, easily accommodated by a single region of the larger. Indeed, that reconciled and redeemed
world was the Donatist church, that "granary" of good Christians to which Jesus
called attention when he pledged that God "will clear his threshing floor and
gather his wheat into the granary, but the chaff he will burn with unquenchable
fire."[72] Augustine returned the world to its standard size and spread the catholic,
or universal, church over it. The passage, he said, prophesied the final judgment.
It did not license Donatists to sift and secede on earth. God's "threshing floor"—
not the "granary"—was the church, a school for sinners, which contained both
wheat and chaff, the good and the wicked, until the very end.[73]

At the end of the council, Augustine seemed satisfied that discussions had gone
pretty much as planned—that is, according to the plan he and his episcopal allies
had filed at the start. That document survives with the conference record and
concedes that a church spread over the world (*diffunditur*) acquires a peculiar
vulnerability. Given the Donatists' charges, there were good reasons to avoid conceding even this, but the Catholics' preliminary plan was intended to keep complaints about individual bishops, however painstakingly researched and persua-
sively repackaged at the conference, from casting their church in the shadow of
particular criminals and specific crimes. So the Catholic executives admitted, if
only by implication, that a church that invited so much of the world to communion could well be—perhaps was asking to be—stained by some of its guests. The
trick was to turn universality into a virtue, and Augustine performed it amazingly
well.[74]

But he did not bring round the Donatists. One hundred years earlier, a contested consecration in North Africa had galvanized the opposition to two mega-
ton institutions, empire and traditional church, into, of all things, a third, and
neither Augustine nor Marcellinus could make it disappear. The council of
Carthage in 411 closed after confirming all previous anti-Donatist rulings.
Augustine continued to write and preach against secessionists. For all that, however, the extinction of Donatism (and of much of Catholic Christianity in the region) awaited the advent of Islam in the seventh century.

The Church and the World

Discussions at the council of Carthage ranged remarkably. Donatists and Catholics quarreled over the origin, history, and character of their battles against each other. They debated the meaning of martyrdom and the makeup of the church. What made the assembly rather unusual, however, was that the government directly determined the outcome. Elsewhere political authorities let their favorite bishops do the precinct work and build consensus around officially sanctioned doctrine and discipline. But Marcellinus stepped right in as arbiter, and the leadership of both churches agreed to it. The Donatists had no choice, but the Catholics did, and we want to see how and why Augustine helped them make it.

We start by backtracking a bit. From the disintegration of the Christian empire, Augustine learned to invest little hope in this world. But during his controversies with the Donatists, he also learned that the churches' executives were well advised to use this world, to cultivate politically influential friends and cooperative public officials. We could argue that he wanted to lay the foundations for something like an imperial church. After all, he did hold that the Catholic Christian church was designed or commissioned to reconcile the whole world to God. Yet he also counseled that the church had to be resigned to the world's resistance, patient as well as militant and universal.

Resistance was deplorable but predictable. Even the best of times stopped short of perfect peace and tranquillity. Augustine tried to correct the expectations of many Christians and those of outspoken pagan critics, all of which attached to the phrase "Christian times." The times, he said, were not Christian not only because neopaganism seemed to be supplanting the piety of the apostles and martyrs but also because Christianity, in time and history, was a religion of unrest, *inquietum*.

> Anyone who hopes for great good here and now is a fool. Does anyone really think that even in the much touted reign of King Solomon peace was fully realized? The sacred book certainly approves Solomon's regime, but only as a shadow of what has been promised. . . . Human affairs are changeable, precarious. Freedom from care is conceded to no one on earth. Dreaded, hostile forces are inescapable. That promised place [of peace] is eternal. . . . We yearn for it through our faith [in God's promise] as we carry on with this pilgrimage full of misery.[75]

De civitate proposed that Christians on pilgrimage cling to God with their faith and desire or yearning, cling to God and to one another in the church. Emancipation from the base instincts that held all hostage—to the extent that it was possible—followed a private struggle. Christians combated concupiscence, their longing for fame and wealth and power, such that their private chambers became war zones. But righteousness was mediated in public by the church. For righteousness was an amnesty, the forgiveness of sins available through the church's sacraments and made effective in "the right climate" of the right church, a climate created and sustained by the Christians who lived charitably with one another and held tenaciously to their religion's highest expectations. Righteousness was not perfect virtue. Perfect virtue, much as perfect peace, was unattainable in this life. Faith and yearning, however, inclined Christians to use the world resourcefully and virtuously and, Augustine stipulated, to be obedient, charitable, humble, self-restrained, and prayerful.[76]

The Donatists distressed Augustine on several counts. We have already heard him fret about their disobedience, arrogance, and catastrophic unkindness to Caecilianists. He also professed to have some difficulty imagining what they prayed for. For they seemed to him to believe they had earned by suffering—and thus securely possessed—nearly everything for which other Christians were praying. Catholics prayed to be made worthy by God of what God both gave to them and expected from them on their pilgrimage, namely, forgiveness and fortitude. They prayed to be made worthy of what they expected from God afterward: perfect peace at their pilgrimage's end. Catholic executives prayed, as had the apostle Paul, that God would make them worthy of their responsibilities to forgive, console, and reveal.[77] But the proud did not know how to pray. They presumed they were worthy, and, worst of all, they thought they had acquired powers of discernment for which even the churches' most discerning executives would never have had the nerve to pray. At the appointed time, "at the close of the age," God's angels would separate good fish from bad, but the Donatists, trying to anticipate, tore "the net," tore apart the church. It was better by far for the present to pray for perseverance and patience and to live in hope.[78]

Augustine also had difficulty imagining what the Pelagians hoped and prayed for. He learned about Pelagius while preparing for the council of Carthage. Fugitives from the Goths were crossing to North Africa with the news that a popular spiritual counselor in Rome was resolutely defending freedom of human choice and all but reducing Christianity to a set of moral imperatives. To Augustine, this position seemed terribly arrogant. If the Pelagians believed that they possessed the wherewithal to overcome sin and the constancy to keep ever after beyond its influence, for what did this Pelagius and his disciples pray? If their fine, free choices were sure to earn them righteousness and eternal reward, for what did they hope?

After listening to Caelestius, one of the more outspoken Pelagian émigrés, Augustine figured he knew what had gone wrong. Pelagius had simply crowded out of his calculations the single consideration that rightly humbled all other Christians, save neopagans and Donatists. He had forgotten all that sacred literature revealed about the pervasiveness and the utterly debilitating effects of sin. And Augustine thought he knew why memory had failed the Pelagians because he shared their contempt for the Manichaeans and because contempt for heretics who discounted human freedom tempted Christians to attribute too much to that freedom. In the 390s, Augustine had himself written against Manichaean pessimism and determinism. He was only then beginning to appreciate how impossible it would be freely and independently to achieve the life and service to which he had been called. By 411, however, the bishop had come to regret his overly optimistic remarks about human freedom and responsibility, remarks to which Pelagians referred as they repeated the very mistakes he had made. They overreacted to the Manichaeans and minimized the extent to which all humans were "mired" in the flesh. In prayer and hope, mired Christians "sighed" upward and forward, acknowledging they were in some measure captives as well as pilgrims in this world, that they were never wholly liberated from their basest instincts, petty jealousies, and worldly preoccupations. But Augustine heard no sighing from Caelestius. Augustine heard nothing that gave him any sense at all that the Pelagians comprehended the gravity of the human predicament. He heard only their self-congratulation and saw only the signs of inordinate self-confidence.[79]

He had his fill of such confidence. Donatists put too great a premium on their powers of discernment; Pelagians overvalued their determination. Whereas the former preempted God's judgment, the latter demoted the divine judge, turning God into a paymaster who distributed handsome—but due—compensation for work well and independently done. Despite passing references to divine sovereignty, the Pelagians so ardently defended human freedom against fatalism that, according to Augustine, they could not recall that salvation was earned *for* them, not *by* them.

> The good that one does comes to light when one knows that justification comes from God's grace and is not a reward for virtue. The apostle said that "God is at work in you, both to will and to work for his good pleasure." All who come from carnal generation to spiritual regeneration come therefore through Christ, who made it clear, when asked, that questions about remission could not be resolved by reason. Even infants must receive the grace of remission, inasmuch as there is no other way to cross to Christ, and no one can be reconciled to God or come to God except through Christ.[80]

But why infants? They had so little time to sin between carnal generation and spiritual regeneration. Caelestius agreed that a ritual dedication was appropriate, but he objected to Augustine's explanation of why infant baptism had to be remission as well as dedication—Caelestius objected, that is, to the idea that sin was transmitted with the flesh. For the Pelagians, sin was a bad but breakable habit that infants had no chance to acquire. So the only baptism that made a substantial difference was one in which adults received the grace that empowered them to overcome habits and temptations, a ritual signaling their mature determination to refashion themselves. Then refashioning themselves, Pelagians fashioned their small congregations into collections of perfectly virtuous Christians.[81]

Augustine balked at what he thought a coarse and sinister perfectionism displayed by both the Donatists and Pelagians. He insisted that churches accustom themselves to abiding imperfections, arguing that Jesus left executives to tend

God's sheep because they needed tending. The Christians strayed. They did not just "cross" to Christ once and for all. At every turn, they needed help to take up their crosses, to accept the grace of remission mediated through the sacraments, and to fortify their faith and expectations. The church was a school for sinners, but it taught them to live with sin, not without it. It taught them to live as pilgrims, to trust history less and eternity more. And to teach them and thus to reconcile the world to God, Augustine's church normally made its peace with the powers of this world. But as "a spiritual earthly city," it could never be completely at peace in this world.[82]

Two political implications impressed Augustine as especially encouraging in the early fifth century. First, Christians skilled in managing conflict should not shy away from public service because as peacemakers on earth, politicians were superb auxiliaries to the churches' executives, who were uniquely charged with a more sublime and soterial peacemaking. Second, churches should invite and use government assistance, for partnerships between the rulers of this world and the representatives of the next seemed a plausible and even agreeable way to begin "pouring" the church over all civilization.

Pastoral implications are more important for our purposes, for they help position Augustine and his school for sinners in the history of early Christian leadership. In 412, pausing over the psalmist's observation that "man is like a breath, his days are like a passing shadow," Augustine registered that a pastor's job was to stop finitude from becoming just another abstraction, to give mortality life in his sermons, and to create and preserve a tension between desperation and expectation. The immediate aim was to teach humility. Far more than an afterthought, however, was Augustine's suggestion that Christians "passed" on pilgrimage for a purpose. The purpose was to subject them to God and to God's instrument, the universal church.[83]

Subjection was never complete. Neither righteousness nor peace on earth was perfect. Mulish perfectionists were extreme examples of the truth they tried to deny—to wit, nobody cleared the vanity in this world until he or she vaulted to the next. To them, Augustine became an apostle of imperfection. He knew that some Christians appeared to have conquered ignorance, that some seemed to have overcome the grossest forms of sin and temptation. But everyone in this world, without exception, was mired in the flesh, he said, and uncertainties or suspicions about immortality muted all their sighs and weighed down all their expectations. He remembered that Solomon, whose peace was nearly perfect, composed Ecclesiastes simply, yet eloquently to explain that nothing was "solid" and "stable" but that all was sacred.[84]

The churches' executives were no Solomons. Nevertheless, they had the words attributed to him and the rest of the sacred texts to guide them. And, Augustine added, they had the martyrs as well. He dismissed the Donatists' charges that he and his episcopal colleagues despised and dishonored the martyrs.[85] Quite the contrary, he replied, Catholic Christians realized that there were no better critics of the perfectionists' pretensions than the illustrious martyrs themselves. In the right hands, martyrs' stories taught humility, shaming wayward, separatist Christians whose self-proclaimed nobility paled by comparison. In the right hands, martyrs' stories, festivals, and shrines encouraged the Christians to have contempt for this world and to prize their alienation in and from it. Finally, in the right hands, the martyrs' legacy was a compelling and an inspiring lesson that calamity in this life regenerated Christians' expectations for the next.[86]

But the bones, shrines, and stories of martyrs too often fell into the wrong hands. Christians seized on the stories or circled the shrines of the martyrs to console themselves and not to confound their ambitions and expectations. That was how Augustine thought of neopagans' devotion to martyrs' monuments and anniversaries, of Pelagians' respect for the martyrs' grit and determination, and of Donatists' idealization of the martyrs' excruciating ordeals. In those wrong hands, then, the martyrs were made to assure that prosperity was protected, that virtues would not go unrewarded, and that the secessionists' hardships attested their holiness. All those wrong hands grabbed at imaginary consolation. Augustine suspected that neopagans, Pelagians, and Donatists never came to grief, so to speak, never even approached the profound self-dissatisfaction that preceded the redemptive reorientation he hoped all Christians would experience.

If his *Confessiones* can be trusted, Augustine had learned firsthand how consciousness responds to long pulls from grief. The death of a dear friend, he remembered, had left him wholly and wretchedly preoccupied with his mortality, meaninglessness, and misery. His agony and despair had taught him how thoroughly his hopes were fixed on earthly, perishable things. And that realization had started his gradual rehabilitation, which we glimpsed at the onset. Heartache awakened displeasure with the world around him and with himself, yet he gladly wished the same on others because he had come to believe that Christians caught in the coils of grief eventually offered their contrition and gave up their "broken spirits" as sacrifices, much as the martyrs had given up their lives.[87]

Augustine understood that executives tending God's sheep would have to do more than just excite and accept the contrition, faith, and yearning of Christians in their flocks. If the church was to be truly universal, its executives would have to try reconciling the world to God, overcoming its ingratitude, and breaking down its resistance.

The resistance the apostle Peter first encountered was his own: He was extremely reluctant to undertake the mission to the gentiles God had assigned him. But what most impressed Augustine was not the apostle's resistance; it was God's response, a vision in which God told Peter to "kill and eat" the animals set before him, repeating the command so there could be no mistake. And then immediately thereafter Peter was alerted to the request from the pagan Cornelius, who asked to be instructed in the faith. That a pagan soldier should be taken into the church, should be "killed" and brought to life, gave Augustine occasion to contemplate that great reversal in the history of Christianity. Although Peter "ate" Cornelius, took him into the body of Christ, later, and through generations, the world very nearly swallowed up the church. Even after the persecutions of the Catholic Christians had ceased, the secessionists in North Africa nibbled and gnawed at the universal church's southernmost limbs or extensions. Neopagans everywhere were charmed away from the center of the Christian faith, lured into an abyss of superstition. Augustine believed the apostle's vision to have been something of a summons, a charge to church executives to reclaim what had been lost and, by all means, to reconcile the rest, "to kill and eat."[88]

The violence of that ghostly vision was rather apt. Sacred literature often marked the limits of divine diplomacy: Peter's God was the same as the psalmist's, renowned for rising in anger and smiting enemies, for "break[ing] the teeth of the wicked." When Augustine came across that passage, he opposed the church's teeth to those of the wicked. *Dentes ecclesiae* were the churches' executives, whose assignment, as Peter's, was "to kill and eat." Their game, of course, was not the sinners but their sin. Executives killed old expectations and superstitions. They chewed, as it were, to prepare the gentiles for their translation into the church, the body of Christ.[89]

My intuition is that Augustine would not have objected to extending this metaphor. For in an imperfect church in an imperfect world, ingestion would invariably lead to indigestion. Virtually every one of the important arguments he offered against the Donatists and so many of his observations in *De civitate Dei* cautioned that the church on earth (and on pilgrimage) would find no rest "until finding rest in God." That portion of the pilgrim city of God in the belly of the Catholic, or universal, church—in its net, on its threshing floor—shared space with the wicked. So when Christians chanted the Bible's psalms of deliverance, they imagined Israel's complaining and groaning and praying as the prophecies of their predicament. Augustine's universal church on earth hungered after a righteousness it had yet to realize and never would, while it struggled to assimilate all those it had eaten. And it never could.[90]

❀ 5 ❀

Authority and Humility

The author of Acts remembered that the apostle Paul had walked past pagans' shrines on his way to preach in Athens. Each shrine had been home to a different god, one of them "to an unknown god." The Athens sermon summed up Paul's protest against such idolatry: "The god who made the world and everything in it, being lord of heaven and earth, does not live in shrines made by men."[1] Had Augustine rid Christianity of neopaganism, the faithful might have accepted that the highest righteousness resided in heaven. On earth, they might have cherished, above all, their greatest expectations—those for the next life—lavishing fewer funds on, and less faith in, those monuments sheltering the remains from this one. But Augustine did not purge neopaganism. The Christians of the fifth and sixth centuries were not all that sure about the distinctions between the hereafter and the here and now. It seems they were reluctant to believe that no god or godly spirit lived in those impressive buildings that patrons and church executives were constructing around Christian worship.

The buildings were filled with aids to faith. Interiors were decorated with re-minders that the humble would be exalted. Jesus himself did not live there, though he frequently visited. Whenever Christians celebrated the eucharist, the very substance of the savior's perfect life, body and blood, touched down on the altars and transformed all who witnessed. Ideally, recollecting his precious promise of resurrection and anticipating reward for faith and patience joined Christians—odds and ends, executives and eccentrics—into a holy community, a holy communion.

It happened fairly often, during festivals and nearly every Sunday as well. In several churches the eucharist was celebrated daily. Priests advised worshipers to approach altars "with clean hands and a pure heart," to tidy up their messy lives. Penitents could not attend until their penances were done, and the evidence sug-gests that Christians took the prohibition and privilege quite seriously. "Participation" in the life of their savior—by their recollection, anticipation, and transformation—was a privilege for which Christians yearned when it was denied them or offered too infrequently. We might imagine them proceeding to the altar and almost certainly awed by the miracle there, but perhaps glancing around at illustrations on church walls. Pope Gregory I referred to wall drawings as a Bible for the unlettered.[2] Not all of the drawings depicted episodes from the sacred texts; some pictured local heroes and heroines of the faith—martyrs, ascetics, and outstanding executives—suffering, healing, and preaching. The Christians were surrounded by their saints while waiting for the eucharist or walking to the altar, and the altar itself often doubled as a tomb for their churches' most memorable martyr or administrator.

To say that memorabilia turned some churches into museums only slightly overstates the case, but the Christians treasured their mementos, be they body parts of local or widely acclaimed celebrities, threads from their clothing, or instruments of torture that had touched them. Relics of that sort were often associated with devotion, although a few of the devout were keenly aware of the danger of excessive veneration, notably Augustine, the church's chief critic of neopaganism. But even he was aware of the power of relics to inspire awe. If only the church could draw on that power, keep awe within proper bounds, and redirect it from the things and heroes of this world into the highest expectations for the next!

Bishops and Bones

Augustine enthusiastically welcomed the bones of the martyr Stephen when they were delivered to Numidia and deposited at one of the shrines near Hippo. Maybe the bishop guessed that stories of healing would draw tourists—pilgrims—within the reach of his sermons; or perhaps he figured that cures and curious occurrences at the shrine would provoke parishioners to reanimate their pious, yet flagging expectations. For whatever reason, Augustine muted the skepticism he had expressed on previous occasions. He preached about bones and wonders and miracles, granting that the relics possessed powers beyond human comprehension. He urged others to write up the cures they witnessed or experienced. One marvel may stand for the many he reported, the story of two travelers from Caesarea in Cappadocia that suggests the subtlety with which he related remedy to redemption.

The two, brother and sister, came to Hippo some weeks before Easter. They had been afflicted with a terrible trembling ever since being cursed by their mother for having mistreated her. But Easter morning, while gripping the rail near Stephen's bones and praying for forgiveness and health, the brother slipped into a trance and fell to the ground. When he raised himself, his limbs were still; the spasms had ceased. Three days later, as Augustine was speaking about the event, shouts were heard from the shrine, where the young man's sister was just then similarly restored to health. The bishop gathered everyone in church and continued his commentary. I wager that he lifted his voice as he mentioned the timing—Easter and three days after—and that he was seen staring in the direction of the shrine and then back again at the altar as he rehearsed how the two

Cappadocians had been raised and restored. Gaze, gestures, and tone of voice no doubt rerouted his parishioners' awe and devotion from Stephen's part in the siblings' miraculous recuperation to Jesus' resurrection and Jesus' part in the redemption of all.[3]

We know Augustine labored to reorient expectations. He wanted Christians to expect far less of martyrs, saints, and bones in terms of immediate, material gain and gratification. Instead of pleading for the intervention of the blessed dead to gratify earthly and often self-indulgent desires for safety and health and honor and wealth, Christians, he said, ought to pray and hope for everlasting reward and peace. But we learned pages ago that Augustine grudgingly accommodated habits and practices of which he demonstrably disapproved. He did not want to run the risk of jarring loose persons who were as yet strapped insecurely to their new religion, Christians hesitant to surrender suddenly and forever their former, pagan prejudices. But Augustine's episcopal colleagues, then and thereafter, faced other challenges. In fact, their convictions were nearly indistinguishable from his accommodations. We can only imagine whether he would have thought they tried too hard to make Christianity too easy.

Late in the sixth century, Gregory of Tours told what has since become an emblematic tale of Gallic accommodation. Locals, he recalled, came every year to a lake in the Aubrac Mountains. They brought wagonloads of cloth and carving with them, and as they feasted for several days, they threw their cargo into the water to appease the spirits. Then they scattered, chased from the scene by a near deadly downpour that arrived punctually to end each annual festival. The bishop tried to discourage them, emphasizing the apparent, stormy proof that God was upset with their superstition. Nonetheless, they were undeterred until that bishop built a shrine on the shore for the relics of Bishop Hilary of Poitiers. Thereupon the locals transferred their loyalties from the lake to the lakefront, from the spirits in nature to one bishop in another bishop's shrine. Instead of heaving their wares into the water, they handed them over to Hilary. And the weather for all subsequent festivals improved.[4]

But bishops generally kept their holiest relics close to them. As important as it might have been to pry "rustics" from their attachments to sacred shrubs, streams, and lakes, it was also critical that bishops and bones protect the cities of Gaul, Italy, Iberia, and North Africa. The age of "centralization and assimilation under the Roman empire" was fatefully coming to an end. The west increasingly belonged to the Vandals, Visigoths, Ostrogoths, Burgundians, and Franks. Authority to resist them, negotiate with them, and submit to them in the fifth and sixth centuries fell to the churches' chief executives, who were often eulogized as their cities' "defenders." They strategically placed relics in their home churches, their cathedrals. And in Clermont, Nantes, Bordeaux, Rheims, and Auxerre, the bishops also built shrines into and atop their fortifications and deployed relics as well at the city gates. Even before Augustine asked Christians not to count on martyrs' memorabilia for earthly protection, Victricius, bishop of Rouen, had spoken for the next generations of executives when greeting a new shipment of relics as if it were a battalion of soldiers.[5]

Victricius anticipated skepticism. The relics were small; his city's crises were bound to be behemoth. It seemed wise to make explicit the assumption on which the cults of relics were based: *Ubi est aliquid, ibi totum est* (wherever a fragment is found, the power and divinity of the whole is present).[6] If the smallest keepsakes were not to disappoint and disappear, bishops would have to make the point often. Paulinus of Nola did so when he sent his friend and fellow bishop Severus "a tiny sliver" of the true cross given him by the bishop of Jerusalem. Along with that sacred splinter, Paulinus dispatched a memorandum that was to be read publicly, no doubt, and as often as "faith demanded." The document detailed the discovery: how God kept the cross on which Jesus was crucified safely buried until the conversion of Constantine, how Constantine's mother paid for the search, how special revelations directed her where to dig, and how a miracle enabled her to distinguish the true cross from the other two on which the thieves had been executed. In conclusion and without reservation, Paulinus pronounced that the cross "suffered no diminution" when broken apart and distributed.[7]

At home in Nola, Paulinus composed poems celebrating the heroics of Felix the Confessor, whose remains and relics were divided among the bishop's church, the local monastery, and at least one nearby shrine. Each year Paulinus's latest verses were recited during the festival commemorating the anniversary of Felix's death. The poems created memories, associating them with the annual festival and with the venerable tokens of the saint's enduring presence. Poems, memories, and memorabilia attested the confessor's patronage and protection.

In 401, Paulinus told the grisly tale of an accident that had wounded a parishioner named Theridius on the eve of a previous year's celebration. After having finished the eucharistic meal, members of the congregation were singing psalms when Theridius decided to stroll in the night air. In a dark corridor leading outside, he bumped into an ornate, unlit lantern suspended from the ceiling. One of its three protruding hooks slashed into his eye and lodged in the socket. Paulinus described the unfortunate victim's predicament with gruesome, anatomical precision and either remembered or scripted Theridius's extended and, under the circumstances, surprisingly eloquent appeal for Felix's help. It confessed the plaintiff's sins, candidly conceding his blindness to justice and imploring Felix to save his sight and soul. The confessor's bones were within earshot. Felix heard and obliged, at least on the first count. According to Paulinus's report, Felix steadied Theridius's hand and thereby achieved, through all the pain, what no seasoned surgeon would have dared.[8]

Paulinus claimed that Felix had also done miraculously well while alive; several biographical poems complement the former's more lurid tales of the latter's cures from the crypt. At the beginning of one, Felix landed in prison, but God arranged for his release and led him to the roadside place where the local bishop, Maximus, had collapsed. With God's additional help, Felix revived Maximus and restored him to his church, whereupon the duly grateful bishop turned benefactor. At

God's command, Maximus blessed Felix, thus bestowing eternal life on the one who had brought him back to this life. Hence, the conclusion of Paulinus's commemorative piece amounts to a role reversal. Its cheerful last lines applaud the reciprocity between confessor and executive. Did Christians of Nola have any inkling that Bishop Maximus's benediction heralded episcopal jurisdiction over the cults of confessors, martyrs, and saints? At some level, they certainly must have been aware that their bishops annually revived Felix, liturgically and narratively, in festivals and poetic tributes.[9]

The lakefront relics, Victricius's saintly "soldiers," and Paulinus's poems accommodated desires for a divine presence. It could be argued that Christianity was flirting with idolatry, that the cults' executive custodians had more or less forgotten what Paul had said: "God does not live in shrines." For bishops colonized holy places, moved bones into their cathedrals, made saints their very special friends and partners in pastoral care. Bishops acquired relics, ordered up illustrations and inscriptions, and composed vignettes and eulogies to emphasize both their patronage and that of their divine patrons.

Peter Brown compared episcopal custodians to electricians "rewir[ing] an antiquated wiring system." "In this process of rewiring," he wrote, "the figure of the martyr himself change[d]"; martyrs became the bishops' and their churches' patrons at the heavenly court. The episcopal electricians moved the bodies and bones so that "more power could pass through stronger, better insulated wires toward the bishop as leader of the community." This was a skill or trade that bears watching in yet another context, where "rewiring" created consensus from conflict in times of crisis.[10]

The city of Tours, for example, was in trouble in the early 570s. No local candidate for episcopal office had distinguished himself amply enough to win both the clerical vote and popular acclaim, so the church finally decided to import its new chief executive. Venantius Fortunatus, the prolific eulogist, later bishop of Poitiers, left word that the king and queen had selected the outsider and pulled strings, as we might have said, to get him elected. And today it is easier to imagine such political influence than to accept another of Fortunatus's explanations—namely, that Saints Julian and Martin brought Gregory to Tours. Yet it turns out that the second and implausible explanation is fairly well attested and Merovingian intervention is not.[11]

Gregory was an exceptionally good choice for Tours. He came from solid ecclesial stock—his relatives served several churches in the region, some as bishops—though he was still a stranger in the Touraine. He anticipated that his nomination was likely to cause a stir, but he was not a timid man. Shortly after his consecration at Rheims, he traveled to Clermont to worship at the nearby tomb of Julian, thought to have been martyred during the early fourth century. The annual festival there had been a family favorite, so Gregory thought of the tomb's tenant as his protector and patron. (Fortunatus called him Julian's *alumnus,* his foster son.) The new bishop of Tours requested and received some threads from a cloth covering the coffin. They were to be his safe convoy into and his defense (*praesidium*) against the rough-and-tumble of the Touraine factions and feuds.

When he arrived at his destination, partisans urged Gregory to build a new church immediately and put their treasure from Clermont on display. But he "rewired" tactfully, secretly setting the threads in the church dedicated to Martin, whom local custom had canonized nearly two hundred years before. In the interim, Tours's cult of Bishop Martin turned the city into a popular pilgrimage site. All factions in the 470s agreed on Martin's value for the region. Offending Martin's many friends would have been a ghastly mistake. A saintly rival might have caused a panic, so Gregory waited—but not long—for a miracle to suggest that Martin had hospitably welcomed Julian and possibly sent for him. A citizen saw a shaft of light from heaven enter the church where Gregory concealed the relics. The light fell directly on them, and that was enough to make Julian appear to be Martin's partner and to make Julian's *alumnus* bishop by consent as well as by title.[12]

On other occasions, straight-ahead stubbornness served bishops well, for the Goths against whom they defended their cities and with whom they negotiated proved to be headstrong neighbors and sovereigns. And to be effective, the churches' executives needed local solidarity and unconditional support. For these, executives ordinarily looked to their communities' cults. Ian Wood suspected that the bishops of Marseilles managed less well than other Gallic executives under trying circumstances because "no major saint-cult [in Marseilles] could be relied on to bolster episcopal power."[13]

Truth be told, however, the dire character of those trying circumstances is often exaggerated by scholars who harp on the barbarity of the so-called barbarians. If Christians and their executives in the fourth, fifth, and sixth centuries had learned of their Germans exclusively from textbooks, specifically from the literature of classical antiquity, we would have to excuse them for having deliberated over whether the barbarians' inhumanity rivaled that of beasts. But all in Gaul learned their Germans from commerce with them and increasingly realized that darkness had not descended on all civilization. By the 470s, Sidonius of Clermont, Faustus of Riez, and quite a number of their episcopal colleagues were concurring that the Germanic tribes, self-styled defenders of the western empire, were not comically primitive or horridly lawless peoples. And these executives also concurred that Catholic Christianity possessed sufficient stamina and popular support to make the best of a barbarous, though not an irredeemably bad, situation.[14]

Maybe confidence of this kind was cosmetic, a brave front in cruel times. But the confidence seems genuine to me, and it might have been responsible, at least in part, for the great popularity of episcopal office among the Gallo-Roman aristocracy. That caste could do dreadfully little about those great and unwanted changes that had closed customary routes through imperial administration to public service. Barbarians were unlikely at first to appoint resident aristocrats to posts their ancestors had occupied under the emperors' deputies. Yet after

Constantine, episcopal office yielded to incumbents much of the power and many of the perquisites to which the elite in Gaul had grown accustomed. The great families conspired to control executive appointments. Brothers succeeded brothers as bishops; sons inherited their fathers' sees; nephews were heirs to their uncles'.

The Goths in Gaul were relatively oblivious to the creation of episcopal dynasties, indifferent to all Catholic Christianity. They brought their own, Arian Christianity from Dacia, north of the Danube River, where Bishop Ulfilas evangelized during the fourth century. The Arian mission originated among the bishops disappointed at the outcome of Nicaea in 325. They temporarily won the government to their side of that savage Christological controversy, getting Constantius to meddle on their behalf, but their more lasting influence was due to Ulfilas, who translated sacred literature into Gothic, thus assuring an alternative to the Nicene consensus wherever the Goths and those they converted prospered. The Vandals were particularly partisan. They expelled Quodvultdeus, the Catholic bishop of Carthage, as soon as they captured the city in 439. The Goths in Gaul, by contrast, were tolerant for long stretches. They left the Gallo-Roman Catholic bishops to their careers and episcopal dynasties, while those bishops, for their part, went about their business: defending their cities, seeing to the celebrity of their cults, asserting their authority over the monasteries, coping with the commotion that attended jealousies within and among the Germanic tribes. And through it all the bishops dreamed of converting both the Arian heretics and the pagans with whom they dealt and despite whom they carried on.

Bishop Remigius of Rheims made his initial overtures to King Clovis during the 480s. The chances for success were slim; Clovis was still a pagan, though family weddings had netted him several sets of Arian in-laws. But after his Burgundian bride associated herself with the bishop's aims, the king was baptized a Catholic Christian. By then, 499, the Franks, over whom Clovis ruled, had taken the Rhine and Loire valleys and were preparing to campaign against the Arian Visigoths. The success of that campaign early in the next century left nearly all of what we call France—and more of northwestern Europe—to Clovis and to the bishops of his adopted faith. Remigius was chiefly responsible for organizing the Catholic executives, expanding the Catholic episcopacy, and orchestrating additional missionary activity.[15]

But all was not well. Episcopal independence seems to have been one casualty of Catholic Christianity's success. Gallic bishops quickly came to resent government interference. The year Clovis died, 511, over thirty executives assembled in Orleans to warn that "secular laws" would not prevent them from managing the churches' lands and revenues as they saw fit. They then consented to divide 50 percent of the daily offerings at their cathedral and parochial churches among their priests and deacons but kept at their own disposal all bequests and endowments.[16] The canons of that and subsequent councils, however, show bishops agonizing over kings' and barons' imperious behavior and often grudgingly acceding to their demands. In 541, King Childebert forced the bishop of Lyons to budget funds as he, the king, wished.[17] And repeated conciliar prohibitions did not stop authorities from imposing bishops with no local connections on Verdun, Chalons, Tours, Le Mans, and Arles. Nonetheless, the frequency of and attendance at the church's councils suggest that Merovingian rule resulted in increased episcopal cooperation. Bishops lost something in terms of independence, but, as one admirer observed, conciliar "courage" and consensus-building were truly impressive. "In council, the episcopate showed up best."[18]

By the sixth century, Rome was noticeably quiet about the conduct of Gallic councils. But that had not always been true. Previously, persons exceedingly displeased with local bishops' decisions or indecisiveness had often registered their discontent with the bishop in the old capital, who was by now called "pope." Because complaints carried across the Alps so vividly acknowledged Rome's appellate jurisdiction, complainants were favorably received at papal court. Pope Celestine, for example, jumped at the chance to pronounce on doctrine in 430 when two laymen from Gaul protested their executives' few and feeble efforts to suppress Pelagianism.[19] But late in the fifth century, correspondence and traffic between Roman and Gallic churches fell off considerably. Through much of the sixth century, the popes communicated with Merovingians—bishops and monarchs alike—infrequently, usually through their vicars, that is, their resident Gallic spokesmen, the bishops of Arles.

To be sure, Rome was still a sacred city. Its stock of holy relics was just about inexhaustible. In 516 when Pope Hormisdas sent Sigismund relics of the apostle Peter, the Burgundian king replied ingratiatingly that such precious gifts "from the very threshold of the apostles" greatly enriched and would certainly protect "your Gaul."[20] The submission that he expressed with the possessive "your Gaul," however, was calculated to obtain other help from Hormisdas. For the Burgundians, who had reconverted to Catholic Christianity, were just then threatened on all sides by the Goths and Franks. The Roman church had no standing army. Its chief executives could not rush troops to flash points far from the old capital, but Pope Hormisdas did have the ear of Emperor Anastasius, whom Sigismund was simultaneously courting. There is nothing wrong with historians rummaging for ulterior motives, for the political purposes behind pious gestures, but here what bears remembering is that the popes' prestige and power in Gaul and elsewhere were in no small measure related to a pope's role as purveyor of relics.[21]

But opposition to commerce of that kind developed among the churches' executives who were promoting local cults. Gregory of Tours told a story about an otherwise inconspicuous deacon from Angers who had been dispatched to Rome to acquire relics of the apostles Peter and Paul. As the deacon was waiting to book passage from Nice, the blessed Hospicius miraculously cured his deaf-and-dumb companion. The deacon turned back, inferring somewhat defiantly, as did Gregory, that holiness on his side of the Alps sufficed. Not all roads in Gaul led to Rome.[22]

The Apostolic See of Rome

For decades, governing the western empire from Rome had been impractical, yet citizens of the old capital must have been shocked as well as disheartened in 402 when Emperor Honorius moved his court to Ravenna. The association between Rome and rule had possessed a certain inevitability, but the new placement looked permanent. The government was safer on the other side of the peninsula, behind the all but impenetrable marshes on the Adriatic coast.

Honorius was fond of Rome; his successor, Valentinian III, even more so. But the two rarely returned to the city and only for ceremonial occasions. In the court's absence, papal political authority increased. The popes' say in many municipal affairs carried greater weight. Occasionally caught—or thought to be—poaching on the prerogatives of others, a few popes came close to forfeiting influence and even office. Pope Innocent I, for example, advocated negotiations with Alaric and once returned from explaining this unpopular position in Ravenna to find another in his place. Innocent, however, did not cry quits; rising to the challenge, he unseated his rival and then continued to extend papal jurisdiction, mostly over the churches to the south.

Innocent was especially irritated by priests' promiscuity. One need not burrow very far into sacred literature, he said, to find exacting standards for clerical behavior. The Old Testament suggested to him that the Levites were vastly, morally superior to the Catholic Christian clergy. And how humiliating it was to be so outclassed by the Hebrews! More to the political point, it was treacherous to let standards slip and subject the church to ridicule. Innocent directed his itinerant representatives to the churches along the Italian peninsula, down to its heel, to remove vulgar, scurrilous, unruly priests from office and to demand that local bishops interrogate candidates for ordination much more conscientiously.[23]

The situation was no better to the north, but a different problem there preoccupied the popes, whose episcopal colleagues in Milan, Aquileia, and, later, Ravenna competed with them for influence. The great peril to Christianity, Innocent told Bishop Decentius of Gubbio, just northeast of Perugia, was diversity in doctrine, liturgy, and discipline. The bishops of smaller churches usually compromised when neighboring churches of far greater consequence disagreed, and these compromises or hybrids increased both the diversity and confusion, bumping Christianity from one phase of disintegration to the next and then to the very brink of anarchy. The pope warned that mixing Roman with Milanese customs and practices led Gubbio farther from the faith of the apostle Peter. Search as Decentius might, he would find no apostle whose pontificate and tomb empowered Milan, or for that matter any other western see, as Peter's pontificate and tomb empowered Rome. Jesus specially designated Peter to watch over religious affairs. Therefore, the Roman church, Innocent's church, was *caput institutionum,* chief or head of all others.[24]

Innocent's successors repeated that claim. At midcentury, Pope Leo I seized an opportunity to apply it to churches in the eastern empire, which were just then caught in a controversy over the divine and human natures of Jesus. The emperor asked Bishop Dioscorus of Alexandria to resolve the dispute at the Council of Ephesus in 449, but the settlement imposed there, accompanied by condemnations and depositions, so unsettled the eastern churches that another council was summoned in 451.

Leo distanced himself from Dioscorus and from the fiasco at Ephesus in a letter to Pulcheria, whose brother called the first council and whose consort, Marcian, succeeded him as emperor and called the second. The pope pardoned everyone who had subscribed to the ill-fated canons of Ephesus provided they repented and consented to a doctrinal formulation he sent to the bishops at Chalcedon for that second conference. He specifically urged on them the belief that the "two natures" were united indeterminately yet "without confusion" in Jesus, the incarnate word of God.[25] Arguably, the Christological disputes, punctuated by personal animosities, so fatigued executives of the eastern churches that they were ready to accept Leo's formula and willing to acquiesce for a time to his claims to paramount doctrinal authority. But Rome's success at Chalcedon owed much more, I suspect, to the pope's excellent relations with Pulcheria and Marcian, whose "extraordinary eagerness" for apostolic truth and the church's welfare he professed to admire and serve.[26]

What followed Chalcedon's adoption of Leo's Christology must have irritated him, for Bishop Anatolius of Constantinople balked at acknowledging Rome's supremacy. He prevailed on his colleagues to confirm before they adjourned that his authority in the east was roughly equal to that of the pope in the west. Leo conceded the fame and "glory" of Anatolius's see. Constantinople, the new capital, Leo said, was a "new Rome." He also explained to Marcian, however, that religious and secular regimes were not inseparable; the apostle Peter did not move east with the capital. And nothing would be steadied or "stable" in Christianity and the empire, as the pope put it, unless his apostolic see, the episcopal see or seat purportedly established by Peter, dignified by his bones, and ruled by his successors, was consulted and obeyed.[27]

But nothing was stable during the remainder of the century. Leo managed to persuade Attila and the Huns to spare Rome in 452, but Gaiseric and the Vandals looted it several years later. In 457, the citizens of Alexandria lynched their Chalcedonian bishop, and opposition to Leo's dual-nature Christology and to those who endorsed it mounted in Egypt, Palestine, and Syria. Gennadius of Constantinople held out for the Chalcedonian settlement during his pontificate, 459–471, but his successor, Acacius, could not.

In Constantinople, the campaign to rehabilitate the council of Ephesus started with an abrupt and, as it turned out, abortive change in the government. After expelling Emperor Zeno from the capital in 475, Basiliscus tried to shore up his leadership, putting erstwhile dissidents in important episcopal sees and thereby creating church executives beholden to him. Bishop Acacius appealed to Rome for help and got more than he bargained for. Pope Simplicius issued his first reply to Basiliscus to alert him, "with the voice of the blessed apostle Peter," that God would preserve only those governments that defended the faith prescribed by Rome (Pope Leo), accepted at Chalcedon, and then endorsed by Emperor Marcian.[28]

When Zeno returned in 476, Simplicius repeated the warning. He said that emperors could summon church councils but should not interfere in any way with episcopal and conciliar deliberations. Since, from the western perspective, Leo and Chalcedon had achieved a definitive consensus, the point seemed purely academic to the bishop of Rome, who made Marcian a model of imperial submission to the church and Chalcedon a model of the church's submission to the pope, the apostle Peter's authoritative voice.[29]

Bishop Acacius was having none of this. The executives at Chalcedon, after all, confirmed that the episcopal sees of Rome and Constantinople were peers and prohibited Pope Leo's legates from reading into the council record any statements celebrating Rome's supremacy. Furthermore, dependence on Rome's voice would have made the formulation of subsequent policy in Constantinople awkward. If peace was to come to the eastern churches, Acacius and Zeno would have to appease the Monophysites, a faction that considered Chalcedon's dual-nature Christology unintelligible. Constantinople feared that Rome could not appreciate how grave the situation was becoming in the east, where religious dissent almost invariably led to political disobedience. Acacius easily persuaded the emperor to approve an edict of reconciliation in 482, which stepped back from the consensus at Chalcedon in the interests of religious and political peace. The edict infuriated Pope Felix III, who succeeded Simplicius and then excommunicated Acacius in 484.

Felix told Zeno that emperors were the church's sons, not its theorists and lawmakers: "Emperors are to be taught, not to teach," either discipline or doctrine. To be sure, the court could "recuperate" those who offended the government, but only the church could absolve and reconcile persons or factions rebelling against God's will, repudiating Leo's and Chalcedon's formulations, and mistakenly redefining Jesus' identity. There would be hell to pay, Felix implied, if the government continued to receive instruction from excommunicates, namely, from Acacius, "who wears the name 'priest' falsely." And there would be hell on earth, he said, if Zeno continued to legislate Christian doctrine without consulting Rome, no matter how irenic or conciliatory his pronouncements.[30]

Gelasius, Pope Felix's principal adviser, was elected to succeed him and proceeded to make short work of Acacius's appeal to the confirmation of Constantinople's autonomy at the council of Chalcedon. His premise was simple: "The apostolic see of Rome" was divinely established to hold all others to "the common faith of the church and its apostolic truth." From that he plausibly inferred that unless a pope approved any council's decision on the jurisdiction of another executive or episcopal see (or the conciliatory gestures of any bishop or emperor), that decision was invalid. Rome had never approved the canon on Constantinople's peer authority. It would not approve adjustments to Chalcedon's dual-nature Christology. Both order and truth depended on papal supervision, Gelasius said, on Roman vigilance against diversity, novelty, and error. He maintained that error was infectious and indelible (*nunquam omnino resolvetur*); it seemed to him that only the emperor's obedience to and conformity with the Roman church could save eastern Christianity.[31]

Despite the advice and instructions of Popes Simplicius, Felix, and Gelasius, the court at Constantinople resourcefully looked for compromises and made concessions in the east. Although leading episcopal sees there were occasionally held by bishops loyal to Chalcedon, the Monophysites were found everywhere and were particularly influential in Egypt and Syria. Rome relented, and after Gelasius's death Pope Anastasius II asked the bishops of Todi and Pesaro to go east and put an end to the war of words. But Anastasius died in 498, too soon to effect much. Thereupon the Roman church itself fell hostage to homegrown factions when two rivals for episcopal office, Symmachus and Laurentius, were simultaneously elected.

For a moment in 499, it looked as if peace and unity might be restored when Laurentius accepted an alternative appointment outside the city, but tempers flared when his friends accused Symmachus of having misappropriated the church's funds to buy popular support. The pope was assaulted on the streets, and the government in Ravenna was forced to intervene. In 502, Theodoric, the Ostrogothic king and nominally the emperor's regent, summoned Italian bishops to a council.

Theodoric had been in Ravenna for nearly a decade. He was an Arian Christian but had generally left Catholic bishops to their own devices until the crisis in Rome got out of hand. He then ordered Symmachus to answer the charges against him and was unbending when many of the bishops called to hear the pope's answers first declined to judge the bishop of so prestigious a see and then petitioned for a change of venue. The council met, as planned, in Rome and cleared Symmachus, but the king apparently overestimated the effectiveness of the acquittal, allowing Laurentius to return to the old capital. Within five years, skirmishes stripped it of the little peace that Theodoric's council had purchased in 502. This time, the king and regent took more direct and drastic measures: Laurentius was expelled and confined to the estate of one of his patrons, and, on word from Ravenna, all the Catholic Christian churches in Rome were handed over to the pope.[32]

Theodoric simply could not tolerate divisions within the church of Italy, save for the one between Arians and Catholics. He worried whether he could attain authority in Ravenna. His Gothic allies were tested on every front across the Alps: The Burgundians had taken Toulouse; Clovis and the Franks besieged Arles. Theodoric suspected that cities in northern Italy were intriguing with likely invaders. To the south, his former allies among the Vandals along the African shore seemed to be in league with the emperor, whose fleets from the east sacked the coastal cities on the peninsula. The king eventually brought the situation in Italy under some control—friendlier contacts with Constantinople moved him to help Hormisdas, Pope Symmachus's successor, repair the church relations that had been wrecked during the pontificates of Felix, Gelasius, and Acacius. Yet east-west diplomacy was a tricky business, and Theodoric lived long enough to see a second deterioration in Ravenna's arrangements with the east. The king was unable to exact a promise from Constantinople that his heirs and territories would go unmolested.

When Justinian became emperor in 527, he was determined to restore the western expanse of the old Roman Empire. He delayed his campaign into Italy to deal with difficulties on the Persian frontier and with discontent in his capital, but by 535, an army commanded by Belisarius had secured Sicily. Imperial troops occupied Rome the year after, although resistance persisted and the city's fate remained uncertain until the winter of 537. In 540, the Goths lost and left Ravenna.

As outstanding a general as he was, however, Belisarius found it impossible to chase the Goths from Italy. They held on to some patches of territory in the north, occasionally reoccupying a few of the cities taken from them, including Rome. But by 555, to the Arians settled in central Italy, the loss of their Gothic patrons must have seemed irreversible. Emperor Justinian was Catholic and devoutly Chalcedonian at first. He gave Catholic executives that material, moral, and political support for which, under the Gothic regimes, they would have had great longing but little hope. Pope Vigilius enlarged his cathedral church at the Lateran, one of Constantine's early gifts to the Christian community.

Money came more easily for a time, a very short time. The popes had fewer financial problems than many of their episcopal colleagues. In Constantinople, a moratorium on ordinations was declared because salaries for priests, deacons, and the junior clergy were draining the church's revenue from daily offerings, rents, and bequests. Too little was left for other expenses. In Rome, however, church executives earmarked one-quarter of all income for salaries—the remaining three-quarters for construction and general maintenance of its buildings, for charity, and for the bishop. Pope Simplicius experimented with the practice in 475. Gelasius confirmed it twenty years later. Thereafter, disbursements in Rome were regulated so that unless more money came into the coffers, more priests meant less for each. Seventy-five percent of the budget was thus protected from the escalating costs for staff. But no shortages were experienced for a while; Rome had ample capital from affluent patrons as well as from the papal estates in Gaul, North Africa, and Sicily, all of which were increasingly accessible thanks to the imperial reconquest. The emperor even nodded assent to papal primacy, giving cause for optimism that Rome and Chalcedon might enjoy unprecedented influence.[33]

But Justinian's assent had been more a casual reference than an open declaration of government policy. The emperor, like Zeno and Acacius before him, thought jurisdiction over church affairs in the east was simply too important to cede to any executive in the west. He ultimately came to assert both the authority of the church's councils in Constantinople to define doctrine and his right and responsibility to direct their deliberations. While trying to make peace with the anti-Chalcedonian factions, his predecessors had inadvertently strengthened the Monophysites' hold over churches from Antioch to Alexandria. Justinian was worried about the prospects for a long and bitter religious conflict, so he tried to find and fix terms for an empirewide Christological consensus. He would have to give up his Chalcedonian prejudices, a sacrifice that pleased his wife, Empress Theodora, who pressed the Monophysite case at court. When Vigilius was summoned to the capital, he probably left Rome thinking that he could stall and outflank Theodora and her associates. He badly miscalculated, was outmaneuvered, and was kept in Constantinople, badgered, intimidated, imprisoned, and finally forced to approve the condemnation of three popular theologians whom Chalcedon and the Chalcedonians accepted as orthodox.

Justinian engineered the condemnation, probably expecting glowing reviews from all sides in the controversy. Chalcedon, after all, seemed in large part to have weathered its enemies' assaults, and three dead theologians did not seem a bad exchange for peace and religious uniformity. The church council called by the emperor in 553 endorsed his compromise. Vigilius, however, had several reservations. He squirmed, resisting, capitulating, retracting, and again resisting. He tried to accommodate both Justinian and the western churches' intense attachments to Chalcedon, only to discover that permission to return to Rome was contingent on his submission to the emperor's will. He must have known that he was returning to face implacable opposition. A North African council had already excommunicated him, the bishops having heard about the concessions preceding his final, unconditional surrender. Only death in 555, weeks before he would have reached Rome, kept Vigilius from the crisis he and Justinian had created in Italy.

Vigilius virtually slipped the papacy into the government's pocket. For years, popes had dictated to the court, to little or no effect. Now a century after Leo, the chief executive of the Roman church was taking dictation. Imagine the predicament of Pope Pelagius I. He had criticized his predecessor's conduct in Constantinople but owed his pontificate to imperial intervention and thus had little choice but to adopt Vigilius's course, repeat Vigilius's justifications, and convince the bishops who thought otherwise that the condemnation of those three theologians had not violated the consensus at Chalcedon. He publicly promised to uphold the canons of that council and lavished praise on Pope Leo, who had helped frame them. Promises and praise solved the first of Pelagius's several problems, getting to and into Rome. But getting the remainder of western Christianity to his side was an unenviable job. Obstacles were everywhere. The churches in Gaul resisted. Leading episcopal sees in Italy, Milan and Aquileia chief among them, opposed the condemnation of 553 and mistrusted Vigilius's and then Pelagius's attempts to amen the emperor and his council without abandoning

Chalcedon. Opposition came to be concentrated in Istria, on the northeast coast of the Adriatic Sea. It reminded Pelagius of the Donatists' intractability, so he often echoed Augustine's curses against secessionists while trying to end the schism.[34]

If the pope's correspondence is any measure, he did not bother to explain in any detail how he and Vigilius before him could have subscribed to both the councils, Chalcedon (451) and Constantinople (553). Instead, Pelagius insisted that Italian churches conform to the doctrine accepted by Italy's preeminent— and only apostolic—see. Pelagius said that custom sanctioned a fine procedure whereby suspicions of episcopal colleagues might be put to rest. Each need simply send two or three of their smarter subordinates to Rome. The pope would see to their continuing education and to their safe return. To laymen who wanted to know why a conference or council could not be called, Pelagius replied that regional, "particular," councils paled by comparison with the council in Constantinople in 553, which had been a sold-out show of solidarity. Over four thousand bishops had attended, he exaggerated; could they all have been mistaken? It was crazy to think their judgment on the heresy of those three controversial theologians was subject to review or reassessment by any local assembly. It was sillier still to think that secessionist executives had a lock on truth.

Curiously, Pelagius appealed to Augustine rather than to Gelasius, to universality against regional specificity, and the pope identified universality with the consensus reached at a single council and confirmed by executives in the other apostolic sees, Antioch and Alexandria. Talk of Roman and papal supremacy was somewhat tame at this time, although the chief executive of the Roman church, the apostolic see, certainly expected western Christians to see doctrine and discipline as he did.[35]

But imperial officials in districts that were dominated by the secessionists were tempted to look the other way. Political instincts kept them from taking unpopular stands. Were they not shrewd to avoid what must have seemed a needless confrontation? For to the untrained eye, religious life in Milan or in Istria carried on much as before. Yet Pelagius tried to impress on leading laymen that bishops contemptuous of Rome could have no real claim on the support of government authorities, whose duty, he told them, was "to extinguish schism by any means." Rome was ready to play hardball and reminded officials of the passage in the gospel of John ordering that branches cut from the true vine be "gathered [and] thrown into the fire." Augustine, applying those words to God's final judgment, had nonetheless made sure that dissidents in the early fifth century paid dearly for their insubordination; a bishop of Rome in the sixth could hardly do less.[36]

The bishops of Ravenna joined those of Rome clamoring for government censure and suppression of the secessionists. Executives in the two cities anticipated overcoming official inertia, if only because both churches generously leased some of their estates in Italy for token sums to statesmen and high-ranking soldiers. Rome put on the block portions of its properties in Sicily, Sardinia, North Africa, and southern Gaul. But the authorities were boundlessly capable of evasion, and the schism defied resolution. In Istria, displeasure with the papacy's betrayals of Chalcedon lasted well into the seventh century; Constantinople's clout in northern Italy did not.

Gregory of Rome, "Bishop of the Lombards"·

Gregory was born around 540, too late to see Belisarius take the old capital but there when Totila and the Goths stormed Rome and took it back in 546. Gregory was also present when they evacuated six years later, leaving a small garrison that Justinian's new field marshal, Narses, easily overpowered. Gregory's family must have followed Narses's next campaigns with interest, particularly his dogged pursuit of the Goths and defeat of a large Frankish expedition in Campania. For the family possessed vast estates in Sicily as well as in the vicinity of Rome, valuing the safe travel and transport that the military operations during the 550s were undertaken to assure. The economic survival of the old capital was often at stake.

We cannot determine exactly what Gregory was doing when Narses captured Verona in 563 and seemed finally to complete Justinian's reconquest two years before the emperor's death. Education—literature, philosophy, law—is the best guess, but subsequent developments suggest that Gregory was also acquiring managerial skills, perhaps on his family's estates and, by 572, in municipal government as well. Meanwhile, Narses attempted to organize the defense of the empire's Italian territories. He sent Sinduald and the Heruls to the Brenner Pass, posting as sentries those mercenaries he most trusted. Narses himself had recruited them twenty years earlier, and, since then Sinduald had been rewarded with rank and riches (*multa beneficia*). Yet the Heruls rebelled in 565; Sinduald was executed for ingratitude.[37]

Narses's next decision was fateful. He invited the Lombards to cross the Alps, to occupy a number of towns in the northeast, and to protect the rest of Italy from Franks, Avars, and others, whose descents, it was feared, would imperil imperial government. Rumors that Narses anticipated recall and licensed the Lombards to exact his revenge originated after they proved unmanageable. The rumors are not to be trusted; it seems certain that the Lombards came as guests in 568, not as invaders.[38]

Harassed by the Avars in Pannonia, modern Hungary more or less, the Lombards liked their new home in Italy well enough to add to it. Maybe they were hastened to do so by Narses's advanced age, doubting whether their arrangement with the empire's agent would outlive him. Possibly the Lombard king Alboin was simply greedy for more of what he had got. Or, conceivably, he did not think much of the chances for the survival of his Lombard confederation—part Arian, part pagan—on the periphery of that portion of the empire dominated by Catholic Christianity. Years before, Bishop Nicetius had pressed the king's wife to convert Alboin ("God sent you to him"), for he startled Catholic Christian executives in Italy when he dispatched Arian missionaries as far south as Rome.[39] But Carlo Guido Mor assumed that Lombard piety was rather unremarkable (*molto superficiale*). He suggested that missionaries or pilgrims may actually have been spies, pawns in the king's scheme to conquer but not necessarily to convert. We know too little to judge, except to say that Alboin's wife died before she completed Nicetius's commission and that the Lombards poured across the Piedmont and down the peninsula immediately after they had turned aggressors. Milan fell to them, bishop and priests having escaped to Genoa in 569. Squads spilled into Tuscany and then occupied Benevento and Spoleto, while Alboin besieged Pavia, later the Lombard capital.[40]

Incensed by Pavia's desperate three-year defense, Alboin vowed to slay all the inhabitants. But legend has it that when the city was taken in 572, the king's horse suddenly dropped at the gates, refused to budge, and held up traffic until Alboin renounced his vow, "for all the people here are Christians."[41] If that horse's tale circulated at the time, it likely brought little comfort to Gregory, who then worked in Rome for the city government. He and his family were fervently Catholic; two of his ancestors had been popes, Felix III and Agapetus. Neither he nor the old capital welcomed prospects for the regeneration of Arian Christianity. Few, if any, looked forward to Lombard tyranny.[42]

Some relief came when Alboin died in 573 or 574 and Lombard barons dismembered the confederation, which turned into a tangle of alliances and antipathies. Camps and duchies covered northern and central Italy, save for Rome, Ravenna, and a narrow corridor between them. Pope Pelagius II sent Gregory to Constantinople as papal ambassador in 579, just as one Lombard army encircled Rome. The new ambassador's first task was surely to solicit assistance, but Constantinople could ill afford an adventure in Italy. It was overwhelmed by crises elsewhere and advised Gregory and Pelagius to play (and pay) off one Lombard baron against another.

Some years before Gregory left Rome, he endowed and joined the monastery of Saint Andrew on one of his family's estates. He reentered when he returned from the east in 586 yet made himself available to the papal chancellery. The Lombard confederation had been reconstituted by then, and the church's diplomats no longer could count on a stock of disaffected Lombards. Pelagius had to supplement Rome's small imperial garrison with Frankish troops. Gregory, however, was assigned to other tasks, specifically to oversee Pelagius's initiatives to end the Istrian schism. Just as officials before and after him, Gregory told the separatists that they had absolutely no justification for dividing the Italian church, that their forbears had none for seceding from Rome. As others before and after him, he finally exchanged unavailing argument for arms, asking the emperor's regent in Ravenna, then called exarch, to compel conformity.

Pope Pelagius II died in 590. The election of a replacement went according to established protocol. There had been rules, as we saw, as early as the third century, rules reformulated at the council of Nicaea and variously and regionally amended as the years passed. Weight was given to the preferences of the local clergy. Propertied citizens could sometimes sway the outcome, as could the patronage of the previous bishop or timely words from the metropolitan, the area's leading church executive. Merovingians required candidates to sue for royal diplomas before accepting election. The consent or acclaim of Christians in the district was occasionally decisive, as it seems to have been in Ambrose's election, yet it was usually an afterthought. To tease from this jumble one or more of the most significant factors in any given episcopal election is difficult and particularly so in contested elections. But there are no signs of a contest in 590. It does not appear that Gregory's partisans had to clear or cope with clerical or popular opposition to his candidacy. The only one unhappy with the choice seems to have been Gregory himself.[43]

Gregory's earliest known biographer, an anonymous monk at Whitby on the Northumbrian coast of England, dramatically decked out the improbable story of his subject's unhappiness, which is worth condensing here because it shows how church executives were expected to handle their promotions. This biographer insisted that Gregory had returned from Constantinople with every intention of spending the remainder of his days in his monastery. He put off ordination. He much preferred reading and conversation with his fellow monks to a priest's pastoral work.[44] When he was elected bishop, he fled, concealed in a barrel. Having made his way into a nearby forest, he waited for the honor and obligation to fall to another, but a beam of light from heaven led the Romans to his hideout and their new pope. To snatch lessons from such episodes was a biographer's trade. Here the monk not only illustrated the irresistibility of God's will but also drew an important conclusion for all involved in episcopal elections as balloters or would-be bishops: The more they resisted their election, the worthier those candidates were, and the more admirably and selflessly they served.[45]

Cato of Clermont was an excellent counterexample. Elected bishop in 551, he delayed his consecration until an endorsement arrived from the Merovingian court. Cato's episcopal colleagues, who traveled some distance, quite understandably were displeased and let it be known, but Gregory of Tours, telling the tale, did not consider the delay or the deference to royalty particularly objectionable. Instead, he rounded on the candidate for assuming that his reputation for piety had procured his election and would guarantee King Theodovald's imprimatur. According to Gregory, the bishop-elect figured that twenty years of exceptionally diligent service as a priest had earned him his stripes, and such self-esteem (*vanae conflatus gloriae*) made it clear that he was the wrong man for the job.[46]

Both stories of election, Gregory's and Cato's, illustrate roughly the same point. The right men for the job confessed their unworthiness, showed creditable humility (but also showed that they knew how little accumulated credits mattered), sensed that their office was less a reward than a burden and a divine trust. Gregory of Rome elaborated in his sketch of the perfect pastor. Humility alone drove some to excuse themselves from office when they thought others better qualified; enlightened humility combined a sense of personal unworthiness with sound doctrine *and* ultimate acquiescence. "They are truly humble in God's eyes," he said,

> if their humility does not make them stubborn, does not make them reject what they were ordered to undertake for the public good. No one who is genuinely humble knows his election was divinely arranged . . . yet refuses it. Submit, then, to God's plans. Be other than obstinate when equipped with talent and required to rule and to be of use to others. One should flee from office in one's heart; nonetheless, one should reluctantly obey.[47]

Gregory practiced what he preached. He circulated among his colleagues the obligatory defamation of character ("I am unworthy and weak"), though he had already submitted to "God's plans." But he also confided to Bishop John of Constantinople that he had not been at all prepared for what he had found on taking office. He had been named to captain an old, horribly battered vessel, and who could tell whether the "the violent storm" would soon abate?[48]

Battles broke out suddenly and often. Carnage came on the Christians when they least expected it (*improvisae clades*). The Lombards were untrustworthy allies and ruthless enemies. Gregory remembered that the Bible predicted havoc and distress—"there will be terrors"—but just then that prediction gave him precious little comfort. He complained that his vessel, the church, was springing leaks and that "every single day our world is cluttered with new and escalating wickedness."[49] After scarcely a year as pope, he wrote again to Constantinople, profoundly disturbed that he had become far more the bishop of the Lombards than the bishop of Rome.[50]

Whatever Gregory meant when he referred to himself as a bishop of the Lombards, he could hardly have imagined that Catholic Christianity in Italy could have pulled through the chaos of the Lombard conquest and civil wars had he turned his back on the intruders. True, bishops did not ordinarily organize their cities' military offensives. Yet they frequently arranged for and financed fortifications and occasionally bargained with the enemy to negotiate an armistice or get the best terms for a surrender. In 592, Gregory concluded a truce with Duke Ariulf of Spoleto. Subsequently, Gregory used the church's networks to explore prospects for peace with Duke Agilulf of Turin once Agilulf had been named to head the Lombard confederation. Through it all and for the remainder of the pontificate, the pope and his chancellery pursued three objectives: the conversion of all Lombards from Arianism and paganism, the prevention of Istrian secessionists from turning the catholicization of Lombardy to good account by winning converts to their cause, and the defense of Rome.

Gregory's and Rome's initiatives for peace with the Lombards outraged Romanus, exarch in Ravenna, who prevailed on the emperor to reprimand the pope. Gregory replied in 595: He was not foolish and unworldly, as the exarch charged; he was only securing what was left of imperial Italy and rescuing Rome, he said, when and while Romanus showed himself unwilling to commit intelligence, troops, and resources to the tasks.[51]

"Not unworldly" is an understatement. Although Gregory mentioned to Bishop Anastasius of Antioch that he would much rather have devoted his time to contemplating their "heavenly home," he did wondrously well as the city's patron and better still, perhaps, as the church's administrator.[52] He apologized for his worldliness, usually to episcopal colleagues but always to himself. He professed to despise the business that kept him from books, sometimes treating administration as a heavy burden and punishment and then, rarely, as one of God's practical jokes. The result, however, was costly labor, not laughter. Investigating alleged improprieties in the churches of south and central Italy, arguing with exarch and emperor, and proffering tenuous truces to the Lombards took a heavy toll on Gregory's health. He was often ill, sometimes incapacitated.

The background worry of this bishop of the Lombards and beleaguered bishop of Rome was that religious discipline was everywhere deteriorating; political chaos and church corruption were bringing Christianity to the verge of collapse. Gregory ruled on simony in southern Gaul and through his legate passed judgment on perjury in Corinth, where the irregularities were so glaring, grave, and disgraceful that he had the bishop there deposed. No comprehensive study of his interventions would make sense on my watch, although select episodes document Gregory's expressed sentiments on episcopal and papal leadership, serve up some of the pressing problems, and communicate the background worry of this bishop of bishops.

Pastoral Rule

Two letters to Cyriacus, the new bishop of Constantinople in 596, summarize Gregory's sense of episcopal obligations. Cyriacus must have announced his election with customary and appropriate self-reproach, for Gregory's reply started with the conventional rejoinders: The worthy candidate confessed his unworthiness; the strong was aware of his own infirmities and unafraid to face them; it was wrong to decline appointment "arrogantly, under a show of humility." Then the pope conceded that Cyriacus, or anyone like him who graduated from service to the church to "pastoral rule" (*animarum regimen*), was accepting a daunting challenge, for contentious, mean-spirited, sharp-tongued priests and bishops had supplied the faithful with a batch of bad examples. Their vices had undermined discipline even as they had tried to enforce it. Better bishops had to be strict in administering justice, he demanded, but they should also be compassionate.[53] Each executive's burden was like that of the faith's great heroes. At Stephen's martyrdom, for example, he had stolen a line from Jesus and implored God to pardon those persecuting him. The martyr mixed indignation ("you stiff-necked people") with compassion and illustrated at the same instant how difficult, yet desirable it was to do so. Given the delinquency of colleagues and its effects on the faithful, Gregory guessed that spirited and disciplined church executives would have plenty of opportunities to practice blending severity with clemency.[54]

To assist them, he wrote an uncomplicated textbook on church discipline and self-discipline. It mapped a middle ground between excessive severity and overindulgence, instructing the bishops to correct sins of pride, sloth, impudence, greed, and intemperance but also to censure undue humility, haste, servility, inordinate liberality, and extravagant abstinence. The pope appreciated that the churches' disciplinarians were peculiarly susceptible to sins associated with self-esteem. He urged them to look for the signs of human frailty in themselves as well as in those they censured. His rule for the rulers of the church was quite simple, "Humility in [your] hearts and discipline in [your] practice." An effective executive, Gregory said, judiciously permitted parishioners to see through the cracks in his tough, censorious exterior, canvassing and marshaling the opinions of others against his sense of self-importance and superiority. The most effective executives tried to see their weaknesses as others saw them but lost neither the ability nor the opportunities to inspire awe and fear for the sake of righteousness. Those cracks should close, in other words, when bishops "thunder[ed]" the dreadful punishments of hell awaiting the arrogant, complacent, and insolent.[55]

To arrogance, complacence, and insolence, Gregory repeatedly opposed humility, vigilance, and obedience. He lifted a passage from the book of Job—"I smiled on them when they had no trust"—and interpreted God's "smile" as the grace "favoring" good deeds. There were two routine ways to lose favor. The Christians who put their deeds and virtues on display to earn others' approval in effect sold over all that was good to the devil. Gregory compared them to those fools who made a show of their wealth, attracted the attention of thieves, and then "walk[ed] into ambush." The arrogant "los[t] the fruits of their labor because they play[ed] for applause." Complacent Christians also failed to look after their treasure. They overcame temptation—for such a conquest was one of the early effects of God's "smile"—but they were "heedlessly secure." They forgot or underestimated the treachery of that secret satanic adversary who capitalized on the bravado of the arrogant. They, too, were overconfident. To relax their guard, to settle for "slack thinking," was to beckon the kind of trouble that vigilance would doubtlessly have kept at bay. The churches' executives therefore should thunder to humble the conceited and arouse the complacent.[56]

The faithful, for their part, ought to obey their churches' executives. Gregory often said so, he once explained, because the Christians of his time simply and maddeningly would not suppress their "murmuring" against authority figures. They could not hear the thunder from the pulpit, as it were, for all their grousing and grumbling. The pope was fond of the place in the Bible where Samuel was said to have been promptly and perfectly obedient to Eli. Gregory rehearsed the story at length to let each instance of obedience catch the fancy of his readers: Eli seemed to call Samuel three times; each time Samuel came without hesitation, although circumstances—Eli's denials that the call was his—would have caused others to pause. Preachers could ask for no more clear-cut indictment of Christians' resentments and small rebellions, all of which reminded Gregory of the mother of all sins, the disobedience in Eden.[57]

From Adam and Eve to the Apocalypse of John, sacred texts commended submission to authority and prophesied the frightening fate of those who defied it. Gregory read his Bible that way and suggested that it was, in its current form, an oblique appeal for authority; so many of its passages perplexed the faithful until they asked for and then accepted an authoritative interpretation. After painstaking study, church executives should be able to help their subjects over many hurdles, obscure allusions and apparent contradictions. Bishop Natalis of Salona too candidly admitted to Gregory that he could spare little time for the study of sacred literature and for his forthrightness got a papal reprimand: Dutiful executives learned that the Bible was "a lantern," and without that lantern, Gregory lectured him, "the dark night of this life" was unbearable.[58]

Gregory wrote winding, looping commentaries on Job, the Song of Songs, 1 Kings, and Ezechiel, all of which survive, and on the Pentateuch, the prophets, Proverbs, and perhaps others, now lost. He also commented on postbiblical miracles in a set of dialogues that have attracted considerable scholarly attention. Some readers refuse to catalog it with the other works; they argue that it is inauthentic, unlike anything the pope did or would have done. But the consensus is that Gregory eagerly collected stories of the miracles of near contemporaries, episcopal colleagues, and monks—as the text itself reports—that he sandwiched interviews with informants between administrative appointments and teaching duties. Then by 593, he had started writing.[59]

The interlocutor, Peter, wants to learn more about saints who raised the dead, expelled demons, changed water to oil, and chased pests from church gardens with their prayers. He settles for stories that are usually light on analysis; Gregory answers by braiding the virtues and marvels of many splendid Christians, treating the marvels as God's advertisements for the excellence of the virtues. Peter asks why those reports of wonder-workers' wonders circulated so widely when each called for secrecy, as Jesus had. Was God powerless to do what his son and saints so explicitly desired? Of course not, Gregory replies: Publicity assuredly was part of God's plan, whereas desires for secrecy were perennial signs of sanctity. From the time of Elijah and Elisha through that of the earliest apostles and into the sixth century, heroes of the faith tried to hush those who witnessed their miracles, and God always got the word out. Publicity was compatible with humility. That was the pattern; the miraculous events as well as the ways they were relayed followed patterns. What happened in 599 might well copy something five hundred or more years before. Indeed, similarity suggested veracity, which is to suggest that the resemblances between first-century and sixth-century miracles would have been taken to argue for the historicity of each set.[60]

The difference was that later miracles were church related. Many miracle workers were church executives. Their stories were told and depicted in the churches, as were the stories of their biblical progenitors; their memorabilia, displayed there; their bodies, buried there. Gregory knew that reputations and relics inspired devotion—and not just devotion to specific saints but also to their virtues and to their church. When Abbot Sabinus on the island of Capri griped about delays in getting the bones of the blessed Agatha transported from the mainland, the pope pushed the project.[61] And he generously distributed relics from Rome's virtually limitless stock, much as his predecessors had. But one request appears to have staggered him: The empress asked to have the head of the apostle Paul shipped to Constantinople. Unlikely, he replied; Peter and Paul were immovable. Lives were lost when it was tried: "No one approaches them to pray without profound fear." Gregory was upset with eastern Christians for coveting cadavers from the old capital. He told the empress that several monks had recently been caught disinterring corpses from an open field. When they were interrogated, they confessed to conspiring to pass them off in Greece as relics of Roman saints. Religious sentiment tempted some to fraud and others to superstition, but the pope did not want to discourage piety in Constantinople. He was sorry to disappoint "the religious desire" of royalty and offered compensation: "Very soon I will send you links in the chains that the apostle Paul wore around his neck and wrists."[62]

Gregory was often prepared to please political authorities, expecting them to confirm the prerogatives of the Roman church. He was agreeable to Queen Theodelinda because she seemed to coax the Lombard confederation from Arian to Catholic Christianity and to grow more and more suspicious of the Istrian secessionists. He obliged the Merovingian queen when she wanted an awkward favor—that Bishop Syagrius of Autun be awarded status surpassing that of his episcopal colleagues—because that request signaled to her subjects recognition of papal jurisdiction over the Gallic church.[63]

But we must abandon the idea that Gregory consistently claimed and exercised sovereignty over the sovereigns of his time, although subsequent apologists for papal imperialism were fond of this notion.[64] True, his collection of miracles has King Totila fall to his knees before Bishop Cerbonius of Populonia. Totila ordered that Cerbonius be clawed to death for having harbored the Goths' enemies, but when the bear was brought forward, it "bent down in humble submission," and Totila, having seen God's hand in such a spectacle, followed that creature's lead.[65] This story corrects the impression that papal cooperation and deference were always for sale. Gregory could demand submission as well as submit. He occasionally scolded and instructed political officials as if he expected their quick and complete compliance, and his tolerance for misrule was limited. His *Moralia* has strong words for self-absorbed princes who

> in so pious an office become the pacesetter[s] for impiety [*impietatis dux*]. One should not accept leadership if he does not know how to lead others to live well. . . . Let those who rule think carefully, for they must live for their subjects as well as for themselves. They must conceal the good they do in the folds of their memory [to give an example of humility], yet they must also supply their subjects with examples of

good behavior. They must discipline the sins of others yet not take pride in either the force or the effect of their judgments.[66]

Slow to correct others, arrogant, and quick to take offense, the imperial regents or exarchs of Ravenna, as Gregory described them, were among those impious "pacesetter[s]." They criticized his truces with the Lombards and passed lightly over his appeals for assistance with Rome's self-defense. They indulged Istrian secessionists, ignoring efforts to reunite Italian catholicism. They did nothing to silence the insolent Ravennate clerics, and their deputies welcomed bribes from affluent pagans to stall the progress of Christianity. On the island of Sardinia, for example, government officials seemed to take their wages and orders from the local pagan reactionaries. To complicate matters there, the metropolitan bishop Januarius was unloved and widely mistrusted. His episcopal colleagues showered Rome with protests. Januarius, they said, was an insufferable, immoral, obtuse, old charlatan. Gregory dispatched investigators and was outraged by what they reported, but his impulses to do more than exhort the exarch to restrain his agents and excommunicate some of the metropolitan's subordinates were held in check for reasons now hard to cull: Januarius's dotage, his metropolitan standing, his intermittent submission to Rome, or Sardinia's distance from the pope's more pressing concerns. Maybe something of which we know nothing kept Gregory's ax from falling.[67]

Gregory was less magnanimous to Bishop Demetrius of Naples, whom he deposed for unspecified crimes. When Neapolitans failed to agree on a replacement in 593, Gregory sent a candidate from Rome who was so put off by the nastiness of Neapolitan disputes that he refused to serve.[68] Gregory tried again and won clerical and popular support for his second nominee. But even afterward, the pope had to monitor Naples closely. It surprised him how often difficulties prompted him to intervene directly to protect his bishop or arrange for the city's defenses or simply secure an exemption for the monks whom the military commander wanted to post as sentries.[69]

Nor should we overlook the crises in Rome. Senior clergy, priests and deacons, resented the administrative influence of Gregory's fellow monks, yet with equanimity and discretion he managed the jealousies his appointments occasioned. His chief problems were material. In 589 the city's population had swollen with refugees from the territories taken by the Lombards; the Tiber had swollen with unusually heavy rains. Floods took Rome's granaries off line. Famine and plague greeted Gregory's election in 590, lingering long thereafter. At the very start of his pontificate, he sped letters to Sicily directing officials to resupply Rome with harvests from the papal estates, but he was never able to muster adequate resources to meet what must have seemed to him the million or more municipal misfortunes. The city's walls were in horrible shape; the exarchs regularly let the pay of soldiers manning them slip dangerously in arrears; the poor required care; captives required ransom—Neapolitans as well as Romans. Gregory subscribed to the four-part division of the church's income, yet emergencies seemed always to deplete his reserves. He dextrously begged donations from private citizens in Constantinople, and he replied to a physician there in 597, as he often did to donors, with precious relics of the apostle Peter.[70]

With so many ordeals, it is no wonder that Gregory missed his monastery, missed the time to contemplate and confer about the perfections of the next life. Yet he was determined to grapple with the sordid realities of this world, a determination he saw as the defining trait of executive leadership in the church. Thus, the tidings of a Donatist revival in the North African province of Numidia were not well and warmly received in Rome. According to Gregory, those latter-day Donatists were dogmatically certain of their incorruptibility and of his church's corruption, but we ought not jump to the conclusion that they closely resembled the separatists who had touched off Augustine's charges two hundred years earlier. Possibly they preached perfection or maybe only railed against the featherweight discipline of their Catholic counterparts—for Gregory also was critical of the administration of the universal church in North Africa. In any event, the pope believed that the "new" Donatists were "wolves" "tearing at" God's flock, dragging Christians from their executives. And worse still, the Donatists' bishops were in line for positions of regional church leadership, while the Catholic bishops seldom ventured from their villas to object. All this triggered Rome's demands for Numidian episcopal resistance and government aid. But because Popes Pelagius I and Vigilius had badly bruised Rome's reputation in the region, the best Gregory could do was rely on the goodwill of an ensemble of well-placed bishops. More was out of the question.[71]

The Bishop of Bishops and "Servant of the Servants of God"

For all his sparring with Istrians, Arians, and Donatists, Gregory is most widely celebrated among English-speaking peoples for the mission he sent to Kent in 596. No timid enterprise, to be sure, although it was not all it is often cracked up to be. Twenty years after arriving, the Roman Catholic Christians were expelled. Nonetheless, we definitely learn something from the design, if not also from the dispatch, about the perceived scope of papal authority.

Bertha was already a Catholic when she crossed from the continent to marry King Ethelbert of Kent. The wedding alerted Gregory to the possibility that papal initiative might net many converts among the *Angli*. He sent Augustine, a monk from Sicily, who was then residing in Rome and was made bishop en route. Word returned within a year that over ten thousand had been baptized at a single festival. The pope was deleriously happy and ordered dozens of others north in 601 to put the finishing touches on his (and on Augustine's) masterstroke. He congratulated his episcopal colleagues in the east for praying for the mission's success so effectively: "If there is great joy in heaven for one penitent, how much more should we suppose there is when a whole people is saved from its error?"[72]

The *Angli* had worshiped rocks and trees, Gregory informed Bishop Eulogius of Alexandria, playing up the strangeness of the "error," which was on the whole not all that peculiar. Although the pope's knowledge of the far northwest was a brew of fact and fiction, he was sure his missionaries "found a people for whom we would not have known to look."[73] But God had guided them, Gregory was confident, and God was responsible for the enterprise and for its achievement. No sooner were the *Angli* "found" and baptized than they were organized, at least in the papal parlors. For Gregory had a clear idea of what he (and God) wanted done, and quite naturally he shared it with Augustine. Gregory appointed his monk and bishop as metropolitan for the southern sector of the island and told him to name a counterpart for the north, who in turn would select twelve bishops to assist him. Gregory was quite explicit about the chain of command. The metropolitan bishops of York in the north would be subject to Augustine in London as long as that first missionary lived. After his death, seniority would determine honorary primacy; strictly speaking, however, neither York nor London would be subject to the other. They would act in concert and complete agreement.[74]

This optimism was rather remarkable, coming, as it did, from the church's chief executive, who well knew that consensus rarely came easily and seldom stayed long. Imagine Gregory bent over a rough map of the territory, marking distant dioceses where there had been none. To be sure, the pope did not actually set diocesan boundaries, yet he did feed Augustine and, through him, the island's Catholics a diet of detailed instructions. For instance, Gregory cautioned them not to leave too many miles between episcopal sees so that travel to and from regional conferences and consecrations would not overtax elderly incumbents. And he tried to guarantee that the practice and theology of the Roman church—such matters as the distribution of income and attribution (and definition) of sin—survived the trip north.[75]

But England was inhospitable and could not be mastered as easily as Gregory imagined. His "map" apparently did not record the extent to which the Celtic Christians, who cared nothing for papal leadership, had gained a foothold along the western coast from Cornwall to Mull and Iona. Moreover, the old Roman roads to Northumbria were unsafe. Augustine dared not implement Gregory's plans for the English Catholic episcopacy. Later in the seventh century, York did welcome its first Catholic bishop; later still, Catholic Christians in Northumbria sought association with Rome.

Gregory gave the eastern churches a very different look. He radiated confidence that Catholic Christianity unified "the whole human race," and in 595 he generously shared the sovereignty over that unity with Bishops Eulogius of Alexandria and Anastasius of Antioch. As if Gregory had every intention of resurrecting the ideals of collegial government that Pope Pelagius I had introduced decades earlier, he trumpeted the authority of the church's three apostolic sees.[76]

Bishop John of Constantinople was the big loser. He had no apostle in his family tree. His asset was his position or pontificate in the capital, and proximity to political power emboldened him to apply the title "ecumenical patriarch" to the office. Gregory's main preoccupation on the eastern front was to deprive the bishops of Constantinople of that dignity. He assured John that all bishops were brothers, forgetting for the occasion his apostolic triumverate, the alleged preeminence of the three apostolic sees. The Bible, Gregory had once said, was a lantern, but the churches' bishops were "stars," whose lives and great learning sparkled in the world's dark sky of sin and error. Their posts, lives, and learning were not fortune's gifts but God's. So it would not be impertinent to ask whether "when you [John] wish to place yourself above them by inflating your title . . . are you not saying, 'I will ascend to heaven and exalt my sun above the stars,' " the words that would have been identified in an instant with the snobbery scripted by the prophet Isaiah for another presumptuous bearer of light, later called Lucifer?[77]

There is no mistaking what Gregory meant here. On the question of shared sovereignty, he was rather imprecise; his explanation, when he cared to give it, was ambiguous. He compared apostolic collegiality among the bishops of Rome, Antioch, and Alexandria to that mysterious sympathy among the members of another sacred three-and-one, the trinity.[78] But Bishop John's title snapped Gregory back to precision. The arguments for Constantinople's paternity were easily dismantled, he said, professing to have been "shocked" by this "ecumenical patriarch's" arrogance. Had John not referred to his own unworthiness immediately after his election? Admirably self-effacing statements had proved John to be worthy, yet his subsequent airs belied their proof and thus disclosed their truth—John was indeed as unworthy as he had confessed. Yet Gregory did not judge that his colleague had rocketed so very far "above the stars" to be beyond recall. A single, sleek imperative from the papal arsenal aimed to bring him down: *Humilitatem dilige*—love humility.[79]

Humility, expressed as obedience and experienced as submission, was not just an administrative convenience for Gregory, who would have been scandalized by the suggestion that a layman's servility served only the leadership of her or his church. For above all, submission saved the submissive souls. This world seemed stable, and during periods of perceived stability Christians generally assumed their laws and landmarks would last forever because they were "fixed" in perception and memory. Yet that was an illusion, Gregory explained; instability was inescapable. This world was perpetually, if imperceptibly, perishing (*ad nihilum transeat; ad nihilum properant*). Only God "stands"; only those who submitted to God and obeyed God's deputies on earth found serenity and stability. The single alternative to obedience and submission was to pass and perish with other ephemera.[80]

Obedience to Rome was obedience to the apostle Peter, to whom Jesus was said to have entrusted "the whole church." Sacred texts afforded all the proof Gregory needed of that latter contention: "Feed my sheep," "strengthen your brethren," and "I will give you [Peter] the keys."[81] Peter's relics were widely distributed; his remains, however, remained in Rome with the popes and with their commissions to "feed" and "strengthen." In and from Rome, Peter was apostle in chief. Later popes would infer from the passages on Petrine authority Rome's right to dictate doctrine. Leo I was their favorite pope; Chalcedon, their favorite council. Gregory, however, was taken with Peter's astounding humility. He imagined the apostle gallantly declining lofty titles and concluded that "bishop" or "pope" should have been enough for his heirs. Yet if another was to be drafted, Gregory had a recommendation: *servus,* servant of all priests who serve God and the church.[82]

But supreme arbiters serve and rule. They serve, that is, by ruling on controversial cases, by granting and withholding special episcopal prerogatives, and by deposing undisciplined bishops. Gregory's exercise of Rome's appellate jurisdiction and his many efforts to exert moral influence were tolerated, even accepted and solicited, to a great extent because he cultivated sentimental attachments to the apostle Peter among the Christians distant in every direction from Peter's tomb. And I gather that Gregory's purposes were advanced more often than obstructed by the indignation he sometimes expressed: "Who can possibly doubt that the church in Constantinople is subject to the apostolic see?"[83] Yet having listened to the servant of those who served God and the church, I estimate that whatever the groundwork for papal autocracy he laid, he put a discernibly less tyrannical spin on pastoral rule than many admirers and critics have alleged.[84]

Gregory managed crisis by crisis. Claude Dagens made a terribly important point about such managerial activity. Dagens said that the pope's "apostolic ardor" was altogether compatible with "an eschatological mentality." His intense interests in maintaining order and in resolving conflicts provisionally held against the passing and perishing of this world. He left the battered vessel he had inherited afloat, if not exactly flush. But then Gregory would surely have said that prosperity, too, would pass because time itself was running out.[85]

Time did not run out, but for our purposes it has. There is only enough left to mention that public officials ran from Rome, leaving the papacy to provide public services, and that buildings ran down and were taken over by the church. The senate's offices and those of the city prefect were transformed into churches and monasteries, as were parts of the imperial palace abandoned by the exarch's representatives. Decades after Gregory's death in 604, Wilfred of Hexham, later bishop of York, was terrifically impressed by the renovations when he came to Rome. Returning to Northumbria, he prevailed in 664 on his clerical colleagues and his king to forsake Celtic Christianity and Columba, its sacred patron, for the observances of Roman Catholic Christianity, its style of episcopal leadership, and its sacred patron, the apostle Peter. Thereafter the perseverance of Anglo-Saxon missionaries on the Continent, the ingenuity of papal executives (which we would not be wrong to call Gregorian), and the countless other circumstances that no final paragraph could inventory gave an empire to Peter and Rome, an empire in rhetoric, if not also in reality. Arguably, Gregory only hoped for a mutually sustaining balance between the church's regional authorities and his own, singularly apostolic see in the west. Nonetheless, that capital of the old empire soon became the capital of Latin Christendom.

Conclusion

How difficult it must have been to take up the apostolic witness to Jesus' presence and promises in contexts quite unlike those of the first apostles. Whereas the first, stalwart apostles had been itinerants—preaching in one place, arousing antagonism, and moving on to another—successors constituted an increasingly settled, administrative, pastoral ministry. The earliest apostles were overtaken by Jesus or, as Paul, overpowered by his memory; they derived authority and a sense of mission from encounters with their savior. Successors, however, got their authority and commissions differently—from their acquaintances with the early apostles, from their abilities usefully to interpret the sacred literature, or from their services to institutions that claimed apostolic origin. We have seen how they derived and distributed authority, and we have been attentive to their "ecclesiastical thinking," which, Hans von Campenhausen remarked, drove the caravan composed of church, book, and bishop "from primitive Christianity to Catholicism." From his perspective, there was something rather sinister about that "thinking," if only because it "incline[d] in the direction of a one-sided preference for office . . . toward an unbalanced ascendancy of office." But stories collected here seem to suggest that he misjudged the angle of incline and the ease with which obstacles to organization were scaled.[1]

Almost from the start, Christians protested that rules, leaders, and growth compromised their new faith. Allegations generated conflicts, which managerial elites tried to resolve. They pronounced ever more authoritatively on the character and meaning of sacred literature and fashioned fresh ideas about the jurisdictions of elders, bishops, and church councils. Dissidents persisted. Wolves of all sorts troubled the flocks. Perhaps the most persistent emphasized inspiration over office. Relentlessly, they reasserted the prestige of prophecy, contrasted purity with popularity, and recalled the virtues of itinerancy, objecting to the managerial strategies of settled ministries. The point of no return was reached, it seems, early in the fourth century when Emperor Constantine declared for Christianity. The bishops, who had been evolving as preeminent strategists and managers since the second century—thanks to Ignatius and Cyprian and circumstance—were recognized and honored by the government as "the politicians of the church."[2]

Constantine and Constantius, his son and sole surviving heir after 350, depended on cooperative church politicians to engineer doctrinal consensus, to provide an adequate confessional base for political solidarity. Either the emperor or his episcopal agents called church councils to establish terms for religious conformity and to discipline nonconformists. Uncooperative bishops, probably dumbfounded to see how readily they could be deposed and replaced, complained that their church had got too cozy with the court. Ambrose of Milan echoed those complaints when, two decades after the fact, he denounced the consensus at the council of Rimini summoned by Constantius in 359. Councils could err; their lay patrons could ask too much; emperors would sin.

Not all Christians agreed, but by the early fifth century the churches' executives were generally conceding that the church on earth had room for sinners as well as for the saved. Augustine gave this comprehensivist principle great range, defending one Christian faction in North Africa against another. The Catholic church, he was confident, was a place for regeneration, not just a place or refuge for the regenerate. Secession from the Catholic, or universal, church was a grave mistake, he snapped; there was no salvation to be had outside it. Augustine, however, harped on the attribute of universality just as the universal empire was coming unglued. In theory, the church was universal but also provisional and "pilgrim." Corruption, conflict, and crisis would always mark its pilgrimage on earth. But in practice, church executives tried to appease patrons and manage conflicts as if the impermanence of all earthly things might not affect executive initiatives, as if the controversies occasioned by corruption, diversity, and novelty might someday cease.

Perhaps as early as the third century but unquestionably by the fifth, select bishops of Rome longed for greater leadership, claiming a special dignity and authority for their see. Their old capital had not consistently been the seat of imperial government since the second century, yet Rome enjoyed a formidable religious reputation. Countless martyrs, notably those venerable apostles Peter and Paul, had ended their days and been entombed in and around the city, making it a favorite, much-frequented pilgrimage site. Its bishops (on later shifts they were called "popes") said they were Peter's deputies, caretakers of the entire pilgrim church. But while Christian antiquity was slipping gracelessly into its middle ages, historical conditions and crises—the Gothic wars, Lombard belligerence, famine, flood, and schism—were restricting the scope of papal activity (albeit not the reach of papal rhetoric). Crises were "decisive," Michael Fiedrowicz said, in getting Pope Gregory I to devote himself largely, though not exclusively, to the moral and administrative reorganization of Italy. At the conclusion of Gregory's story (and ours), however, we are at the beginning of another, for the roots of medieval papal imperialism lay here in late Christian antiquity.[3]

I culled stories to illustrate where and how some "ecclesiastical thinking" brushed the ground and to suggest where, why, and how that ground was contoured by controversy. I stressed duress, but much that is fundamental for a complete understanding of the duress under which the apologists for executive management and the churches' executives themselves framed policy and practice cannot be known. Christian demography (the size of congregations before official acceptance of the new faith and the rates of conversion thereafter) is very difficult to determine, as are the nature and extent of spiritual training and exercise that were independent of organized Christian communities at any given time. Correspondence, chronicle, and apology seldom sounded out religious indifference. They only ambiguously probed mild disaffection. They clearly opened fire on outspoken protest, virulent nonconformity, and secession, but sources strenuously revised as they reported. All this argues for great caution as we approach the final lines. Nevertheless, enough has been described here (and elsewhere) to conclude that commerce and conflict with nonconformists shaped religious conformity. Efforts to discipline and exclude them raised questions and prompted answers about the competence to discipline and exclude. Efforts to reconcile and reintegrate them were coded in comprehensivist ecclesiastical thinking about authority and management.

Notes

INTRODUCTION

1. Dudley Fenner, *A Defense of the Godlie Ministers Against the Slaunders of Dr. Bridges* (London, 1587), pp. 89–90.

2. Annabel Patterson, *Reading Holinshed's "Chronicles"* (Chicago, 1994), p. 47.

3. Of those compendious texts, the most packed is probably W.H.C. Frend, *The Rise of Christianity* (London, 1984), to which the collection honoring Frend is a fine, topical supplement: Ian Hazlett, ed. *Early Christianity: Origins to A.D. 600* (Nashville, 1991). Of other introductory texts, I recommend Henry Chadwick, *The Early Church* (Harmondsworth, 1967); Peter Brown, *The World of Late Antiquity from Marcus Aurelius to Mohammed* (London, 1971); and Robin Lane Fox, *Pagans and Christians* (New York, 1987). For more detailed commentaries on each of the elements herein, see, respectively, R. F. Evans, *One

and Holy: The Church in Latin Patristic Thought (London, 1972); Bruce Metzger, *The Canon of the New Testament: Its Origin, Development, and Significance,* 2d ed. (Oxford, 1988); and Hans Freiherr von Campenhausen, *Ecclesiastical Authority and Spiritual Power in the Church of the First Three Centuries* (London, 1969). Johannes Quasten, *Patrology,* 4 vols. (Westminster, Md., 1983–1988), is an excellent reference work. Jaroslav Pelikan, *The Christian Tradition: A History of the Development of Doctrine,* vol. 1 (Chicago, 1971), usefully covers the territory largely left untouched here. More specialized studies are listed in Suggestions for Further Reading, which compass only titles available in English. My notes, however, record debts to secondary sources in other languages. The first time I refer to each primary source, I cite the original language edition consulted and an accessible English translation when one exists.

4. Peter Novick, *That Noble Dream: The "Objectivity Question" and the American Historical Profession* (Cambridge, 1988), pp. 589–592.

CHAPTER 1

1. Luke 12:32. For emancipation or deliverance, see Luke 2:29–32.

2. Matthew 6:33.

3. Note, however, the argument that the relationship with God "is essentially an individual affair" in John's gospel. See James G. Dunn, *Unity and Diversity in the New Testament: An Inquiry into the Character of Earliest Christianity* (Philadelphia, 1977), pp. 118–119.

4. Matthew 15:1–20, 23:23–24.

5. Matthew 23:16, 23:33. See also Shaye J.D. Cohen, *From the Maccabees to the Mishnah* (Philadelphia, 1987), pp. 125–126, 148–149.

6. For power-sharing, see Matthew 23:8–12.

7. 1 Corinthians 4:15–16.

8. 1 Corinthians 14:18–19, 16:15–18. For authority and ecstatic utterance in the Corinthian community, see Wayne A. Meeks, *The First Urban Christians: The Social World of the Apostle Paul* (New Haven, 1983), pp. 118–123, 134–136. For laborers, see Heinrich Greeven, "Propheten, Lehrer, Vorsteher, bei Paulus: Zur Frage der 'Ämter' im Urchristentum," in *Das kirchlicher Amt im Neuen Testament,* ed. Karl Kertelge (Darmstadt, 1977), pp. 347–349.

9. Compare 1 Corinthians 12:28 with Romans 12:6–8.

10. Philippians 1:1. "Deacons," *diakonoi,* probably connoted "those who [also] serve."

11. Acts 14:23.

12. See, for example, the remarks of Irenaeus, bishop of Lyons from the late 170s to the end of the century, in *Adversus haereses* 1.22.5, *SC,* vol. 264, translated recently as *St. Irenaeus of Lyons: Against the Heresies* (New York, 1992). For "after my departure," see Acts 20:29–30.

13. Galatians 2:11–14.

14. Jerusalem exercised no supervision over the missionary initiatives recorded in Acts. Consult Augustin George, *Études sur l'oeuvre de Luc* (Paris, 1978), pp. 384–385; and Dunn, *Unity and Diversity,* pp. 356–358. For Judaizing tendencies, see Philip Francis Esler,

Community and Gospel in Luke-Acts: The Social and Political Motivations of Lucan Theology (Cambridge, 1987), pp. 105–109.

15. 1 Timothy 5:17–19.

16. Titus 1:5–7; and 1 Timothy 3:1–7.

17. 2 Timothy 3:1–8, referring to Exodus 7:11 and supplying the names of Pharaoh's sorcerers from Jewish tradition.

18. In this connection, see John Howard Schütz, *Paul and the Anatomy of Apostolic Authority* (Cambridge, 1975), pp. 279–280. For the case for cumulative institutionalization, see Margaret Y. MacDonald, *The Pauline Churches: A Socio-historical Study of Institutionalization in the Pauline and Deutero-Pauline Writings* (Cambridge, 1988), esp. pp. 203–220, discussing the pastoral letters.

19. See Marlis Geilen, "Zur Interpretation der paulinischen Formel ἡ κατ' οἶκον ἐκκλησία," *Zeitschrift für die neuetestamentliche Wissenschaft und die Kunde der älteren Kirche* 77 (1986):119–120, 124–125, discussing Romans 16:5 and 1 Corinthians 16:9.

20. 1 Corinthians 10:16–17.

21. 1 Corinthians 11, 14:26–33. See also Gerd Thiessen, *The Social Setting of Pauline Christianity* (Philadelphia, 1982), pp. 150–151, 166–167.

22. Matthew 16:19, 18:18; and John 20:23.

23. For the arrow and archer, see Walter Bauer, *Rechtglaübigkeit und Ketzerei im ältesten Christentum* (Tübingen, 1934), translated as *Orthodoxy and Heresy in Earliest Christianity* (Philadelphia, 1971), p. 236.

24. For dependable orthodoxy in Rome, see Bauer, *Orthodoxy,* p. 128. For a useful discussion of Bauer, conflict, and consensus, see John G. Gager, *Kingdom and Community: The Social World of Early Christianity* (Englewood Cliffs, N.J., 1975), pp. 76–88.

25. Clement, letter to Corinthians, 15.1–5, *SC,* vol. 2, translated in *ACW,* vol. 1.

26. Clement, letter to Corinthians 37.2–3.

27. Clement, letter to Corinthians 19.1–3, 44.6.

28. Bauer, *Orthodoxy,* pp. 102–104.

29. Clement, letter to Corinthians 3.3, 21.5, 45.1.

30. In this connection, consult Gerbert Brunner, *Die theologische Mitte des ersten Klemensbriefes* (Frankfurt, 1972), p. 119.

31. Clement, letter to Corinthians 44.3, 57.1–2.

32. Clement, letter to Corinthians 21.6, 44.1–4, 47.5, 54.2.

33. *The Shepherd of Hermas,* Vision 3.9; Similitudes 8.7, 9.27, translated in LCL, *The Apostolic Fathers,* vol. 2. For the list of bishops, see Irenaeus, *Adversus haereses* 3.3.3, *SC,* vol. 211.

34. See Peter Lampe, *Die stadtrömischen Christen in den ersten beiden Jahrhunderten: Untersuchungen zur Sozialgeschichte* (Tübingen, 1987), pp. 334–345.

35. See Ignatius, letter to Rome 2.2, 4.3, *SC,* vol. 10, recently translated, with all the others cited here, in William Schoedel, *Ignatius of Antioch: A Commentary on the Letters of Ignatius of Antioch* (Philadelphia, 1985).

36. See Ignatius, letters to the churches of Smyrna 4.2, Magnesia 11.1, and Philadelphia 10.1–2, as well as his correspondence with Polycarp 8.1.

37. Ignatius, letter to Philadelphia 2.1–2.

38. Ignatius, letter to Smyrna 8.1–2.

39. Ignatius, letter to Polycarp 4–6.

40. Ignatius, letter to Philadelphia 3.3–4.1. See also his letters to Magnesia 6–7 and Ephesus 3.2.

41. See Ignatius, letter to Smyrna 7.1.

42. See Ignatius, letters to Magnesia 6.1 and Tralles 3.1–2.

43. Ignatius, letter to Philadelphia 7–8.1.

44. Robert Joly, *Le dossier d'Ignace d'Antioche* (Brussels, 1979), pp. 75–85. My argument with Joly, however, should not be taken to propose that Ignatius had other than "an uphill struggle . . . to ensure the kind of social control he wanted bishops to practise" (p. 179). For that struggle, see Harry O. Maier, *The Social Setting of the Ministry as Reflected in the Writings of Hermas, Clement, and Ignatius* (Waterloo, Ont., 1991), pp. 170–181.

45. See Polycarp, letter to Philippians 7, *SC*, vol. 10, translated in LCL, *The Apostolic Fathers*, vol. 1.

46. Luke 24:1–12, 24:16, 24:27, 24:37, 24:44–45.

47. Irenaeus, *Adversus haereses* 3.14.3; and Tertullian, *Adversus Marcionem* 4.5.5–6, *CCSL*, vol. 1, translated as *Five Books Against Marcion* (Oxford, 1972). For Tertullian's career, see Chapter 2.

48. See, for example, Romans 6:4.

49. 2 Corinthians 3:3–6, 11:13.

50. Galatians 6:15.

51. R. Joseph Hoffman, *Marcion: On the Restitution of Christianity. An Essay in the Development of Radical Paulinist Theology in the Second Century* (Chico, Calif., 1984), pp. 135–153. For a reevaluation of Gnosticism, see Simone Petrément, *A Separate God: The Christian Origins of Gnosticism* (San Francisco, 1990), which may be trusted as an introduction to the scholarly consensus it repudiates.

52. 2 Timothy 3:16.

53. For a translation of the Fragment, see Harry Gamble, *The New Testament Canon: Its Making and Meaning* (Philadelphia, 1985), pp. 93–95.

54. See Geoffrey Hahneman, *The Muratorian Fragment and the Development of the Canon* (Oxford, 1992), notably pp. 32–35.

55. Ptolemaeus, letter to Flora 4.1, 5.7, *SC*, vol. 24.

56. See Justin, *First Apology* 30, *PG*, vol. 6, translated in *FC*, vol. 6.

57. See Justin, *First Apology* 56, 58.

58. Justin, *Dialogue with Trypho* 114–115, *PG*, vol. 6, translated in *FC*, vol. 6.

59. Justin, *Dialogue* 17.

60. Justin, *First Apology* 16.

61. See Helmut Koester, "The Text of the Synoptic Gospels in the Second Century," in *Gospel Traditions in the Second Century: Origins, Recensions, Text, and Transmission*, ed. William L. Petersen (Notre Dame, Ind., 1989), pp. 28–32; and Helmut Koester, *Ancient Christian Gospels: Their History and Development* (London, 1990), pp. 360, 370–371, 399.

62. Irenaeus, *Adversus haereses* 3.11.8, *SC*, vol. 211.

63. See Klaus Koschorke, *Die Polemik der Gnostiker gegen das kirchliche Christentum* (Leiden, 1978), pp. 252–253, citing *The Second Logos of the Great Seth*.

64. Irenaeus, *Adversus haereses* 1.28.1.

65. Irenaeus, *Adversus haereses* 3.2.2.

66. Irenaeus, *Adversus haereses* 1.30.13–14, 5.20.1, *SC*, vol. 153.

67. Irenaeus, *Adversus haereses* 3.12.9.

68. Irenaeus, *Adversus haereses* 4.26.5, *SC,* vol. 100.

69. Consult Gilbert Vincent, "Le corps de l'heretique: La critique de la gnose par Irénée," *Revue d'histoire et de philosophie religeuses* 69 (1989):418.

70. Irenaeus, *Adversus haereses* 3.2.2.

CHAPTER 2

1. Jerome, *De perpetua virginitate B. Mariae* 17, *PL,* vol. 23, translated as *On the Perpetual Virginity of the Blessed Mary Against Helvidius, FC,* vol. 53.

2. Tertullian, *De praescriptione haereticorum* 39.1, citing 1 Corinthians 11:19, *CCSL,* vol. 1, translated as *The Prescription Against Heretics,* in *ANF,* vol. 3.

3. Tertullian, *De praescriptione* 15–19.

4. Tertullian, *De praescriptione* 20.4–8.

5. Tertullian, *De praescriptione* 37.1; and Tertullian, *Adversus Marcionem* 4.5.1, citing Galatians 6:16.

6. For useful assessments of Tertullian's rules, see René Braun, *Deus Christianorum: Recherches sur le vocabulaire doctrinal de Tertullien,* 2d ed. (Paris, 1977), pp. 446–453; L. William Countryman, "Tertullian and the *Regula Fidei,*" *The Second Century* 2 (1982):208–227; and Eric F. Osborn, "Reason and the Rule of Faith in the Second Century A.D.," in *The Making of Orthodoxy: Essays in Honor of Henry Chadwick,* ed. Rowan Williams (Cambridge, 1989), pp. 43–44, 53–57.

7. Consult Renato Uglione, "La gradualità della rivelazione in Tertulliano," in *Crescita dell'uomo catechesi dei padri,* ed. Sergio Felici (Rome, 1987), pp. 141–144.

8. See Cyprian, letter 20.2.2, *CCSL,* vol. 3B, translated in *ACW,* vol. 43.

9. Tertullian, *Apologeticum* 37.2, 42.8, *CCSL,* vol. 1, translated as *The Apology,* in *ANF,* vol. 3; and Tertullian, *De fuga in persecutione* 12.8, *CCSL,* vol. 2, translated in *ANF,* vol. 4.

10. Tertullian, *Apologeticum* 39.2; and Tertullian, *De spectaculis* 1.4, *CCSL,* vol. 1, translated as *The Shows,* in *ANF,* vol. 3.

11. Tertullian, *De anima* 9.4, *CCSL,* vol. 2, translated as *A Treatise on the Soul,* in *ANF,* vol. 3.

12. Paul Mattei, "Le schisme de Tertullien: Essai de mise au point biographique et ecclésiologique," in *Homage a René Braun,* ed. Jean Granarolo and Michele Biraud (Nice, 1990), vol. 2 pp. 133–135. For the legacy of prophecy, see Justin, *Dialogue* 87; and Tertullian, *Adversus Marcionem* 5.8.11. For the charges against Montanists in Asia Minor, see Eusebius, *Church History* 5.16–18, *SC,* vol. 41, translated in *FC,* vols. 19–20. For assimilation in North Africa, see Douglas Powell, "Tertullianists and Cataphrygians," *Vigiliae Christianae* 29 (1975):38–40, 52–54.

13. Tertullian, *Apologeticum* 39.3.

14. Tertullian, *De spectaculis* 3.2–4, citing Psalm 1:1.

15. Tertullian, *Adversus Marcionem* 5.18.7–8.

16. Tertullian, *De corona* 13, *CCSL,* vol. 2, translated as *The Chaplet,* in *ANF,* vol. 3.

17. Tertullian, *Adversus Hermogenem* 23, *CCSL,* vol. 1, translated as *Against Hermogenes,* in *ANF,* vol. 3.

18. Tertullian, *De praescriptione* 7.6–8. See also Tertullian, *Apologeticum* 47.5.

19. Tertullian, *Adversus Valentinianos* 2.1, citing Colossians 2:8, *CCSL*, vol. 2, translated as *Against the Valentinians*, in *ANF*, vol. 3.

20. See Tertullian, *Adversus Praxean* 3.1, 9.1, *CCSL*, vol. 2, translated as *Against Praxeas*, in *ANF*, vol. 3. For the polemical contexts that influenced Tertullian's various estimates of simplicity, consult Georg Schöllgen, *Ecclesia Sordida? Zur Frage der sozialen Schichtung frühchristlicher Gemeinden am Beispiel Karthagos zur Zeit Tertullians* (Münster, 1984), particularly pp. 272–276.

21. Tertullian, *Apologeticum* 24.3; and Tertullian, *De anima* 20.1.

22. Tertullian, *De praescriptione* 7.3; and Tertullian, *Adversus Hermogenem* 8.2. Consult also Otto Kuss, "Zur Hermeneutik Tertullians," in *Neutestamentliche Aufsätze: Festschrift für Prof. Josef Schmid zum 70. Geburtstag*, ed. Otto Kuss et al. (Regensburg, 1963), pp. 140–144. Among more recent studies, see Jean-Claude Fredouille, "Bible et apologétique," in *Le monde latin antique et la Bible*, ed. Jacques Fontaine and Charles Pietri (Paris, 1985), pp. 483–485; and Mark S. Burrows, "Christianity in the Roman Forum: Tertullian and the Apologetic Use of History," *Vigiliae Christianae* 42 (1988):209–235.

23. Tertullian, *Adversus Valentinianos* 27.2, 29.4.

24. Tertullian, *Ad nationes* 2.11, *CCSL*, vol. 1, translated in *ANF*, vol. 3.

25. Tertullian, *Apologeticum* 47.

26. Tertullian, *De monogamia* 11.13, *CCSL*, vol. 2, and *De pudicitia* 19.3–4, *CCSL*, vol. 2, translated as *On Monogamy* and *On Modesty*, in *ANF*, vol. 4.

27. Tertullian, *De resurrectione mortuorum* 27.4–6, *CCSL*, vol. 2, translated as *On the Resurrection of the Flesh*, in *ANF*, vol. 3. For wineskins, see Matthew 9:17 and Mark 2:22; for celestial bodies, see 1 Corinthians 15:40–41.

28. Tertullian, *De resurrectione* 21.

29. Tertullian, *De anima* 43.9–12; for souls in ether and in lunar limbo, 42, 54.

30. Tertullian, *De anima* 33.8–9; and Tertullian, *Ad nationes* 1.19.3–4. But Jean-Claude Fredouille, *Tertullien et la conversion de la culture antique* (Paris, 1972), pp. 337–357 found Tertullian's assessments of philosophy more balanced, less bitter (*raideur*).

31. Tertullian, *De resurrectione* 3.4–7.

32. Tertullian, *Apologeticum* 21.8; and Tertullian, *De carne Christi* 22, *CCSL*, vol. 2, translated as *On the Flesh of Christ*, in *ANF*, vol. 3.

33. Tertullian, *De carne Christi* 9.6–7.

34. Tertullian, *Adversus Marcionem* 5.5.9.

35. Tertullian, *Adversus Judeos* 14.2–3, *CCSL*, vol. 2, translated as *An Answer to the Jews*, in *ANF*, vol. 3.

36. Tertullian, *Adversus Marcionem* 4.35.14–15.

37. In this connection, see Tertullian, *Apologeticum* 6.9–10, 10.6–7; Tertullian, *Adversus Praxean* 14; and Tertullian, *Adversus Marcionem* 1.11, 1.18.2–3. Consult also Renato Uglione, "L'antico Testamento negli scritti Tertullianei sulle seconde nozze," *Augustinianum* 22 (1982):169–171.

38. Tertullian, *De anima* 1.1–4.

39. Tertullian, *De praescriptione* 8.8, citing Matthew 7:7.

40. Tertullian, *De praescriptione* 14.5.

41. Tertullian, *Adversus Praxean* 18.

42. Tertullian, *Scorpiace* 8.8, *CCSL*, vol. 2, translated in *ANF*, vol. 3; and Tertullian, *De fuga in persecutione* 6.1–2, citing Matthew 10:23.

43. Tertullian, *Adversus Marcionem* 4.11.5–6, citing Luke 5:33.

44. Tertullian, *Adversus Marcionem* 4.25.14–15, citing the lawyer in Luke 10:25–26.

45. For times and causes, see Tertullian, *Adversus Praxean* 13.5; and Tertullian, *De resurrectione* 30.1. Review also R.P.C. Hanson, "Notes on Tertullian's Interpretation of Scripture," *Journal of Theological Studies* 12 (1961):273–279; Thomas P. O'Malley, S.J., *Tertullian and the Bible* (Utrecht, 1967), pp. 132–133, 151–152, 172; J. H. Waszink, "Tertullian's Principles and Methods of Exegesis," in *Early Christian Literature and the Classical Intellectual Tradition: In honorem Robert M. Grant,* ed. William R. Schoedel and Robert L. Wilken (Paris, 1979), pp. 27–30; and Paolo Siniscalco, "Appunti sulla terminologia esegetica di Tertulliano," in *La terminologia esegetica nell'antichità,* ed. Carmelo Curti et al. (Bari, 1987), pp. 103–122. Review also Hanson, "Notes on Tertullian's Interpretation," 273–279 ("realism and restraint"); Hans Freiherr von Campenhausen, *The Formation of the Christian Bible,* trans. J. A. Baker (Philadelphia, 1972), pp. 276–277 ("down to earth").

46. Tertullian, *Adversus Judeos* 2.

47. John 16:12.

48. Tertullian, *De monogamia* 11.

49. Tertullian, *De monogamia* 2.2–4.

50. Tertullian, *De monogamia* 3.8.

51. Tertullian, *De baptismo* 17.2, *CCSL,* vol. 1, translated as *On Baptism,* in *ANF,* vol. 3.

52. Tertullian, *Ad nationes* 1.7; and Tertullian, *De paenitentia* 2, *CCSL,* vol. 1, translated as *On Repentance,* in *ANF,* vol. 3.

53. Tertullian, *De pudicitia* 2.3–4.

54. Tertullian, *De pudicitia* 13.14, 14.20–21, 16.6.

55. Tertullian, *De pudicitia* 9.22.

56. Tertullian, *De virginibus velandis* 1.4, *CCSL,* vol. 2, translated as *On the Veiling of Virgins,* in *ANF,* vol. 4.

57. Tertullian, *De pudicitia* 21.5.

58. Tertullian, *De pudicitia* 21.10, 21.16, citing Matthew 16:19.

59. Tertullian, *De virginibus velandis* 16.1–2.

60. Tertullian, *De virginibus velandis* 1.7, 3.2.

61. Tertullian, *De pudicitia* 1.3. In this connection, see Paul Monceaux's still valuable *Histoire littéraire de l'Afrique chrétienne* (Paris, 1901), vol. 1, pp. 285–286, for the claim that Tertullian was out to make all Christians ascetics.

62. Tertullian, *De exhortatione castitatis* 10.1, *CCSL,* vol. 2, translated as *Exhortation to Chastity,* in *ANF,* vol. 4.

63. Peter Brown, *The Body and Society: Men, Women, and Sexual Renunciation in Early Christianity* (New York, 1988), pp. 79–81. See also Claude Rambaux, *Tertullien face aux morales des trois premiers siècles* (Paris, 1979), pp. 309–314; and Francine Cardman, "Tertullian on Doctrine and the Development of Discipline," *Studia Patristica* 16.2 (1985):139–140.

64. Tertullian, *De praescriptione* 8.14, 13.5, 20.4–6, 28. Therefore, it cannot be claimed that Tertullian's early arguments "neither depend on nor presuppose" spiritual intervention, as Dimitri Michaelides suggests. Compare Jakob Speigl, "Herkommen und Fortschritt im Christentum nach Tertullian," in *Pietas: Festschrift für Bernhard Kötting,* ed. Ernst Dassman and K. Suso Frank (Münster, 1980), pp. 172–173, 176; and Dimitri Michaelides, *Foi, écritures, et tradition* (Paris, 1969), p. 69.

65. Tertullian, *De virginibus velandis* 1.7.

66. Tertullian, *De pudicitia* 21.17.

67. Tertullian, *Adversus Praxean* 1.5.

68. Tertullian, *De pudicitia* 1.12: See also Vittorino Grossi, "A proposito della conversione di Tertulliano al Montanismo, *De pudicitia* 1.10–13," *Augustinianum* 27 (1987):57–70.

69. Tertullian, *Adversus Praxean* 10.8.

70. Tertullian, *De praescriptione* 12.

71. Tertullian, *Adversus Marcionem* 5.2.

72. Consult Bernhard Kötting, "Zur Frage der *Successio Apostolica* in fruhkirchlicher Sicht," in *Ecclesia Peregrinans: Das Gottesvolk unterwegs* (Münster, 1988), vol. 1, pp. 517–530.

CHAPTER 3

1. Eusebius, *Historia ecclesiastica* 5.28.3–4, LCL.

2. Hippolytus, *Refutatio omnium haeresium* 9.12, *PTS*, vol. 25, translated as *The Refutation of All Heresies,* in *ANF*, vol. 6.

3. Manlio Simonetti, "Roma cristiana tra II e III secolo," *Vetera Christianorum* 26 (1989):126–130.

4. E. R. Dodds, *Pagan and Christian in an Age of Anxiety* (New York, 1970), pp. 133–34.

5. Charles Norris Cochrane, *Christianity and Classical Culture* (Oxford, 1940), pp. 152–155. Cyprian, letter 75.1, citing Isaiah 2:2, *CSEL*, vol. 3.2, translated in *ACW*, vol. 47. For translations of Cyprian's other correspondence, see *ACW*, vol. 43 (letters 1–27), vol. 44 (28–54), vol. 46 (55–66), and vol. 47 (67–82).

6. John Chrysostom, *De sacerdotio* 3.5–6. *SC*, vol. 272.

7. Luigi I. Scipioni, *Vescovo e populo: L'esercizio dell'autorità nella chiesa primitiva (III secolo)* (Milan, 1977), pp. 66–67, 130–132; and Alexandre Faivre, *Naissance d'une hiérarchie: Les premières étapes du cursus clérical* (Paris, 1977), p. 80.

8. Eusebius, *Historia* 6.34, 6.41.

9. Cyprian, letter 58.4; and Cyprian, *De lapsus* 3, *CSEL*, vol. 3.1, translated as *The Lapsed,* in *ACW*, vol. 25.

10. Cyprian, letter 8.

11. Cyprian, letter 16.2; and Cyprian, *De bono patientiae* 17, *CCSL*, vol. 3A.

12. Cyprian, letter 15.1–2, citing 1 Corinthians 11:27.

13. Cyprian, letter 19.2.

14. Cyprian, *De lapsus* 17, citing Jeremiah 17:5.

15. Cyprian, letter 20.2.

16. Cyprian, letter 20.3.

17. Cyprian, letter 55.3.

18. Cyprian, letter 55.20.

19. Cyprian, letter 55.29.

20. Cyprian, letter 59.5.

21. Cyprian, letter 48.3–4.

22. Cyprian, letters 67.4–5, 68.2, citing Acts 1:15–26.

23. Cyprian, letter 3.3, citing Matthew 8:4 and John 18:22–23. See also Jakob Speigl, "Cyprian über das *judicium Dei* bei der Bischofseinsetzung," *Römische Quartalschrift für christliche Altertumskunde und Kirchengeschichte* 69 (1974):37–41.

24. Joseph A. Fischer, "Das Konzil zu Karthago im Herbst 254," *Zeitschrift für Kirchengeschichte* 93 (1982):237.

25. Cyprian, letter 67.9.

26. Cyprian, letter 65.1.

27. Cyprian, letter 72.2.

28. Cyprian, letter 68.1–5.

29. For Cyprian's irritation (*agacement*), see Roger Gryson, "Les elections ecclésiastiques au IIIᵉ siècle," *Revue d'histoire ecclésiastiques* 68 (1973):376.

30. Cyprian, *De ecclesiae catholicae unitate* 4, *CCSL*, vol. 3, translated in *ACW*, vol. 25; and Cyprian, letter 71.3.

31. Enzio Gallicet, "Cipriano e la chiesa," in *La concezione della chiesa nell'antica letteratura cristiana*, ed. Aldo Ceresa-Gastaldo (Genoa, 1986), pp. 29–30. Consult also Werner Marschall, *Karthago und Rom: Die Stellung nordafrikanischen Kirche zum apostolischen Stuhl in Rom* (Stuttgart, 1971), pp. 86–89, 100–102.

32. Cyprian, letter 76.1.

33. Eusebius, *Historia* 7.13, 7.28–30, 8.1.6.

34. See Robin Lane Fox, *Pagans and Christians* (New York, 1986), pp. 591–595.

35. Eusebius, *Historia* 9.9.

36. Eusebius, *Historia* 8.6.10, 8.9.2–3.

37. See Rowan Williams, *Arius: Heresy and Tradition* (London, 1987), pp. 33–36, 259.

38. Eusebius, *Historia* 8.13.12–14.

39. See Peter Iver Kaufman, *Redeeming Politics* (Princeton, 1990), pp. 14–28. See also Bernhard Kriegbaum, "Die Religionspolitik des Kaisers Maxentius," *Archivum Historiae Pontificae* 30 (1992):50–54.

40. Eusebius, *Historia* 10.2.

41. See Augustine, *Contra Cresconium grammaticum* 4.7.9, *CSEL*, vol. 52.

42. Klaus Girardet, "Das Reichskonzil vom Rom (313): Urteil, Einspruch, Folgen," *Historia* 41 (1992):114–116.

43. Exodus 7:1.

44. Athanasius, *Contra Arianos* 11, *PG*, vol. 25, translated in *NPF*, vol. 4.

45. For blame, see Hilary of Poitiers, *De synodis* 78, *PL*, vol. 10, translated as *On the Councils*, in *NPF*, 2d series, vol. 9.

46. Timothy Barnes, *Athanasius and Constantius: Theology and Politics in the Constantinian Empire* (Cambridge, Mass., 1993), pp. 131–32. For obsessive pursuit, see John Matthews, *The Roman Empire of Ammianus* (London, 1989), p. 446.

47. *Collectanea antiariana Parisina* A.1.3, discussing John 14:28, in *CSEL*, vol. 65.

48. See Charles Pietri, "La politique de Constance II: Un premier Césaropapisme ou l'imitatio Constantini?" in *L'Église et l'empire au IVᵉ siècle*, ed. Albrecht Dihle (Geneva, 1989), pp. 119–124.

49. Sulpicius Severus, *Chronica* 2.38, *CSEL*, vol. 1, translated in *NPF*, vol. 11.

50. Athanasius, *Apologia ad Constantium* 20, citing 1 Kings 21, PG, vol. 25, translated as *Defense Before Constantius*, in *NPF*, 2d series, vol. 4.

51. See R.P.C. Hanson, *The Search for the Christian Doctrine of God* (Edinburgh, 1988), pp. 329–334. For Gallus and Silvanus, see Ammianus Marcellinus, *Rerum gestarum libri qui supersunt* 14.7, 14.11, 15.5 (Paris, 1968), translated as *The Later Roman Empire* (New York, 1986).

52. Athanasius, *Historia Arianorum* 33–34, *PG,* vol. 25, translated in *NPF,* 2d series, vol. 4.

53. For Sirmium, see Manlio Simonetti, *La crisi ariana nel IV secolo* (Rome, 1975), pp. 230–232.

54. *Collectanea antiariana Parisina* A.5.1.3.

55. Sulpicius Severus, *Chronica* 2.43; and Ambrose, *Expositio evangelii secundum Lucam* 5.71, citing Luke 6:26, *SC,* vol. 45.

56. Hilary, *Contra Arianos vel Auxentium Mediolanensem* 1, *PL,* vol. 10. See also Simonetti, *Crisi ariana,* pp. 314–325.

57. See *Collectanea antiariana Parisina* A.1.4; and Hilary, *De synodis* 1–2.

58. Hilary, *Ad Constantium Augustum, liber secundus* 4–7, *PL,* vol. 10.

59. Sulpicius Severus, *Chronica* 2.45.

60. Hilary, *Liber in Constantium imperatorem* 7, *SC,* vol. 334.

61. *Collectanea antiariana Parisina* B.4.1.2.

62. Auxentius's answer to Hilary is appended to the latter's *Contra Arianos* 13–15. For the charges, see 15: "Hilarius et Eusebius contendunt ubique schismata facere."

63. Hilary, *Contra Arianos* 14.

64. Hilary, *Contra Arianos* 8, 11.

65. Hilary, *Contra Arianos* 12. See also Yves-Marie Duval, "Ambrose, de son élection à sa consecration," in *Ambrosius Episcopus,* ed. Giuseppe Lazzati (Milan, 1976), pp. 250–251.

66. Hilary, *Contra Arianos* 4.

67. Hilary, *Contra Arianos* 3. See also Harry O. Maier, "Private Space as a Social Context of Arianism in Ambrose's Milan," *Journal of Theological Studies* 45 (1994):76–77. For the contexts of alternative and private worship, see Josef Schmitz, *Gottesdienst im altchristlichen Mailand: Eine liturgiewissenschaftliche Untersuchung über Initiation und Messfeier während des Jahres zur Zeit des Bischofs Ambrosius* (Bonn, 1975), pp. 248–251. For the apostolicity of Hilary and Eusebius, see Rufinus, *Historiae ecclesiasticae libri duo* 1.30, *PL,* vol. 21. For the administrative energy of the late empire episcopacy, consult Alan Wardman, *Religion and Statecraft Among the Romans* (Baltimore, 1982), pp. 153–156.

68. Paulinus of Milan, *Vita sancti Ambrosii* 3, CUAPS, vol. 16.

69. Neil B. McLynn, *Ambrose of Milan: Church and Court in a Christian Capital* (Berkeley, 1994), pp. 43–51.

70. Consult the text of their statement published by Marcel Richard, "La lettre *Confidimus Quidem* du Pape Damasus," *Annuaire de l'Institut de Philologie et l'Histoire Orientales et Slaves* 11 (1951):326–327; and discussed in Charles Pietri, *Roma Christiana: Recherches sur l'église de Rome de Militade à Sixte III,* 2 vols. (Rome, 1976), 1:734–736.

71. Ambrose, *De fide* 2.12.101, *CSEL,* vol. 78.

72. Ambrose, *De fide* 1.4.32, citing Isaiah 6:3.

73. Ambrose, *De fide* 2.14.127, citing Mathew 17:5 and John 16:15.

74. Ambrose, *Lucam* 1.12–13, *SC,* vol. 45. See also Daniel H. Williams, "Ambrose, Emperors, and Homoians in Milan: The First Conflict over a Basilica," in *Arianism After Arius: Essays in the Development of the Fourth-Century Trinitarian Conflicts,* ed. Michael R.

Barnes and Daniel H. Williams (Edinburgh, 1993), pp. 138–139, who suspected that the Arians worshiped at the church during sequestration.

75. *Codex Theodosianus* 16.1.1, 16.5.6 (Berlin, 1905); and Ambrose, *De spirito sancto* 1.1.20–21, *CSEL*, vol. 79, translated in *FC*, vol. 44.

76. Ambrose, letter 21.17, *CSEL*, vol. 82, translated in *FC*, vol. 26.

77. Ambrose, letter 20.19–20; and Ambrose, *Lucam* 9.31–32, *SC*, vol. 52.

78. Ambrose, *Expositio Psalmi CXVIII* 13.2, citing Deuteronomy 4:24 and Luke 12:49, 24:32, *CSEL*, vol. 62.

79. Ambrose, *De viduis admonitio* 1.14.83, *PL*, vol. 16, translated as *Concerning Widows*, in *NPF*, vol. 10; and Ambrose, *De officiis ministrorum* 1.33.170–172, 2.21.109, *PL*, vol. 16, translated as *On the Duties of the Clergy*, in *NPF*, vol. 10. For faith as *plantatio*, see Giuseppi Toscani, *Teologia della chiesa nel sant'Ambrogio* (Milan, 1974), pp. 386–391. For Ambrose's episcopal network and church growth, see Michael Zelzer, "Ambrosius von Mailand und das Erbe der klassischen Tradition," *Wiener Studien: Zeitschrift für klassischen Philologie und Patristik* 100 (1987): 223–226; Santo Mazzarino, *Storia sociale del vescovo Ambrogio* (Rome, 1989), pp. 21–30, 39–45; and Rita Lizzi, "Ambrose's Contemporaries and the Christianization of Northern Italy," *Journal of Roman Studies* 80 (1990):164–167, 172.

80. For the council as tribunal and inquisition, see Thomas Gerhard Ring, *Auctoritas bei Tertullian, Cyprian, und Ambrosius* (Würzburg, 1975), pp. 215–220.

81. For Palladius's blunder, see *Gesta episcoporum Aquileia adversum haereticos Arrianos* 11–14, 36, *SC*, vol. 267. See also Ambrose, letter 10. Precedents for what Ambrose considered Palladius's miscue are inventoried by Manlio Simonetti, "Giovanni 14:28 nella controversia ariana," in *Kyriakon: Festschrift, Johannes Quasten*, ed. Patrick Granfield and Josef A. Jungmann (Münster, 1970), vol. 1, pp. 151–161. Yves-Marie Duval, "Le sens des débats d'Aquilée pour les nicéens: Nicée, Rimini, Aquilée," *Antichità Altoadriatiche* 21 (1981):81–87 put exegesis in the context of the conciliar debate.

82. Ambrose, *Oratio de obitu Theodosii* 34, CUAPS, vol. 9; and Ambrose, *De sacramentis* 6.4.19, *SC*, vol. 25, translated in *FC*, vol. 44.

83. Ambrose, letter 51.6.

84. Ambrose, letter 41.26–28; and McLynn, *Ambrose*, pp. 304–309.

85. Ambrose, letter 51.13–14.

86. Ambrose, *De paenitentia* 1.5.22–26, 1.16.87, 2.5.34–37, *SC*, vol. 25.

87. Chromatius, sermon 41.7, *SC*, vol. 164.

CHAPTER 4

1. Augustine, *Confessiones* 5.14.24, 6.4.6, *CSEL*, vol. 33, translated in *FC*, vol. 21.

2. Augustine, *Confessiones* 6.11.19.

3. Augustine, *De vera religione* 3.3–5, *CSEL*, vol. 77.2, translated as *True Religion*, in LCC, vol. 6.

4. Augustine, *Confessiones* 6.6.9.

5. Augustine, *Confessiones* 8.2.5.

6. Augustine, *Confessiones* 8.12.29, citing Romans 13:13–14.

7. Augustine, *Soliloquia* 1.1.5, 1.11.19, *CSEL*, vol. 89, translated in *FC*, vol. 5.

8. Augustine, *Confessiones* 9.6.14.

9. Augustine, letter 21, *CSEL*, vol. 34, translated in *FC*, vol. 9.

10. Augustine, *In Johannis evangelium tractatus* 53.7, *CCSL*, vol. 36; and Augustine, sermon 355.6, *PL*, vol. 39.

11. Augustine, *Confessiones* 8.3.6.

12. Augustine, *Contra Cresconium grammaticum* 3.80.92, *CSEL*, vol. 52.

13. Augustine, *Confessiones* 1.1.1.

14. Augustine, *De doctrina Christiana* 3.3–5, *CCSL*, vol. 32, translated as *On Christian Doctrine*, in *FC*, vol. 2. On this count, see Cornelius Mayer, "Augustins Lehre vom *homo spiritalis*," in *Homo Spiritalis*, ed. Cornelius Mayer and Klaus Heinz Chelius (Würzburg, 1987), pp. 59–60.

15. Augustine, *De civitate Dei* 5.24, *CSEL*, vol. 47–48, translated as *The City of God*, in *NPF*, vol. 2.

16. Zosimus, *Historia nova* 3.6–8 (Hildesheim, 1963), translated for the Australian Association for Byzantine Studies (Canberra, 1982).

17. See Maria Cesa and Hagith Sivan, "Alarico in Italia: Pollenza e Verona," *Historia* 39 (1990): 371–372; and J.H.W.G. Liebeschuetz, *Barbarians and Bishops: Army, Church, and State in the Age of Arcadius and Chrysostom* (Oxford, 1990), pp. 57, 69–72.

18. For Gibbon, see Jaroslav Pelikan, *The Excellent Empire: The Fall of Rome and the Triumph of the Church* (San Francisco, 1987), pp. 79–89.

19. Augustine, *Enarrationes in Psalmos* 90.4, *CCSL*, vol. 39, translated in *NPF*, vol. 8.

20. Augustine, *In Johannis evangelium tractatus* 6.17, 7.6.

21. Augustine, *Enarrationes in Psalmos* 90.6.

22. Augustine, sermon 296.6, *PL*, vol. 38; and Augustine, *Sermo de sancto Joanne Baptista* 8.13, *PL*, vol. 46.

23. For *l'étroitesse spirituale*, see Pasquale Borgomeo, *L'Église de ce temps dans la prédication de saint Augustin* (Paris, 1972), pp. 108–112.

24. Augustine, sermon 273.8.8, *PL*, vol. 38.

25. Augustine, letters 17.4, 29.3–6, *CSEL*, vol. 34.

26. Prudentius, *Peristephanon liber* 2.465–468, 12.1–66, LCL (1953), vol. 2.

27. Augustine, *Contra Faustum Manichaeum* 20.21, *CSEL*, vol. 25, translated in *NPF*, vol. 4; Augustine, sermon 296.8–9, and Augustine, *De civitate Dei* 8.27.

28. Augustine, *De cura pro mortuis* 2.4–3.5, *CSEL*, vol. 41, translated as *Care for the Dead*, in *FC*, vol. 27.

29. Augustine, *De cura pro mortuis* 4.6.

30. Augustine, *De cura pro mortuis* 18.22, citing Luke 21:33; and Augustine, sermon 105.7.10, *PL*, vol. 38.

31. See Gaetano Lettieri, *Il senso della storia in Agostino d'Ippona: Il 'saeculum' e la gloria nel 'De civitate Dei'* (Rome, 1988), pp. 248–253; Ramsay MacMullen, *Christianizing the Pagan Empire* (New Haven, 1984), pp. 74–85; and Victor Saxer, *Morts, martyrs, reliques en Afrique chrétienne aux premiers siècles* (Paris, 1980), pp. 129–130, 197–198.

32. Augustine, *De urbis Romae excidio* 8.9, *CCSL*, vol. 46; and Augustine, letter 29.9–10.

33. Augustine, *De civitate Dei* 14.9.

34. Augustine, *De civitate Dei* 19.20.

35. Augustine, *De civitate Dei* 15.6, 15.18.

36. Serge Lancel, *Actes de la conference de Carthage en 411* (Paris, 1972), vol. 1, pp. 159–164.

37. Augustine, *Ad Donatistas post Collationem* 24.41, *PL,* vol. 43.

38. Lancel, *Actes* 3.165.

39. Augustine, *Post collationem* 10.13, citing 1 Corinthians 5:19; and *Actes* 3.258, citing Jeremiah 23:28 and Ezekiel 32:26.

40. Augustine, *Contra epistulam Parmeniani* 3.3.17, *CSEL,* vol. 51; Augustine, *Contra Cresconium* 3.81.93; and Augustine, sermon 392.6, *PL,* vol. 39.

41. Augustine, *Contra litteras Petiliani* 2.7.14, *CSEL,* vol. 52, translated as *Reply to the Letters of Petilianus,* in *NPF,* vol. 4.

42. Augustine, letter 108.19, *CSEL,* vol. 34.

43. Augustine, *Contra litteras Petiliani* 3.38.44.

44. Augustine, letter 35.2, *CSEL,* vol. 34.

45. Jean-Paul Brisson, *Autonomisme et christianisme dans l'Afrique romaine* (Paris, 1958), pp. 337–341; and Emin Tengstrom, *Donatisten und Katholiken: Soziale, wirtschaftliche, und politische Aspekte einer nordafrikanischen Kirchenspaltung* (Göteburg, 1964), pp. 43–52, 71–78.

46. Augustine, letter 185.15–16, *CSEL,* vol. 57.

47. Augustine, letter 76.3, *CSEL,* vol. 34.

48. Augustine, *Contra epistulam Parmeniani* 2.4.8, 2.7.13, citing Jeremiah 17:5.

49. *Actes* 3.102.

50. *Actes* 3.230.

51. Augustine, *In Johannis evangelium tractatus* 13.13; and Augustine, *Tractatus de testimoniis scripturarum contra donatistos et contra paganos,* 1–4, citing Matthew 8:11, Psalms 2:8; 72:11, and John 19:23, printed in *Revue des études augustiniennes* 37 (1991):42–46.

52. Augustine, *Contra litteras Petiliani* 2.36.84, citing Galatians 6:5.

53. I borrow the phrase from Gerald Bonner, "Pelagianism and Augustine," *Augustinian Studies* 23 (1992):34.

54. Augustine, sermon 46.1.2, 46.13.31, citing Philippians 2:21, *PL,* vol. 38.

55. Augustine, *Contra Cresconium* 3.8.8, citing 1 Corinthians 3:7.

56. Augustine, *Contra litteras Petiliani* 2.101.233.

57. Augustine, *De baptismo* 4.12.18, *CSEL,* vol. 51, translated in *NPF,* vol. 4.

58. Augustine, *Contra litteras Petiliani* 1.3.4; and Augustine, *Contra Cresconium* 2.21.26.

59. Augustine, *Contra Cresconium* 2.26.31.

60. Augustine, *Contra Cresconium* 2.28.35.

61. Augustine, *De baptismo* 1.16.25; and Augustine, *Enarrationes in Psalmos* 55.20, *CSEL,* vol. 39. For Augustine's indignation, see Remi Crespin, *Ministère et sainteté: Pastorale du clergé et solution de la crise Donatiste dans la vie et la doctrine de Saint Augustin* (Paris, 1965), pp. 190–93, 204–206.

62. Augustine, *Contra litteras Petiliani* 2.19.43, citing 1 Peter 3:15.

63. Augustine, sermon 46.17.41, *PL,* vol. 38.

64. Augustine, letter 185.22, 185.33. Consult also Ernst Ludwig Gräsmuck, *Coercitio: Staat und Kirche im Donatistenstreit* (Bonn, 1964), pp. 182–183, which calls this "the axiomatic assertion" in Augustine's vindication of coercive Christianity.

65. Augustine, letter 185.8–10, citing Matthew 5:10.

66. Augustine, letter 93, *CSEL,* vol. 34.

67. Augustine, letter 128, *CSEL,* vol. 44.

68. Augustine, *Post collationem* 41–43.

69. Augustine, letter 141.2,9, *CSEL,* vol. 44.

70. *Actes* 3.40–41. For a more favorable account of Donatist tactics, see Maureen A. Tilley, "Dilatory Donatists or Procrastinating Catholics: The Trial at the Conference of Carthage," *Church History* 60 (1991):7–19. Consult also W.H.C. Frend, *The Donatist Church,* 2d ed. (Oxford, 1985), pp. 278–289. Jean-Louis Maier, *Le dossier du Donatisme* (Berlin, 1989), vol. 2, pp. 104–173, documented imperial and Caecilianist measures against Donatism during the decade before the council.

71. Augustine, *Breviculus Collationis cum Donatistis* 3.18.35, citing 2 Corinthians 5:19, *CSEL,* vol. 53.

72. *Actes* 3.258, 3.276, citing Matthew 3:12 and Luke 3:17.

73. *Actes* 3.261.

74. *Actes* 1.55.

75. Augustine, *De civitate Dei* 17.31.

76. Augustine, *De civitate Dei* 12.9, 19.27.

77. Augustine, *Contra litteras Petiliani* 2.106.241, citing Colossians 4:2–4.

78. Augustine, sermon 251.3–4, citing Matthew 13:47–50, *PL,* vol. 38; and Augustine, *Enarrationes in Psalmos* 64.9, *CSEL,* vol. 39.

79. Augustine, *Enarrationes in Psalmos* 84.9; and Augustine, *De gratia Christi et de peccato originali* 2.6.6, *CSEL,* vol. 42, translated as *On the Grace of Christ and Original Sin,* in *NPF,* vol. 5. See also Otto Wermelinger, *Rom und Pelagius: Die theologische Position der römischen bischöfe im pelagianischen Streit in den Jahren 411–432* (Stuttgart, 1975), pp. 155–58, 278–282; Aimé Solignac, "Pelage et pelagianisme," in *Dictionnaire de spiritualité, ascétique, et mystique: Doctrine et histoire* (Paris, 1986), vol. 12.2, cols. 2926–2936; and Elizabeth Clark, *The Origenist Controversy: The Cultural Construction of an Early Christian Debate* (Princeton, 1992), pp. 207–215.

80. Augustine, *De peccatorum meritis et remissione et baptismo parvulorum* 1.33.62, quoting Philippians 2:13, *CSEL,* vol. 60.

81. See Peter Brown, "Pelagius and His Supporters: Aims and Environment," in his *Religion and Society in the Age of Augustine* (London, 1972), pp. 193–200.

82. See Paolo Brezzi, "Una civitas terrena spiritualis come ideale storico-politico di Sant'Agostino," *Augustinus Magister* 2 (1954):921; Mariette Cavenet, "Culture paienne et foi chrétienne aux racines de l'Europe: La *Cite de Dieu* d'Augustin," *Gregorianum* 74 (1993):9–13; and, especially, Luigi Alici, "Interiorità e speranza," in *Interiorità e intenzionalità nel 'De civitate Dei' di Sant' Agostino,* ed. Remo Piccolomini (Rome, 1991), pp. 64–67.

83. Augustine, *Enarrationes in Psalmos* 144.4, *CSEL,* vol. 40.

84. Augustine, *Enarrationes in Psalmos* 39.10, *CSEL,* vol. 38; and Augustine, *De civitate Dei* 20.3. To say Augustine was something of an apostle of imperfection is not to agree with Robert Markus that Augustine offered a vindication of "Christian mediocrity." Consult Robert Markus, *The End of Ancient Christianity* (Cambridge, 1992), pp. 50–53; and Peter Iver Kaufman, "Augustine, Martyrs, and Misery," *Church History* 63 (1994):12–14.

85. Augustine, *Breviculus* 3.8.12.

86. Augustine, *De civitate Dei* 19.20; and Augustine, sermon 169.9.11, *PL,* vol. 38.

87. Augustine, *Confessiones* 4.4–6; Augustine, *De civitate Dei* 11.28; and Augustine, sermon 80.8, *PL,* vol. 38. See also Norbert Fischer, "Augustins Weg der Gottessuche," *Trierer theologische Zeitschrift* 2 (1991):96–98.

88. Augustine, *Enarrationes in Psalmos* 34.26, citing Acts 10:9–48, *CSEL,* vol. 38.

89. Augustine, *Enarrationes in Psalmos* 3.7, *CSEL*, vol. 38.

90. Augustine, *Enarrationes in Psalmos* 139.2, *CSEL*, vol. 40. Note also Borgomeo, *L'Église de ce temps,* pp. 170–173.

CHAPTER 5

1. Acts 17:22–24.

2. Gregory I, letters 9.208, and 11.10, *CCSL*, vols. 140–140A; select letters are translated in *NPF,* vol. 12.

3. Augustine, *De civitate Dei* 22.8.

4. Gregory of Tours, *Liber in gloria confessorum* 2, *MGH, SRM,* vol. 1, translated as *Glory of the Confessors* (Liverpool, 1988).

5. For accommodation and evangelization, see C. E. Stancliffe, "From Town to Country: The Christianisation of the Touraine, 370–600," in *The Church in Town and Countryside,* ed. Derek Baker (Oxford, 1979), pp. 54–59. For the end of assimilation, see James J. O'Donnell, *Cassiodorus* (Berkeley, 1979), pp. 1--11. For Victricius, see Luce Pietri, "Culte des saints et religiosité politique dans la Gaule du Ve et du VIIe siècle," in *Les fonctions des saints dans le monde occidental* (Rome, 1991), pp. 355–357.

6. Victricius of Rouen, *De laude sanctorum* 10–11, *CCSL*, vol. 64.

7. Paulinus of Nola, letter 31.3–6, *CSEL*, vol. 29, translated in *ACW*, vol. 36.

8. Paulinus of Nola, *Carmina* 23, *CSEL*, vol. 30, translated in *ACW*, vol. 40.

9. Paulinus of Nola, *Carmina* 15.

10. Peter Brown, *The Cult of Saints: Its Rise and Function in Late Antiquity* (Chicago, 1981), pp. 37–39, 54, 60–61. See also Raymond van Dam, *Leadership and Community in Late Antique Gaul* (Berkeley, 1985), pp. 194, 214–216, 234–236.

11. Venantius Fortunatus, *Carmina* 5.3, *MGH, AA,* vol. 4.

12. Gregory of Tours, *Liber de passione et virtutibus sancti Juliani martyris* 34, *MGH, SRM,* vol. 1, translated in Raymond van Dam, *Saints and Their Miracles in Late Antiquity* (Princeton, 1993).

13. Ian Wood, *The Merovingian Kingdoms, 450–751* (London, 1994), p. 86.

14. For Faustus, Sidonius, and the 470s ("by now, barbarians had become an accepted part of the Gallic landscape" [p. 119]), see Ralph Whitney Mathisen, *Roman Aristocrats in Barbarian Gaul: Strategies for Survival in an Age of Transition* (Austin, 1993), pp. 119–121. Walter Goffart, "The Theme of 'The Barbarian Invasions' in Late Antique and Modern Historiography," in *Das Reich und die Barbaren,* ed. Evangelos K. Chrysos and Andreas Schwarcz (Vienna, 1989), pp. 87–107, is an excellent reminder that "the underlying theme of relations between Rome and the barbarians in late antiquity was not antagonism and strife but mutual need and cooperation" (p. 97). Nevertheless, for literary shading of barbarous darkness, consult Yves Albert Dauge, *La barbare: Recherches sur la conception romaine de la barbarie et de la civilisation* (Brussels, 1981), esp. pp. 585–592.

15. Georg Scheibelreiter, *Der Bischof in merowingischer Zeit* (Vienna, 1983), pp. 144–145.

16. *Concilium Aurelianense,* 511, 14 and 23, *CCSL*, vol. 148A.

17. *Concilium Aurelianense,* 549, 15, *CCSL*, vol. 148A.

18. J. M. Wallace-Hadrill, *The Frankish Church* (Oxford, 1983), pp. 107–109.

19. Coelestine I, letter 21.1, *PL*, vol. 50.

20. Sigismund's letter, mistakenly registered to Pope Symmachus, is printed with the works of Bishop Avitus of Vienne in *Epistularum ad diversos, libri tres* 1.27(29), *MGH, AA*, vol. 6.2.

21. For Sigismund's appeals to Anastasios, see Georg Scheibelreiter, "*Vester est populus meus*: Byzantinische Reichsideologie und germanisches Selbstverständnis," in *Das Reich und die Barbaren*, ed. Chrysos and Schwarcz, pp. 206–207.

22. Gregory of Tours, *Historia Francorum* 6.6, *MGH, SRM*, vol. 1, translated as *The History of the Franks* (New York, 1969). For Gregory's reservations about Rome and St. Peter, see Van Dam, *Leadership and Community*, pp. 182–183.

23. Innocent I, letter 2.9.12, citing Leviticus 21:12, *PL*, vol. 20.

24. Innocent I, letter 25.2, citing Matthew 16:18–19.

25. Leo I, letter 95.4, *PL*, vol. 54.

26. Leo I, letter 126. Compare Stephen Otto Horn, *Petrou Kathedra: Der Bischof von Rom und die Synoden von Ephesus (449) und Chalcedon* (Paderborn, 1982), pp. 250, 283–284.

27. Leo I, letter 104.3.

28. Simplicius, letter 56.8–12, *CSEL*, vol. 35.

29. Simplicius, letter 60.

30. Felix III, *Epistola sive tractatus, PL*, vol. 58 (cols. 950–952).

31. Gelasius, *De anathematis vinculo, PL*, vol. 59 (cols. 102–103). See also Walter Ullmann, *Gelasius I (492–496): Das Papsttum an der Wende der Spätantike und zum Mittelalter* (Stuttgart, 1981), pp. 126–127, 202–204, 209.

32. John Moorehead, *Theodoric in Italy* (Oxford, 1992), pp. 118–119.

33. For disbursements, see A.H.M. Jones, "Church Finances in the Fifth and Sixth Centuries," *Journal of Theological Studies* 11 (1960):91–93.

34. Pelagius I, letters 10.3, 35.7, 52.8, *Pelagii I Papae epistulae quae supersunt*, ed. Pius M. Gasso and Columba M. Batlle (Montserrat, 1956).

35. Pelagius I, letter 59.6–8.

36. Pelagius I, letter 24.15–18, citing John 15:6.

37. Paul the Deacon, *Historia Langobardorum* 2.3, *MGH, SRL*, translated as *The History of the Lombards* (Philadelphia, 1907; reprint ed., 1974).

38. Paul the Deacon, *Historia* 2.5. Consult also Neil Christie, "Invasion or Invitation? The Longobard Occupation of Northern Italy, A.D. 568–569," *Romano-Barbarica* 11 (1991):86–87, 103–106.

39. *Epistolae Austrasicae* 8, *MGH, EMK*, vol. 1.

40. For the Lombards' "superficial" piety, consult Carlo Guido Mor, "Bizanti e Langobardi sul limite della laguna," *Grado nella storia e nell'arte*, ed. Mario Mirabella Roberti (Udine, 1980), vol. 1, pp. 245–246.

41. Paul the Deacon, *Historia* 2.27.

42. Wilfried Menghin, *Die Langobarden: Archäologie und Geschichte* (Stuttgart, 1985), pp. 94–99.

43. Jean Durliat, "L'Évêque et sa cite en Italie byzantine," in *L'Évêque des l'histoire de l'église*, ed. Jean de Viguerie (Angers, 1984), pp. 21–22.

44. *De vita atque ejus virtutibus* 2, with a translation as *The Earliest Life of Gregory the Great* (Lawrence, Kans. 1968).

45. *De vita* 7.

46. Gregory of Tours, *Historia* 4.6–7.

47. Gregory I, *Liber regulae pastoralis* 1.6, *PL*, vol. 77, translated in *NPF*, vol. 12.

48. Gregory I, letter 1.4.

49. Gregory I, *Homiliarum in evangelia, libri duo* 1.1.1, referring to Luke 21:10; Gregory I, *Homiliarum* 1.1.5; and Gregory I, *Moralia in Job* 22.21.52, *CCSL*, vol. 143A.

50. Gregory I, letter 1.30.

51. Gregory I, letter 5.36. Gregory's negotiations are chronicled in Jeffrey Richards, *Consul of God: The Life and Times of Gregory the Great* (London, 1980), pp. 187–194; and, with greater detail, in Georg Jemal, "Gregor der Grosse und die Stadt Rom (590–604)," in *Herrschaft und Kirche: Beiträge zur Enstehung und Wirkungsweise episcopaler und monastischer Organisationsformen,* ed. Friedrich Prinz (Stuttgart, 1988), pp. 123–130.

52. Gregory I, letter 1.7.

53. Gregory I, letter 7.4–5.

54. Gregory I, *Homilia in Hiezechihelem Prophetam* 2.6.4, citing Acts 7:51, 7:60, *CCSL*, vol. 142.

55. Gregory I, *Liber regulae pastoralis* 2.6; and Gregory I, letter 2.40.

56. Gregory I, *Moralia* 8.48.82, 20.3.8, citing Job 29:24, *CCSL*, vols. 143, 143A, respectively.

57. Gregory I, *In librum primum regum* 2.126–127, citing 1 Samuel 3:4–9, *CCSL*, vol. 144.

58. Gregory I, *Moralia* 27.15.30, *CCSL*, vol. 143B; Gregory I, letter 2.44; and Gregory I, *Liber regulae pastoralis* 3.24.

59. Gregory I, *Dialogorum libri quatuor* 1.10.11–16, *PL*, vol. 77, translated in *FC*, vol. 39. With all the subtlety of a monsoon, the readers who accepted Gregory's authorship drenched their commentary on sanctity and the sensational in late antiquity with the skepticism that became fashionable many centuries later: A pope well versed in worldly affairs, they said, could not possibly have believed what Gregory's collection of stories replayed as recent history. No tarpaulin in my shed can keep the dialogues dry, which is to say that I cannot prove the miracles occurred or that Gregory believed they did. I do not know whether he was credulous or condescending, as skeptics allow, or whether a choice between the two extremes is unavoidable. For now, however, we do well to accept what little the text gives us of Gregory's design and inquire about its relevance to our concern with authority. To sample a case for inauthenticity, see Francis Clark, *The Pseudo-Gregorian Dialogues,* 2 vols. (Leiden, 1987), notably 2:749–754.

60. Gregory I, *Dialogorum* 1.19.6–7. See also Carole Straw, *Gregory the Great: Perfection in Imperfection* (Berkeley, 1988), pp. 67–73; Claude Dagens, *Saint Grégoire le Grand: Culture et expérience chrétiennes* (Paris, 1977), pp. 230–233; and William D. McCready, *Signs of Sanctity: Miracles in the Thought of Gregory the Great* (Toronto, 1989), pp. 95–96, 204–205.

61. Gregory I, letter 1.52.

62. Gregory I, letter 4.30.

63. Gregory I, letter 8.4.

64. See Kaufman, *Redeeming Politics* (Princeton, 1990), pp. 86–87.

65. Gregory I, *Dialogorum* 3.11.

66. Gregory I, *Moralia* 24.25.54, *CCSL*, vol. 143B.

67. Gregory I, letters 4.26, 9.11.

68. Gregory I, letter 3.15.

69. Gregory I, letters 9.53, 9.76, and 9.163.

70. Gregroy I, letter 7.25.

71. Gregory I, letters 1.72, 2.39, 4.35.

72. Gregory I, letter 11.36, citing Luke 15:7.

73. Gregory I, letter 8.29.

74. Gregory I, letter 11.39: *Non sibimet discrepando.*

75. Gregory I, letter 11.56a.

76. Gregory I, letter 5.41.

77. Gregory I, letter 5.44, citing Isaiah 14:13.

78. Gregory I, letter 7.37.

79. Gregory I, letter 5:44.

80. Gregory I, *Moralia* 5.34.63, *CCSL,* vol. 143.

81. John 21:17, Luke 22:31, and Matthew 16:19, respectively.

82. Gregory I, letter 5.37.

83. Gregory I, letter 9.26.

84. See Jemal, "Gregor der Grosse," pp. 143–145.

85. Dagens, *Saint Grégoire le Grand,* pp. 365–366.

CONCLUSION

1. Hans Freiherr von Campenhausen, *Ecclesiastical Authority and Spiritual Power in the Church of the First Three Centuries* (London, 1969), pp. 295–297.

2. Averil Cameron, *The Later Roman Empire* (Cambridge, Mass., 1993), pp. 57–61.

3. Michael Fiedrowicz, *Das Kirchenverstandnis Gregors des Grossen: Eine Untersuchung seiner exegetischen und homiletischen Werke* (Freiburg, 1995), pp. 370–371, 381. For papal imperialism, see Kaufman, *Redeeming Politics,* pp. 79–104.

Suggestions for Further Reading

CHAPTER 1

John Tunstead Burtchaell, *From Synagogue to Church: Public Services and Offices in the Earliest Christian Communities* (Cambridge, 1992), is a challenge to the consensus on progressive institutionalization—the consensus identified with Hans Freiherr von Campenhausen, *Ecclesiastical Authority and Spiritual Power in the Church of the First Three Centuries* (London, 1969)—but Burtchaell's arguments favoring early executive leadership are generally unconvincing. His historiographical chapters, however, are excellent and show why historians and theologians so readily imagined "a golden age of inspired, unorganized discipleship."

Morna D. Hooker's *Continuity and Discontinuity: Early Christianity in Its Jewish Setting* (London, 1986), as the title suggests, considers a theme fundamental to Chapter 1. Supplement her lively presentation with Francis Watson, *Paul, Judaism, and the Gentiles* (Cambridge, 1986), which emphasizes Paul's advocacy of sectarian gentile communities. See also Shaye Cohen, *From the Maccabees to the Mishnah* (Philadelphia, 1987); and John K. Riches, *The World of Jesus: First-Century Judaism in Crisis* (Cambridge, 1990). For the so-called social world of early Christianity, see Wayne Meeks, *The First Urban Christians: The Social World of the Apostle Paul* (New Haven, 1983); Wayne Meeks, *The Moral World of the First Christians* (Philadelphia, 1988); Gerd Thiessen, *The Social Setting of Pauline Christianity* (Philadelphia, 1982); E. A. Judge, *The Social Pattern of Christian Groups in the First Century* (London, 1960); Abraham Malherbe, *Social Aspects of Early Christianity* (Philadelphia, 1983); and appropriate articles in the first two volumes of E. P. Sanders, ed., *Jewish and Christian Self-Definition* (London, 1980–1981). Contributions to our understanding of the social world often turn on controversial interpretations of canonical texts. Stephen Barton's "Critical Study of the Field" catches many more of them in its net than I have here, so consult his survey in the *Journal of Theological Studies* 43 (1992):399–427. But add to his ample catch Nicholas Taylor, *Paul, Antioch, and Jerusalem: A Study in Relationships and Authority in Earliest Christianity* (Sheffield, England, 1992).

Religious authority in the early second century is usefully discussed in Barbara Ellen Bowe, *A Church in Crisis: Ecclesiology and Paraenesis in Clement of Rome* (Minneapolis, 1988); James S. Jeffers, *Conflict at Rome: Social Order and Hierarchy in Early Christianity* (Minneapolis, 1991); and Harry O. Maier, *The Social Setting of the Ministry as Reflected in the Writings of Hermas, Clement, and Ignatius* (Waterloo, Ont. 1991). For a striking commentary on early canonical development, see Bart Ehrman, *The Orthodox Corruption of Scripture: The Effect of Early Christological Controversies on the Text of the New Testament* (Oxford, 1993), an exceptional contribution to the history of proto-orthodoxy. Ehrman's identification of corruptions and controversies bears directly on my chapter's too few remarks about the Docetists and Gnostics, for whom review Karl Rudolph, *Gnosis: The Nature and History of Gnosticism* (Edinburgh, 1984); and Elaine Pagels, *The Gnostic Gospels* (New York, 1980), which occasionally crosses from assessment to advocacy. Simone Petrément, *A Separate God: The Christian Origins of Gnosticism* (New York, 1987), is a daring reevaluation of Gnostic origins and themes.

In the words of R.P.C. Hanson, the Bible "is a body of historical evidence against which all doctrine and all that implies doctrine must be matched," *Tradition in the Early Church* (Philadelphia, 1963). Irenaeus and possibly Justin Martyr would probably have agreed, although for Justin, consult Eric Francis Osborn, *Justin Martyr* (Tübingen, 1973); and Oskar Skarsaune, *The Proof from Prophecy: A Study in Justin Martyr's Proof-Text Tradition, Text-Type, Provenance, Theological Profile* (Leiden, 1987), specifically the section on "the new law going out from Zion." Chapters by W. C. van Unnik, Richard Norris, and William R. Schoedel in William R. Schoedel, ed., *Early Christian Literature and the Classical Tradition, In Honorem Robert M. Grant* (Paris, 1979), prompt interest in Irenaeus and late-second-century religious culture. See also William R. Schoedel, "Theological Method in Irenaeus," *Journal of Theological Studies* 35 (1984):31–49; and the remarks in Mary Ann Donovan's survey, "Irenaeus in Recent Scholarship," *The Second Century* 4 (1984):219–244.

CHAPTER 2

The *Revue d'études augustiniennes* annually publishes an annotated survey of the latest works on Tertullian (along with those on Cyprian and Augustine). For trends, however, consult Robert D. Sider, "Approaches to Tertullian: A Study of Recent Scholarship," *The Second Century* 2 (1982):228–260.

Chapter 2 extends my earlier efforts to measure the effects of Tertullian's various polemics on his theology, for which see Peter Iver Kaufman, "Tertullian on Heresy, History, and the Reappropriation of Revelation," *Church History* 60 (1991):167–179. For coverage, however, it is wisest to start with Timothy D. Barnes, *Tertullian: A Historical and Literary Study,* 2d ed. (Oxford, 1985), although Gerald Lewis Bray, *Holiness and the Will of God: Perspectives on the Theology of Tertullian* (Atlanta, 1979), is a useful, if somewhat fatiguing, introduction to Tertullian's "struggle for sanctification." Peter Brown, *The Body and Society: Men, Women, and Sexual Renunciation in Early Christianity* (New York, 1988), pp. 76–82, also discusses the "techniques" commended by Tertullian to Christians looking to achieve "clarity of soul."

To place Tertullian's apology and polemics in the context of Roman religions and history, see the articles in English by Paul Keresztes, Stephen Benko, and R.P.C. Hanson published in *Aufstieg und Niedergang der römischen Welt,* ed. Wolfgang Haase (Berlin, 1979), 2.23.1–2. Peter Cramer, *Baptism and Change in the Early Middle Ages* (Cambridge, 1993), pp. 46–63, illustrates the "daring of Tertullian's rationalism" (and includes in its early chapters remarks that are useful for our discussion of Hippolytus, Ambrose, and Augustine). Other works on Tertullian, however, show how hard it is to pin labels on him—rationalist, biblicist, historicist. See Ellen Flesseman–van Leer, *Tradition and Scripture in the Early Church* (Assen, the Netherlands, 1954); Robert D. Sider, *Ancient Rhetoric and the Art of Tertullian* (Oxford, 1971); and Mark S. Burrows, "Christianity in the Roman Forum: Tertullian and the Apologetic Use of History," *Vigiliae Christianae* 42 (1988):209–235. Two of Sider's other studies relate directly to this chapter's concern: "Structure and Design in *De resurrectione mortuorum,*" *Vigiliae Christianae* 23 (1969):177–196; and his fine contribution on Tertullian's Paulinism to *Paul and the Legacies of Paul,* ed. William S. Babcock (Dallas, 1990).

W.H.C. Frend capably comments on "Montanism: Research and Problems," *Rivista di storia e letteratura religiosa* 20 (1984):521–237. Review also Christine Trevett's survey of "proto-Montanist" sympathies, "Apocalypse, Ignatius, and Montanism," *Vigiliae Christianae* 43 (1989):313–338.

CHAPTER 3

To begin a more general study of Christianity from the third through the early fifth century, we might well ask how easy or hard it was for Christianity after Constantine to appropriate the culture, which, as Robert Markus remarks, "came to be seen as the preserve of pagan religion." To that end, see his *The End of Ancient Christianity* (Cambridge, 1990); and Peter Brown, *Power and Persuasion in Late Antiquity: Towards a Christian Empire* (Madison, 1992). Of course, appropriation assumes some degree of Christianization, "a rather piecemeal process" in the fourth century, according to Michele Renee Salzman. See her "How the West Was Won: The Christianization of the Roman Aristocracy in the West in the Years After Constantine," in *Studies in Latin Literature and Roman History,* ed. Carl Deroux (Brussels, 1992) vol. 6, pp. 451–479; and two of Ramsay MacMullen's important studies: *Christianizing the Roman Empire:* A.D. *100–400* (New Haven, 1984), and "What Difference Did Christianity Make?" *Historia* 35 (1986):322–343. For the persistence of paganism, see also Arnoldo Momigliano, ed., *The Conflict Between Paganism and Christianity in the Fourth Century* (Oxford, 1963).

Cyprian has not been particularly well served in English since the 1970s, and even during that decade the crop was not abundant. Peter Hinchliff, *Cyprian of Carthage and the Unity of the Christian Church* (London, 1974), is a running account of the rigorists and "laxists" in North Africa, yet it runs around and not into or through the scholarly controversies as it documents how and why "the cold disciplinarian became the hero of Christian Carthage." Michael M. Sage, *Cyprian* (Philadelphia, 1975), goes to greater lengths to feature Cyprian's talents as an administrator. Michael Andrew Fahey, *Cyprian and the Bible: A Study in Third-Century Exegesis* (Tübingen, 1971), a contribution to the history of scriptural interpretation, is light on the pastoral context. Among Maurice Bevenot's invariably useful articles in English, see "*Primus Petro datur:* St. Cyprian and the Papacy," *Journal of Theological Studies* 5 (1954):19–35, and "Cyprian and His Recognition of Cornelius," *Journal of Theological Studies* 28 (1977):346–359.

For the history of fourth-century doctrinal conflict and conflict containment, R.P.C. Hanson, *The Search for the Christian Doctrine of God: The Arian Controversy, 318–381* (Edinburgh, 1988), is irreplacable. Many of the protagonists, of course, have found shrewd interpreters. Rowan Williams, *Arius, Heresy, and Tradition* (London, 1987), is principally concerned with the theological and philosophical antecedents but is helpful as well with historical context. Consult also Charles Kannengiesser, *Holy Scripture and Hellenistic Hermeneutics in Alexandrian Christology: The Arian Crisis* (Berkeley, 1982); and Christopher Stead, "Arius in Modern Research," *Journal of Theological Studies* 45

(1994):24–36. For Athanasius, see James D. Ernest, "Athanasius of Alexandria: The Scope of Scripture in Polemical and Pastoral Context," *Vigiliae Christianae* 47 (1993):341–362. And for the apologetic dimensions of Eusebius's *Church History,* see the chapters contributed by Arthur J. Droge, Charles Kannengiesser, and Robert M. Grant to *Eusebius, Christianity, and Judaism,* ed. Harold W. Attridge and Gohei Hata (Leiden, 1992). To put Christian apology, political theology, and Christological conflict in the context of fourth-century history, see Averil Cameron's balanced account of *The Later Roman Empire* (Cambridge, Mass., 1993); and John F. Matthews, *The Roman Empire of Ammianus* (London, 1989). Some works by Timothy D. Barnes are critical for further consideration of the issues at stake herein—principally *Athanasius and Constantius* (Cambridge, Mass., 1993) but also *Constantine and Eusebius* (Cambridge, Mass., 1981) and Barne's previously published papers collected in the Variorum series, *From Eusebius to Augustine* (London, 1994).

Harry O. Maier, "Private Space as the Social Context of Arianism in Ambrose's Milan," *Journal of Theological Studies* 45 (1994):72–93, "define[s] orthodoxy spatially" and suggestively while introducing the conflict that brought Ambrose to power and lasted through the early part of his pontificate. Neil McLynn, *Ambrose of Milan: Church and Court in a Christian Capital* (Berkeley, 1994), puzzles over the familiar scholarly problems and arrives at some strikingly inventive and arresting resolutions. I have found Daniel H. Williams's articles useful while preparing my chapter—particularly his chapter on the first basilica conflict in Milan, published in a collection he edited with Michel R. Barnes, *Arianism After Arius: Essays on the Development of the Fifth-Century Trinitarian Conflicts* (Edinburgh, 1993). But Williams's articles are to some extent superseded by his *Ambrose of Milan and the End of the Arian-Nicene Conflicts* (Oxford, 1995), which arrived on my desk as this inventory was being drafted.

CHAPTER 4

Peter Brown's biography *Augustine of Hippo* (Berkeley, 1967), has acquired a deserved renown and influence. Studies included in *Religion and Society in the Age of Saint Augustine* (London, 1977), "partner" his profile of the bishop excellently, as do the lively and informative sections on Augustine in his *The Cult of Saints* (Chicago, 1981), and *The Body and Society: Men, Women, and Sexual Renunciation in Early Christianity* (New York, 1988).

John Rist recently demonstrated admirable skill in drawing "genuinely Augustinian themes" within reach of general readers in *Augustine: Ancient Thought Baptized* (Cambridge, 1994). Still profitable sources, however, are Christopher Kirwan's work on time and free will in *Augustine* (London, 1989); Henry Chadwick's day tour *Augustine* (Oxford, 1986); and Paula Fredriksen's provocative papers on Augustine's thought, notably her splendid "Paul and Augustine: Conversion Narratives, Orthodox Traditions, and the Retrospective Self," *Journal of Theological Studies* 37 (1986):3–34, and "Beyond the Body/Soul Dichotomy: Augustine on Paul Against the Manichees and the Pelagians," *Recherches Augustiniennes* 23 (1988):87–114. The polemical and pastoral contexts of Augustine's thinking are explored by Brown but also in Gerald Bonner, *St. Augustine of Hippo: Life and Controversies* (London, 1963); and in Frederik van der Meer, *Augustine, the Bishop* (London, 1961). Robert J. O'Connell lately published select *Soundings in St.*

Augustine's Imagination (New York, 1994), suggestive studies of "how Augustine's mind worked."

There is nothing quite comparable for Augustine's early career to George Lawless, *Augustine of Hippo and His Monastic Rule* (Oxford, 1987), though J. J. O'Donnell's editorial remarks in the recent *Confessions* (Oxford, 1992), are immensely helpful, as are Frederick Russell's remarks on Manichaean influence in " 'Only Something Good Can Be Evil': The Genesis of Augustine's Secular Ambivalence," *Theological Studies* 51 (1990):698–717. Estimates of ambivalence and of Augustine's various comments about political culture fill the literature. F. Edward Cranz's contributions, specifically his "The Development of Augustine's Ideas on Society Before the Donatist Controversy," *Harvard Theological Review* 47 (1954):255–316, repay study, despite the superb work that followed. Of that, see Robert Markus, *Saeculum: History and Society in the Theology of Saint Augustine,* 2d ed. (Cambridge, 1989); and Jeremy DuQuesnay Adams, *The "Populus" of Augustine and Jerome: A Study in the Patristic Sense of Community* (New Haven, 1971). For Augustine's responses to 410, see Theodore DeBruyn, "Ambivalence Within a Totalizing Discourse: Augustine's Sermons on the Sack of Rome," *Journal of Early Christian Studies* 1 (1993):405–442 and Peter Iver Kaufman, "Augustine, Martyrs, and Misery," *Church History* 63 (1994):1–14. The explanations for Augustine's views on social control in Elaine Pagels, *Adam, Eve, and the Serpent* (New York, 1988), are intriguing, if less than convincing.

W.H.C. Frend tests the Donatists' impressive grip on North African Christianity in a comprehensive treatment of *The Donatist Church,* 2d ed. (Oxford, 1985). Geoffrey Grimshaw Willis, *Saint Augustine and the Donatist Controversy* (London, 1950), is still useful, but J. E. Atkinson corrects the prevailing image of the Donatist Circumcellions inherited from Augustine and Optatus of Milevus in "Out of Order: The Circumcellions and the Codex Theodosius 16.5.52," *Historia* 41 (1992):488–499. Maureen Tilley, *The Donatist World,* is scheduled for publication in 1996.

Other subjects contemplated in this chapter are pursued elsewhere. Having put the Pelagians' answers in the context of Origen's questions about God's justice and goodness, Elizabeth Clark comes up with some striking conclusions in *The Origenist Controversy: The Cultural Construction of an Early Christian Debate* (Princeton, 1992). Christopher Ocker uses some newly discovered correspondence to good effect to shed light on "Augustine, Episcopal Interests, and the Papacy in Late Roman Africa," *Journal of Ecclesiastical History* 42 (1991):179–201. Consult also Gerald Bonner, "Augustine and Millenarianism," in *The Making of Orthodoxy: Essays in Honor of Henry Chadwick,* ed. Rowan Williams (Cambridge, 1989), pp. 235–254; and Heikki Kotila, *Memoria Mortuorum: Commemoration of the Departed in Augustine* (Rome, 1992). Joseph T. Lienhard, Earl C. Muller, and Roland J. Teske, eds., *Collectanea Augustiniana: Augustine, Presbyter Factus Sum* (New York, 1993), an assortment of essays, indulges several interests addressed herein and many more.

CHAPTER 5

Averil Cameron, *The Mediterranean World in Late Antiquity,* AD *395–600* (London, 1993), is the most readable and reasonable general introduction I have come across, but there is much to recommend the second volume of A.H.M. Jones's magisterial *Later Roman Empire*

(Oxford, 1964). Richard Krautheimer, *Three Christian Capitals* (Berkeley, 1983), rivals neither, yet supplements either and both. Chapters collected in John Drinkwater and Hugh Elton, eds., *Fifth-Century Gaul: A Crisis of Identity* (Cambridge, 1992), chronicle the various invasions and enduring uncertainties but also furnish interesting snapshots of all kinds of curiosities. Several contributors elsewhere lavish special attention on church leadership and diplomacy. From Ralph Whitney Mathisen, *Ecclesiastical Factionalism and Religious Controversy in Fifth-Century Gaul* (Washington, D.C., 1989), for example, we learn that conflict was personal and political rather than doctrinal, and from his *Roman Aristocrats in Barbarian Gaul: Strategies for Survival in an Age of Transition* (Austin, 1993), we discover the effects of political displacement on the Gallo-Roman episcopacy and watch the development of episcopal dynasties. Yet Raymond van Dam's wonderful studies more directly relate to themes featured in this chapter. I suspect that *Leadership and Community in Late Antique Gaul* (Berkeley, 1985), and *Saints and Their Miracles in Late Antique Gaul* (Princeton, 1993), are as close as a historian can come to appreciating "the power of relics." Nonetheless, for "a strategy of Christianization in which the power of rhetoric was more highly esteemed than the potency of relics," revisit "post-Roman Gaul" with William E. Klingshirn, *Caesarius of Arles: The Making of a Christian Community in Late Antique Gaul* (Cambridge, 1994). The arguments for an "ascetic takeover" of the church in Robert A. Markus, *The End of Ancient Christianity* (Cambridge, 1990), offer yet another perspective on Caesarius and evangelization in late antiquity.

Brian Brennan, "The Image of the Merovingian Bishop in the Poetry of Venantius Fortunatus," *Journal of Medieval History* 18 (1992):115–139, introduces Gregory of Tours, Venantius' patron and the prolific hagiographer to whom this chapter's discussions of bishops and bones is indebted. For Gregory, and for the other historians who have illumined these reputedly dark ages, consult Walter Goffart, *The Narrators of Barbarian History (AD 550–800): Jordanes, Gregory of Tours, Bede, and Paul the Deacon* (Princeton, 1988).

Conflicts between intruders and imperial defenders in Italy sometimes set limits on the extension of episcopal authority but occasionally afforded opportunities for the effective assertion of papal power. For general information, see Walter Emil Kaegi, *Byzantium and the Decline of Rome* (Princeton, 1968). Also have at hand John Moorhead, *Justinian I, Emperor of the East* (London, 1994). The fortunes of the papacy can be followed in Bernhard Schimmelpfennig, *The Papacy* (New York, 1992), chaps. 2–3. Walter Ullmann's opinionated approaches to the "growth of papal monarchy" are never dull. His article on "Leo I and the Theme of Papal Primacy," *Journal of Theological Studies* 11 (1960):25–51, is a fine specimen that bears on this chapter's concerns, as does Arthur McGrade's more nuanced article on Leo I and Gelasius, "Two Fifth-Century Conceptions of Papal Primacy," *Studies in Medieval and Renaissance History* 7 (1970):3–43. But Karl Morrison's impeccably crafted judgments on papal apology, above all, deserve the status of required reading. See particularly the early pages of his *Tradition and Authority in the Western Church, 300–1100* (Princeton, 1969). For the popes themselves and church diplomacy, review Jeffrey Richards, *The Popes and Papacy in the Early Middle Ages* (London, 1979).

Richards also composed a creditable account of leadership during Gregory I's pontificate, *Consul of God: The Life and Times of Gregory the Great* (London, 1980). Whereas Richards supplies the politics, Carole Straw has the better ear by far for the pope's pastoral theology; *Gregory the Great: Perfection in Imperfection* (Berkeley, 1988), is a genuinely fresh and exciting assessment of the thought world that may well explain much about styles of executive leadership. Consult also William McCready, *Signs of Sanctity: Miracles in the Thought of Gregory the Great* (Toronto, 1989); and the superb thought world section of Clare Stancliffe, *St. Martin and His Hagiographer: History and Miracle in Sulpicius Severus* (Oxford, 1983).

About the Book and Author

*B*eginning with the organizational difficulties that faced the postresurrection communities of Jesus' followers and concluding nearly six centuries later as many regional representatives of the universal church came increasingly under the influence of Roman bishops, *Church, Book, and Bishop* is the story of leadership—its successes and frustrations. It is a book about the managerial elites largely responsible for overcoming the theological, political, and social obstacles to organization.

Through a series of scenes drawn from clerical life, Peter Iver Kaufman identifies and illustrates these executive strategies for conflict management and consensus-building. Whereas many accounts of this period emphasize nonconformity and conflict, Kaufman studies the distribution and exercise of authority that made it possible to articulate the conformists' positions effectively and to achieve an appreciable measure of institutional coherence.

This story is told in a way that will appeal not only to scholars of the early church and their students but also to generalists interested in the development of Latin Christianity. It will be especially useful as a supplement to courses on the history of Western civilization and on the history of Christian traditions.

Peter Iver Kaufman is professor of religious studies at the University of North Carolina–Chapel Hill. He is the author of *Redeeming Politics; Prayer, Despair, and Drama: Elizabethan Introspection; The Polytyque Churche: Religion and Early Tudor Political Culture;* and *Augustinian Piety and Catholic Reform* as well as over thirty articles on church history.

Index